CRYSTAL PALACE F.C.

CRYSTAL PALACE F.C.
CRYSTAL PALACE F.C.
CRYSTAL PALACE F.C.
CRYSTAL PALACE F.C.
CRYSTAL PALACE F.C.
CRYSTAL PALACE F.C.
CRYSTAL PALACE F.C.
CRYSTAL PALACE F.C.
CRYSTAL PALACE F.C.
CRYSTAL PALACE F.C.
CRYSTAL PALACE F.C.
CRYSTAL PALACE F.C.
CRYSTAL PALACE F.C.
CRYSTAL PALACE F.C.
CRYSTAL PALACE F.C.

FRONT COVER: The 1905 and 1994-95 Crystal Palace team photos span the ninety years of the Club.

CLOCKWISE: Stars from two eras, ninety years apart: Archie Needham, Palace's top scorer in 1905-06 and versatile Wilfred Innerd are with their modern day successors, ace striker Chris Armstrong and Palace's England man, John Salako.

CRYSTAL PALACE FOOTBALL CLUB 1905-1995

The History of the Club

BY

REV NIGEL SANDS MA

with photography by Neil Everitt

SPORTING & LEISURE PRESS
WHITTLEBURY, NORTHANTS, ENGLAND
MCMXCV

PUBLISHED BY SPORTING & LEISURE PRESS
AND PRODUCED BY KEY COMPOSITION,
SOUTH MIDLANDS LITHOPLATES, CHENEY & SONS,
HILLMAN PRINTERS (FROME) LIMITED AND WBC BOOKBINDERS

ISBN 0 86023 555 6

FIRST PUBLISHED IN 1995
SECOND IMPRESSION 1996

Contents

ACKNOWLEDGEMENTS

It would be quite impossible to mention everyone who has helped in the assembling of the material which now comprises the ninety year history of Crystal Palace Football Club as encapsulated in this volume, but there are those friends and fellow supporters of our Club to whom I owe particular gratitude and without each of whom this book would lack some of its lustre, dignity and appeal.

Kenneth and Andrea Pleant graciously and trustingly loaned me the vintage memorabilia collected by George Pleant before the Great War and this was of enormous assistance in illustrating the early pages of this book, while Colin Duncan has once more devoted meticulous care to the reading and correcting of the proofs. Mr and Mrs 'Dickie' Davies kindly allowed me access to their comprehensive collection of football books and those dedicated Palace statisticians Tony Bowden, David Keats and Paul Firmage have once again provided invaluable help.

I am also delighted to acknowledge the important contribution to this history made by Ian King, who devoted great care and much time in assembling the career details of every Palace player since 1905, and by John McBride, whose statistical output in footballing matters is quite astonishing and whose record of every Palace League and major Cup result is a feature of unique appeal and interest.

Then, as every contemporary Palace fan knows, modern-day Palace publications owe much to the brilliance of Neil Everitt, our Club's renowned photographer, and we are all again indebted to him for his pictures.

Finally, it is always possible in a book like this one that photographs have inadvertently been reproduced, following their use in a previous Palace publication, without acknowledgement. If this should be discovered, please accept the author's apologies and let him or the publisher know, so that this omission may be rectified in any subsequent impression.

DEDICATION

Because this volume deals with the entire history of Crystal Palace FC it inevitably looks backward to what is past. But I am a Palace supporter through and through, and of almost fifty years standing, so that, however interesting and important the Eagles' past exploits may be, I look to the Club's prospects, wish it well, and long for its success and continued progress.

Accordingly, the only fitting dedication for this book must be 'Crystal Palace Football Club — its future, its further development and its destiny'.

FOREWORD – *BY STEVE COPPELL*

I am delighted, as one of my first tasks upon returning to Crystal Palace, to be invited to pen a brief Foreword to this important Club book.

Every football club likes to possess a well written, authoritative club history and Nigel Sands deserves the thanks of all Eagles supporters for providing precisely that with this volume which spans the entire ninety years of Crystal Palace FC. No doubt it will give our fans hours of interesting reading and be referred to for many years to come.

It is also the aim and intention of the players, coaches and myself to quickly add another successful chapter for 'The Rev' to record and I know that I can count on the backing of all our supporters in bringing that to fruition.

AUTHORS' PREFACE

I am delighted to be able to offer this history of Crystal Palace FC, the Club that I love and have followed since I was a small schoolboy in the first season after the War. I have enjoyed the writing and assembling of it and I hope that it will furnish great pleasure and interest to its readers as well as providing an invaluable source of reference to us all.

I am sure that Palace supporters will understand that, in order to keep the content to manageable proportions, the level of detail I have been able to provide here is inevitably much less than it has been in some of the other books in this series. Where further information is required I can only refer enquirers to those other volumes, and any which may follow this one, or invite them to contact me, *via* the football club.

This history owes a considerable debt to those fans and people connected with the Club who have encouraged me in the writing I do for and about the Palace. I am grateful to them all.

ABOVE: Mr Sydney Bourne, first chairman. LEFT: Mr William McGregor, chairman of Aston Villa and founder of the Football League. (Pic Terry Weir, Aston Villa FC) RIGHT: The Crystal Palace — original home of Crystal Palace FC. BELOW: Action from the 1901 FA Cup Final at the Crystal Palace with Brown netting for Tottenham against Sheffield United. There's football history here too — notice the old-style pitch-markings. RIGHT: Mr Edmund Goodman when appointed Secretary to Crystal Palace FC.

PALACE PIONEERS

Professional football arrived relatively late in the genteel southern suburbs of London at the Crystal Palace, but it eventually did so in the early years of the twentieth century as a result of the spectacular FA Cup Finals and England Internationals hosted at the Crystal Palace Exhibition Ground after 1895. The 1901 Final drew an amazing crowd of 110,000 to the Palace and it began to be realised that a side playing there regularly could capture sufficient support to be viable.

In 1904 the FA declined to sanction a proposal to this effect from the Crystal Palace company, but twelve months later approved the formation of an independent club which bore the Palace name and played its homes matches there. The general manager of the Palace, Mr J. H. Cozens, and his predecessor, Mr Gillman had both been enthusiastic and the former approached Aston Villa, already a pedigree club in the Football League and twice winners of the FA Cup at the Palace. Chairman of Villa at that time was Mr William McGregor, founding father of the Football League. He fully endorsed the idea and wrote in the *Football Star* in December 1904 'The high water mark of prosperity in the metropolis has not been reached and I believe a really good team at the Crystal Palace would be a tremendous draw'. McGregor also recommended a young, assistant secretary at Villa, Edmund Goodman, for the task of organising both the new Club and its team. It was a brilliant acquisition which remains among the best 'transfers' the Palace club has ever made.

Edmund's own promising football career had been abruptly terminated when he suffered a knee injury which necessitated amputation at the age of just nineteen. For his first two seasons with his new club he was too deeply immersed in the hard secretarial graft of administration to spend sufficient time with the players, as manager, but Palace's first manager, Mr John Robson, was appointed under his guidance and he found the Club's superb first chairman, Mr Sydney Bourne.

The manner in which Mr Goodman secured the support and involvement of Mr Sydney Bourne as Chairman is not only interesting but a clear indication of his shrewdness. Mr Goodman revealed that he scrutinised the books of the Crystal Palace company which dealt with the FA Cup Finals and, among the list of those who always took a number of tickets, was Mr Bourne. Mr Goodman contacted him, put the notion of the new club to him, found him fully supportive and, quite soon, had persuaded Mr Bourne to become a director.

Sidney Bourne had been an all-round sportsman and had played football for twenty-two years after leaving school. A Londoner born and bred, he played for a team known as 'The Mosquitoes' in the early 1880s, later for Champion Hill, then Lyndhurst in Hampshire. In his early days he was an eager and aggressive forward but, as time went by, he dropped back to half-back, then to full-back and finally to goalkeeper!

Having helped Edmund Goodman in the foundation of the Crystal Palace Club, when the Palace left the Southern League for the Football League in 1920 Mr Bourne was made a life member of the former for the service he had given since 1905. He continued as chairman of Crystal Palace until his death in 1930, was the last of the original directorate to remain associated with the Club and was, to the end, an interesting, colourful and most respected personality.

So far then, everything had proceeded most satisfactorily: the new Club was approved by the FA; it had appointed Mr Goodman as its Secretary and persuaded Mr Jack Robson, formerly in charge of Middlesbrough, to come south to manage the playing side. But then application was made for admission to the Southern League — only to be denied (by one

TEAMS.

ASTON VILLA.			NEWCASTLE UNITED.		
1	George	Goal.	12	Gosnell	Forwards.
2	Spencer	Backs.	13	Veitch	
3	Miles...		14	Appleyard... ...	
4	Pearson	Half-Backs.	15	Howie	
5	Leake		16	Rutherford ...	
6	Windmill		17	Macwilliam ...	Half-Backs.
7	Brawn	Forwards.	18	Aitken	
8	Garratty		19	Gardner	
9	Hampton		20	Carr	Backs.
10	Bache		21	Maccombie... ...	
11	Hall		22	Lawrence	Goal.

Colours—**Claret and Light Blue.** *Colours*—**Black and White Stripes.**

Referee ... ... Mr. P. R. HARROWER (London).

Linesmen ... Messrs. G. W. WALKER (Beds) and W. H. BELLAMY (Lincs).

ABOVE: The team line-ups for the 1905 Final as shown in the match programme. BELOW: The first-ever Crystal Palace team group taken in 1905 with manager John Robson standing far left; back: J. Robson (manager), Mr T. C. Walters, Mr A. Daniels (directors), J. Thompson, W. Oliver, A. Grant, R. Rose, H. Astley, M. Edwards, Mr A. P. Cufflin, Mr S. Bourne (directors), E. Goodman (secretary), A. Birch (trainer); front: G. Thompson, R. Hewitson, A. Needham, W. Watkins, E. Birnie, W. Innerd, G. Walker, R. Roberts; sitting: R. Harker, C. Wallace.

vote, it was later revealed) and thus it became necessary for the Palace to compete in its 2nd Division which comprised only 13 clubs, either reserve teams from sides in the 1st Division or lesser known clubs like Grays United and St Leonards United.

The financial implications were considerable, but the seriousness of the situation will be better appreciated by today's reader when it is realised that several clubs had already tried to prove themselves in the Southern League in its earlier years, only to fail and withdraw. St Albans, Shepherds Bush and Maidenhead had all gone to the wall, and in this same season that the Palace joined, there was another, local club, Southern United from Nunhead, who did so — and then resigned the following April.

Whether it was purely because we could not play in the Southern League 1st Division or whether we would have done so anyway is unknown, but Mr Goodman also sought and secured admission to the United League. This competition did provide matches against the first elevens of the other Southern League clubs, although it was played largely mid-week, but Palace took part for two seasons and, in fact, our first competitive game was in the United League, away to New Brompton (later to become Gillingham) on Friday 1 September 1905 — and we won 3-0 with goals from 'Dickie' Roberts, Ted Birnie and Dick Harker.

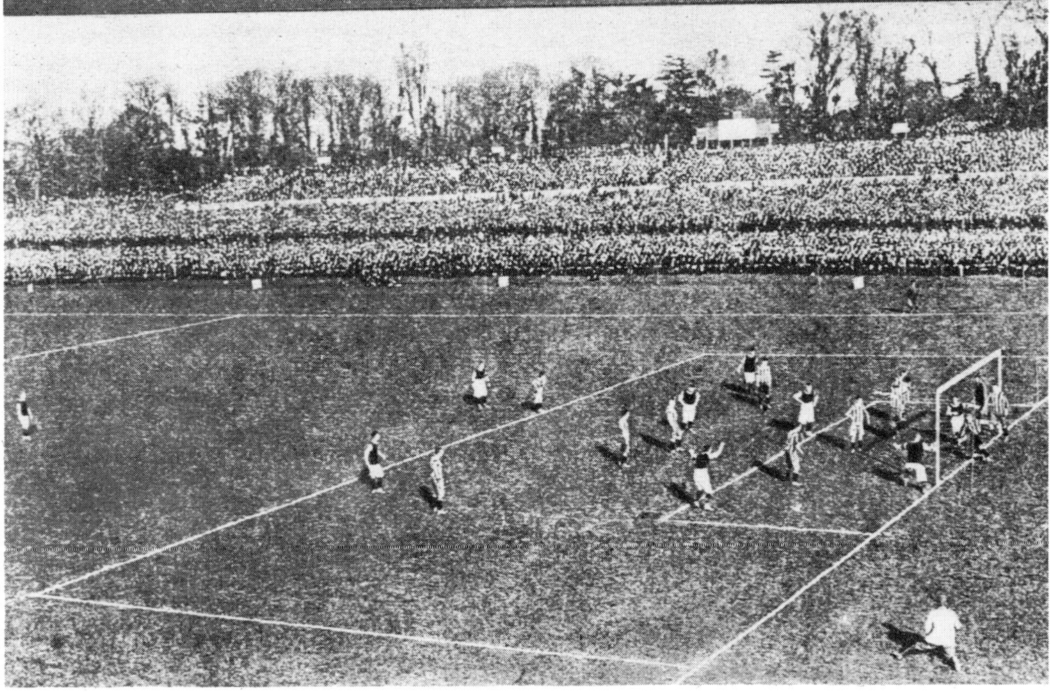

The pitch-markings have changed by the 1905 Cup Final: (above) Harry Hampton scoring one of Aston Villa's two goals which defeated Newcastle and the raid which ended with the other.

ABOVE: A view of the 1911 FA Cup Final between Bradford City and Newcastle at the Crystal Palace. BELOW: Palace's 1908-09 squad.

The Prelude

The majority of the players assembled in the late summer of 1905 by John Robson were from the north of England or the Midlands. Captain was to be Ted Birnie, himself a Geordie and formerly with Newcastle United, and it was the skipper who uttered the rallying call to his playing colleagues at the commencement of the proceedings: 'We must win nearly every Southern League match and then they will have to have us in the First Division'.

That was effectively what Ted Birnie and his boys did — but not before the shock of failing at the first such hurdle! Twenty-four hours after the United League victory at New Brompton, Palace were hosts to Southampton Reserves in the Southern League 2nd Division but, in spite of romping to a 3-0 lead before half-time, they contrived to lose the game by 3-4; then came a United League defeat at Watford a few days later. However, the tide was turned by a Southern League victory at Swindon (Reserves, of course) and thenceforth the Palace's first season became a triumphant cavalcade.

Fulham Reserves, champions of the Second Division the previous term, were trounced 5-0, while from 30 September to 18 November ten consecutive victories were recorded, including the Club's first success in the FA Cup on 7 October when we secured a 7-0 victory, which we have never (yet?!) bettered in that most ancient and distinguished of all competitions, against Clapham.

Another huge victory (7-1) was secured in the preliminary round of the FA Cup when we were paired with Chelsea. In view of the fact that they also had a Football League fixture that afternoon, Chelsea chose to send a largely reserve side to the Palace for the Cup-tie and were humiliated for their folly, while the other outcome was that the FA legislated that any club competing in the Cup must in future field its strongest side.

A further Cup victory, if a much narrower one, by a single goal over Luton Town, took the Palace into the (old) 1st round proper of the competition after Christmas and here they engaged Blackpool in two 1-1 draws, first at Bloomfield Road, then at the Palace, before going down to the powerful Football League side by a single goal in the second replay at Villa Park.

Attendances in the spring of 1906 were reaching 4,000 for the most attractive fixtures. This was largely due to the fact that Palace was locked in an enthralling race for the championship of the Southern League 2nd Division with Leyton, and it was for the game between the two clubs over in Essex that there is the first recorded evidence of hundreds of Palace fans travelling to support their new side in an away fixture. The match was won 2-1, with Charlie Wallace and Archie Needham scoring the goals that secured the title.

By this time the Glaziers' first 'star' player was emerging in the person of George Woodger. Still an amateur, Woodger was one of only two local lads to appear for us in the first season. He was an inside or centre-forward of the highest quality and his delicate, ball-playing skills quickly earned him the quaint nickname 'Lady', and of course a special place in the affections of Palace supporters.

Upon the Palace entering the 1st Division of the Southern League, Woodger turned professional and continued to progress as a valuable goalscorer while still developing those amazing ball skills. His best season for us was unquestionably 1907-08 when he was appointed England's reserve against Scotland.

Thus the first season of Crystal Palace FC became a resounding triumph: champions of their division in the Southern League, runners-up in the United League and having demonstrated playing ability and support in major FA Cup-ties and selected friendly games against senior and distinguished opponents.

Wilfred Innerd took over as Palace's captain for 1906-07 after Ted Birnie departed to Chelsea and the Palace made further progress — though not, ironically, in the Southern League. To put it at its best we struggled there, eventually finishing next to bottom in nineteenth place. However, elsewhere we were superb. We won the United League title, while in the FA Cup we fared brilliantly and it must be doubtful whether any other club has done so well in that competition within two seasons of its foundation. The draw for the 1st round required us to travel to Newcastle, who were among the foremost sides in the country in that first decade of the century. League champions and FA Cup-finalists the previous season, unbeaten at home for more than a year and fielding several current internationals in their team, the Magpies were favourites to win by the biggest margin of the round!

Perhaps the Palace's greatest asset in this tie was that a number of our team, like Horace Astley, winger Charlie Wallace and goalkeeper Bob Hewitson, hailed from the north-east, skipper Wilfred Innerd had actually played for Newcastle teams and so had Dick Harker and winger 'Dickie' Roberts.

It was inevitable that the Palace would have to endure a lot of Newcastle pressure, and this they did successfully but, just four minutes before half-time, the seemingly impossible occurred when Horace Astley eluded the converging full-backs, then rounded Scottish international goalkeeper Jimmy Lawrence to provide the Palace with the lead. And nothing Newcastle could do after the break retrieved the situation so that we were able to provide one of the greatest FA Cup upsets of all time.

Nor was this tremendous victory achieved in isolation. Southern League champions, Fulham, were disposed of by a similar margin in a Crystal Palace replay after a scoreless match at Craven Cottage, and Brentford went the same way in round three after the game at the Palace had remained goal-less. This took the Palace into the quarter-finals where they were paired with Everton, the Cup holders and another club which had already earned a mighty tradition.

A record crowd of some 35,000 turned up at the Palace, in spite of miserable drizzling rain, to witness the confrontation. The Toffees had no fewer than nine internationals in their side but, as at Newcastle, with barely a few minutes to go before half-time, Horace Astley put the Palace ahead. Everton regained their composure during the break and managed an equaliser around the hour so that the last thirty minutes provided the most compelling entertainment — 'a finer contest than many Cup Finals' according to one seasoned observer.

The replay at Goodison Park could really only go one way after Everton secured an early goal, was all over when we were three down after half an hour and eventually finished 0-4, but by now the Palace had gained a fine reputation as a club that could extend and even beat the greatest sides in the land — and that, after just two seasons, was quite remarkable!

The Glaziers re-inforced that reputation with further FA Cup successes in the ensuing two years. In spite of being drawn away each time in 1907-08, they secured creditable outright victories in difficult tests at Coventry (4-2) and Plymouth (3-2) before bowing out to Grimsby (0-1) in deplorable conditions, so that Palace fans had to wait till the following season for another stunning FA Cup victory.

This time it was the Cup holders themselves, the mighty Wolves no less, who became our victims in a 1st round replay after a 2-2 draw up at Molineux. In front of a 30,000 crowd — not bad for a Wednesday afternoon in mid January, even allowing for early closing day — a superb Cup-tie evolved. Both sides forged ahead only to be pulled back and extra time became necessary. In the 103rd minute that remarkable goalscorer Jimmy Bauchop (who had secured our pair of goals in the first game) restored our lead, but it was in the dying moments of the match that Archie Needham scored one of the finest goals in all Palace history. He received the ball in the centre circle, inside our half, and ran at the Wolves' defence, striding through tackles as well as the strength-sapping mud, before lashing it into the net and falling exhausted in the Wolves penalty area and there accepting the acclaim of the fans and the congratulations of his team-mates. It was a wonderful goal, scored by a fine club servant who had been with the Palace from the very beginning, and Palace fans who saw it were still reminiscing about it six or seven decades later!

Crystal Palace FC embarked upon its third season with Mr Goodman assuming responsibility for the playing side as well as continuing as secretary. There were changes in the playing staff too, chief among which was goalkeeper, for Bob Hewitson departed to Oldham, thus presenting Mr Goodman with a considerable problem. But how brilliantly he solved it.

The new manager drafted in a tall, good-looking and studious young man who was to become our first-choice goalkeeper until the 1st World War curtailed the Southern League competition, Joshua (usually nicknamed 'Joe') Johnson, and he played so many games for the Club in those years (295) that he is still among the leading all-time Palace appearances.

Another new face was that of Bill Davies, a winger of craft and guile, who joined us from Stoke City and gained the Palace club's first international honour during this 1907-08 season, when he was capped for Wales against Scotland on 7 March.

Harry Collyer was another great Palace personality in the early years. Sporting his distinctive 'Pentonville' hair cut, he drew huge praise from the pundits for his safe and stylish role at right back. So much did Harry impress that he was given a trial for England in 1909-10 and he appeared several times for the Southern League in representative fixtures.

In spite of a poor start the Palace managed to finish 1907-08 in a praiseworthy fourth place: George Woodger accumulated an impressive 13 goals, popular 'Dickie' Roberts weighed in with eight from the wing in spite of missing the last third of the season through injury, and new signing Jimmy Bauchop from Norwich hit six from the last eight games.

Jimmy was a tough character: a proven goalscorer wherever he went, he never stopped long at any of his clubs (and he played for at least nine!), he also possessed something of a short temper and became Palace's first player to be dismissed when he was sent off in September 1908 in a London Cup match against local rivals Croydon Common.

Palace were joined for 1908-09 by a sparkling little winger in the person of ex-Plymouth, Villa and Albion star, George Garratt. George was a tricky customer out on either flank, tough, strong and unselfish — and so reliable that he seldom missed a match through injury and played 185 League and Cup games for us. He also gained several minor representative honours and became a great favourite in his five years at the Palace.

George Woodger became Palace's third captain when Wilfred Innerd returned to his native north-east in the summer of 1909 and a series of impressive results soon put the Club among the leading contenders for the Southern League title. Chief among these was the 6-0 rout of Southend in September in which J. W. Williams scored five goals. Palace in fact had a new striking partnership for 1909-10 in Williams and George Payne. Williams could play in any forward position and had joined us from Birmingham City. He soon proved highly popular with the Palace fans, who christened him 'Ginger' on account of his auburn hair, but some of the local press gave him the epithet 'The Palace Terrier' which most aptly described his neat, eager and busy style, his snappy tackle and zest for goals. So well did he fare with us that he gained Welsh International honours and 1909-10 was his first and best season with us, although he played regularly for four and a half years.

George Payne came to us from Tottenham and in 1909-10 he was an astonishing marksman with 25 Southern League goals from just 34 outings — 21 of them before Christmas, including hat-tricks in consecutive games in October and four against New Brompton in November!

Although the Palace became the only side to beat champions-to-be Brighton, at their Goldstone Road ground in that season, we were nothing like such a strong side in the second half of the season and slipped, eventually to finish seventh — respectable enough and a considerable improvement on 1908-09 certainly, but disappointing nonetheless in view of the splendid showing and high hopes raised earlier in the term.

The 1909-10 side contained three new defenders, all of whom would go on to become invaluable members of later, more successful Palace teams, and a new half-back who was to become an inspirational captain.

The first of the defenders was already known before his arrival at the Palace because he had starred with Croydon Common, who had won the Southern League 2nd Division championship in 1908-09. Bob Spottiswood was a wing-half, fierce and determined. He missed just one Southern League game for us in 1909-10, gained Southern League honours, went on to make 189 appearances for the Club before the War and helped to form one of our best-ever half-back lines with two other new men, Jimmy Hughes and Harry Hanger.

Big Jimmy Hughes was a powerful bulwark of a centre-half and it is no co-incidence that our best seasons in the Southern League were achieved while he was marshalling our defence. Dominant in the air, strong in the tackle and able to deliver a stream of stylish, sweeping passes to either wing, it was no surprise that he too was chosen to play for the Southern League. Only the Great War prevented him from amassing a huge total of appearances for us — as it was, with four seasons lost to hostilities, Jimmy played 209 first-class games for us with remarkable consistency.

Harry Hanger came to the Palace for the 1909-10 season from Bradford City and this cultured wing-half became a splendid club captain after George Woodger's departure in October 1910. He was popular with his colleagues as well as with the fans and his inspirational captaincy helped lead the Club to within an ace of the Southern League championship in 1914.

Last of the new players of note in 1909-10 was left-back Joe Bulcock, who made an immediate impact, and was chosen to represent the Southern League against the Football League at Stamford Bridge in April before going to South Africa with an FA touring side. Like the others, Joe was to provide sterling service to the Palace and helped to form some of our best defences in the early days.

It was obvious, virtually from the start of the 1910-11 season, that George Woodger would not long remain a Palace player. Clearly of a class above most of the Southern League, George yearned for full England recognition, and the only way he could gain it would be to play for a major Football League club, so it was no surprise when he moved to 1st Division Oldham on 30 September for a fee variously described at between £450 and £800 — a substantial enough sum for those days — and he did eventually fulfil his ambition to play for England.

Woodger's replacement at centre-forward, Charlie Woodhouse, netted on his debut on 1 October when we beat Leyton 5-4 at the Palace in a splendid game. Charlie was a strong, rumbustious leader of the attack. He played in every remaining Southern League game in 1910-11 and finished as our top scorer by a distance, with 15 goals from his 33 matches. He had come to us from Halesowen.

Another newcomer at this stage who was to become a Palace regular up to the War, was inside forward Charlie Hewitt, a bustling bundle of energy with considerable experience. Once George Woodger had left us, it was Charlie who became the great supplier for the wing wizardry of George Garratt, but he was also a useful goalscorer, hitting 39 Southern League goals for us.

It was probably Palace's strongest Southern League squad to date that was available to Mr Goodman for 1910-11 and the team did well. We secured four 'doubles', yet nobody beat us twice, although there was the odd statistic whereby we failed even to score in any of the four matches against the two relegated clubs, Southend and Portsmouth. Came the last game of the season and the Palace could have finished runners-up to champions Swindon, but a heavy defeat at Northampton consigned us to fourth position, with the Cobblers themselves taking second place.

Early in the 1911-12 season Palace suffered a heavy blow with the death of ace scorer Charlie Woodhouse, but we again began the season with the look of potential champions. For example, Norwich were trounced 6-0 at the Palace in one of Charlie's last games, during which he scored twice and Palace hit five goals in a twenty minute spell in the second half. We won 4-2 at Southampton in November and put five past Exeter in December without reply.

Ted Smith, Charlie Woodhouse's replacement, had as stunning a start to a career at a new club as any player. Arriving from Hull City, Ted made his debut at West Ham on 30 December. Both he and Dick Harker notched hat-tricks in a fabulous 6-1 win (still, easily, our best performance at Upton Park); then the following week he repeated the feat to help Palace beat Bristol Rovers 4-1. Ted was that sort of centre-forward. Goals simply flowed from his boots and his head and there was little defenders could do to stop him. He was to go on to score 109 times in the Southern League for us, and to become club captain in the Football League after the War. Altogether he hit 124 goals for us in League and Cup competitions and only Peter Simpson has ever done more.

And yet, still the Palace could not get within sight of the Southern League title. We finished brightly enough with only one defeat in the last six games, but could only reach seventh place this time.

However, Mr Goodman was aware of the quality of his team and there was little he could do to improve it for 1912-13, although a useful arrival who could fill a variety of roles was Ernie York, who made 28 appearances in four different positions, and we were occasionally favoured with the distinguished England amateur international half-back, Rev Kenneth Hunt, who had played against us for Wolves in the great Cup-tie back in 1909 and been lavish in his praise of his team's conquerors afterwards.

Harry Collyer and Joe Johnson received Benefit games, during this season the Palace won the London Challenge Cup for the first time, beating West Ham in the replayed final at Tottenham by a goal to nil with 'Ginger' Williams netting the vital strike, and no fewer than five players were called to represent the Southern League in inter-league contests.

George Garratt left us during the close season of 1913 for Millwall, but Mr Goodman let him go without a qualm, because two young wingers were coming swiftly to the fore — John Whibley and Ben Bateman, who won three amateur international caps during the 1913-14 season. Their considerable contribution was largely after the War but they were valuable members of the 1913-14 Palace side which came unbearably close to the Southern League championship.

Another player emerging into the spotlight was full-back Horace Colclough, who took his chance brilliantly when Joe Bulcock was injured in only the second game of the season. Horace was a magnificent full-back. He had joined us from Crewe in 1912 and, once he was in our side, there was no displacing him. He gained Palace's first full England international honour when he represented his country against Wales at Cardiff (2-0) on 16 March 1914, and he was yet another Palace player to earn Southern League representative honours.

1913-14 was Palace's best in the Southern League: we retained the London Challenge Cup by beating Tottenham (who included Jimmy Bauchop) 2-1, the winner scored by Bill

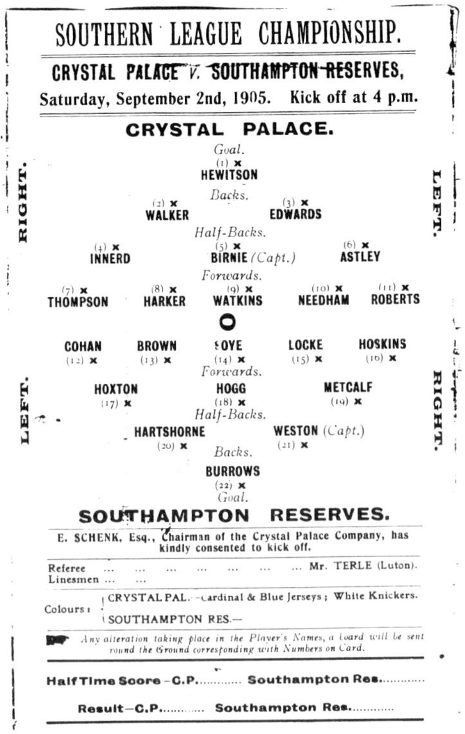

SOUTHERN LEAGUE CHAMPIONSHIP.

CRYSTAL PALACE v. SOUTHAMPTON RESERVES,

Saturday, September 2nd, 1905. Kick off at 4 p.m.

CRYSTAL PALACE.

RIGHT. LEFT.

Goal.
(1) × HEWITSON

Backs.
(2) × WALKER (3) × EDWARDS

Half-Backs.
(4) × INNERD (5) × BIRNIE (*Capt.*) (6) × ASTLEY

Forwards.
(7) × THOMPSON (8) × HARKER (9) × WATKINS (10) × NEEDHAM (11) × ROBERTS

O

COHAN (12) × BROWN (13) × FOYE (14) × LOCKE (15) × HOSKINS (16) ×

Forwards.
HOXTON (17) × HOGG (18) × METCALF (19) ×

Half-Backs.
HARTSHORNE (20) × WESTON (*Capt.*) (21) ×

Backs.
BURROWS (22) ×

Goal.

LEFT. RIGHT.

SOUTHAMPTON RESERVES.

E. SCHENK, Esq., Chairman of the Crystal Palace Company, has kindly consented to kick off.

Referee ... ... Mr. TERLE (Luton).
Linesmen ... ...

Colours: CRYSTAL PAL.—Cardinal & Blue Jerseys; White Knickers.
SOUTHAMPTON RES.—

Any alteration taking place in the Player's Names, a board will be sent round the Ground corresponding with Numbers on Card.

Half Time Score—C.P. .... Southampton Res. ....

Result—C.P. .... Southampton Res. ....

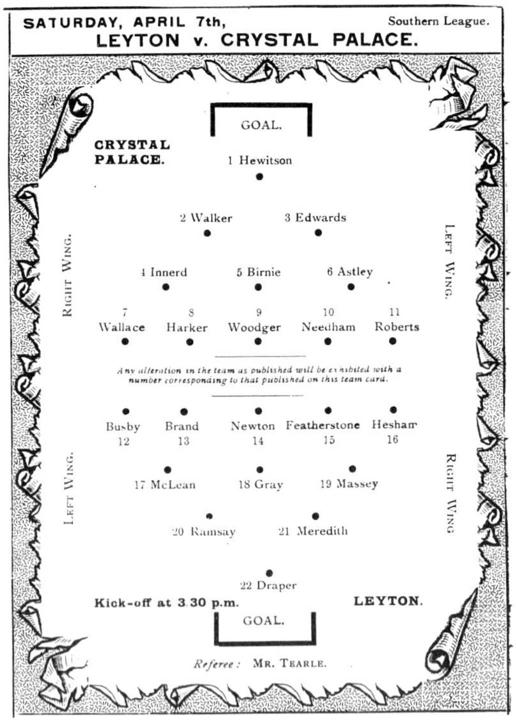

SATURDAY, APRIL 7th, Southern League.

LEYTON v. CRYSTAL PALACE.

GOAL.

CRYSTAL PALACE.

1 Hewitson

2 Walker 3 Edwards

4 Innerd 5 Birnie 6 Astley

RIGHT WING. LEFT WING.

7 Wallace 8 Harker 9 Woodger 10 Needham 11 Roberts

Any alteration in the team as published will be exhibited with a number corresponding to that published on this team card.

Busby 12 Brand 13 Newton 14 Featherstone 15 Hesham 16

LEFT WING. RIGHT WING.

17 McLean 18 Gray 19 Massey

20 Ramsay 21 Meredith

22 Draper

Kick-off at 3.30 p.m. LEYTON.

GOAL.

Referee: MR. TEARLE.

LEFT: The programme for our initial Southern League match, and RIGHT: for the match at Leyton on April 7 1906 where Palace clinched the championship of the division by beating their closest rivals.

Davies, to become the first Club to claim that trophy twice in succession, but it was the League title we wanted and which we so nearly won. By early 1914 it was clear that the race was between ourselves and Swindon Town. It was always close and the lead changed hands (or should we say, 'feet'?!) several times, but in the last month of the season Swindon had a slightly better goalscoring record, so that the last Saturday was reached with them ahead of us only on goal-average, and everything hinged on the results of the final matches of the season. We were at Gillingham, Swindon at Cardiff.

Truth to tell we did not play at all well at Gillingham and fell behind in the first half. Ted Smith put us level when he ran from inside his own half, but we could not get a winner — and then learnt that Swindon had fought out a 0-0 draw in Wales. The Club and its supporters were bitterly disappointed to be denied the highest honour by such a slender margin, but true sportsmanship was revealed in the way that a telegram was immediately sent off from our headquarters to Swindon bearing our congratulations to the Robins on winning the championship in spite of our best efforts.

The Palace probably had a more difficult time in 1914-15 than most clubs. The Admiralty requisitioned the Crystal Palace and closed it to the public in February 1915, so that we could no longer play there. Several Southern League clubs offered their grounds to complete the home fixtures but the directors decided to move across to the Herne Hill running track, where distinguished amateurs West Norwood had their base.

With little real support Ted Smith kept on scoring goals for us and it was as well that he did. He notched up 21 out of our none too grand total of 47 which was probably the only creditable thing about 1914-15 at the Palace, although future skipper Albert Feebery had arrived and was making a reasonable deputy for Harry Hanger at left-half.

Perversely, (but not untypically) the Palace had their best spell of the entire term, comprising four straight wins, late in the season in April, but this was long after it was clear that the best we could hope to achieve was a place near the top of the lower half of the division (we actually finished 15th out of twenty clubs), and by then virtually everyone's interest lay in a far greater contest being fought out in Europe.

ABOVE: Four Palace heroes from the 1905-06 championship season in contemporary cigarette cards. CENTRE: A wonderul cartoon depicting Palace's amazing victory at Newcastle in the FA Cup in January 1907. The 'Glazier' figure is a play on the distinctive towers at each end of the great Crystal Palace building. Another hugely impressive victory followed at Brentford in round three . . . to pair Palace with Everton in the quarter final. Palace approached the tie with confidence! BELOW: A goalmouth incident from the Palace-Swindon encounter at the Crystal Palace in October 1913. Palace captain Harry Hanger is airborne and the immortal Harold Fleming of Swindon and England is immediately to his left, while the head of Palace pivot Jimmy Hughes is visible behind three players.

LEFT: Horace Astley — scorer of the 1907 FA Cup goals which beat Newcastle and took Everton to a replay. CENTRE: Action from the Palace-Everton Cup-tie at the Crystal Palace. Horace Astley's opportunism records the opening goal for Palace. BELOW: Ted Smith scoring with a diving header against Reading at the Crystal Palace in November 1913 (5-1). Bill Davies, who provided the cross, is over on the right wing. RIGHT: Three Palace stars who featured in our splendid Southern League teams before the 1st World War: 'Ginger' Williams, a mighty popular winger or centre-forward, full-back Harry Collyer and prolific goalscorer, Ted Smith.

World War I

Football during the hostilities was frowned upon, to say the least, by the authorities and as a result coverage of the sport is tantalisingly brief in the newspapers of the period. Some clubs actually suspended operations entirely for the duration of the War but the Palace administration does not appear to have even considered such a step. The formation of the London Combination for the 1915-16 season, with the provision of matches against the top Football League sides in the metropolis, was a positive reaction and unquestionably welcomed by ourselves and the other Southern League clubs in the capital.

Naturally, most of the players became engaged in war work of some kind although sometimes this turned out to the Club's advantage, as for example in the case of Horace Colclough, who was still available to play for the Palace until October 1916 because he was serving somewhere in the vicinity as a despatch rider in the Royal Engineers. However, most of the familiar names were missing and, like all the other clubs, use was made of players from other League teams who were stationed nearby. Frequently, as the War progressed, there were Palace sides which did not contain a single pre-war Palace player.

It was inevitable that there would be more than the occasional farcical result: Palace's worst came towards the end of the war with a 0-11 hiding inflicted by West Ham in April 1918, in which Sid Puddefoot hit seven goals for the Hammers. Twice we conceded eight goals; twice again it was seven. Our best was a 10-1 victory over Reading in March 1916.

Taken overall, the Palace performed creditably enough for a Southern League side in the London Combination, although it would be futile to deny that the balance of results went against us. Our best overall performance in the four years of competition was to finish sixth in a fourteen match supplementary tournament in the spring of 1916 — but the mood of footballers and football authorities at that dreadful time can be best understood in the context of the deaths of Club captain Harry Hanger and former favourites 'Ginger' Williams and Joe Bulcock.

However, as far as Crystal Palace FC was concerned there was some better news during the War — the Club found a new home. The Nest opposite Selhurst Station had been the ground of Croydon Common since 1908 but the Robins had ceased to function after the end of the 1915-16 season and the Nest remained untenanted for two years until the Palace took out a lease from the London, Brighton and South Coast Railway Company, dated 27 June 1918, and played the last of the 1st World War seasons there.

It was poignant that, during that 1918-19 season, half a dozen or so games were played for the Palace by a strong and highly capable full-back, formerly at the Nest with Croydon Common — Jack Little. Jack was a regular member of the Common team which won the championship of the Southern League 2nd Division in 1914, with the remarkable record of only conceding 14 goals in 30 games, and he was to become an integral part of the Palace defensive line-ups right through to 1926, so that well over half his 242 League appearances for us were actually in Division Two of the Football League — and that after he had played in every game in the 3rd Division championship season of 1920-21.

Finding a worthy post-war successor to Joe Johnson, Palace's superb goalkeeper between 1907-15, was obviously going to be an enormously difficult task, but Palace manager, Edmund Goodman, actually discovered an even better one!

Jack Alderson hailed from Crook, in County Durham, but was stationed at Woolwich in the latter stages of the War and it was while he was there that he guested for the Palace during the late winter and spring of 1919, and signed professional forms for us immediately after leaving the Forces.

LEFT: Jack Little. RIGHT: Palace's new home from 1918. An early picture of The Nest. BELOW: The famous painting by R. Caton Woodville of the attack on the German defences by the East Surrey Regiment on 1 July 1916, dribbling a football through 'no-man's land'. This heroic band must have included supporters of Crystal Palace FC.

Tall, lean, and almost cadaverous, Jack was a goalkeeper of the highest class. He played 205 first-class games for us and is one of only two Palace goalkeepers to have gained a full England cap. Jack helped to form one of Palace's best-ever defences in 1920-21, when we won the 3rd Division championship, and that was to be our best defensive record for over half a century. He became a phenomenal penalty-saver later in his career with us in Division Two and, in an era when media coverage was restrained at best, the praise that was showered on Jack also demonstrates his greatness.

The high spot of Jack's career in one sense was the international cap he earned for England against France in Paris (4-1) in May 1923, but in another it was perhaps on a far less spectacular occasion, at a Palace game soon after the end of the War. A youthful soldier, struck dumb from shell-shock in the trenches, was behind Jack's goal when one particularly brilliant piece of goalkeeping so enthralled him that his speech was instantly restored.

'The Nest' at Selhurst, formerly tenanted by Croydon Common. Here's a Jim Mercer cartoon about the Robins.

"OVER THE TOP— AND THE BEST OF LUCK."

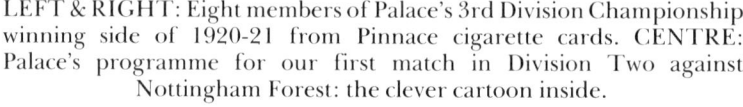

LEFT & RIGHT: Eight members of Palace's 3rd Division Championship winning side of 1920-21 from Pinnace cigarette cards. CENTRE: Palace's programme for our first match in Division Two against Nottingham Forest: the clever cartoon inside.

Palace Progress

Naturally, it was back to Southern League duty for Crystal Palace FC in August 1919 and inevitably we started with a line-up bearing small comparison with the ones of the immediate pre-war days, although captain was again the prolific Ted Smith. Partly due to Ted's 19 goals from 31 appearances Palace fared well in the Southern League championship, but Ted's efforts were now augmented by dapper little Scottish Junior International inside-forward, John Conner, who totted up 18 League goals. As a result the Palace finished third in the Southern League in May 1920, just two points behind champions Portsmouth.

But perhaps the feature of the immediate post-war Palace side most remembered was the defensive triumvirate of Jack Alderson in goal, Jack Little at right-back and Ernie Rhodes on the left. Ernie had been at the Palace longer than his two colleagues, having joined us in the summer of 1913, but it was only now that he made his major contribution. Those who saw these three men play together tell of an understanding that bordered on the uncanny: they were first in the same Palace line-up for our second game of the 1919-20 season and none of them missed a single fixture in League, Cup or friendly matches for one hundred games! Ernie was strong, in the mould of traditional '20s full backs, but he was always cool under pressure and had a keen eye for the volleyed clearance, so that it was entirely fitting when the Football League honoured him with a place in one of its representative sides in the autumn of 1921.

It was agreed in May 1920 that the clubs in the Southern League first division should comprise a new Football League third division for 1920-21. In fact Cardiff City (who finished 1919-20 one place below the Palace!) were admitted to the second division while Grimsby Town, who had been bottom of the second, joined the Palace and the rest in division three and Palace made it a triumphant entry!

It has to be admitted there was no immediate indication of success for, when the 1920-21 season opened on 28 August, the Palace were down in South Wales at Pennydarren Park, home of Merthyr Town, where they lost by the odd goal in three. The mid-week home game, against Plymouth — the first Football League fixture to be hosted at the Nest — remained scoreless, but the Palace then made their intentions and abilities clear for all to see with a run of six consecutive victories.

However, come early November, with the Palace well to the fore in the race for the title, possible disaster struck. A midweek match against Southend at the Nest saw the Palace in considerable difficulties. Skipper Ted Smith had to spend some time off the field after an injury, Southend played a pretty physical game with their right-back, Reid, twice cautioned by the referee (rare in those days, and virtually equivalent to a dismissal today). In the end the Palace were unable to get back on terms and we lost 2-3 but the frustration was too much for some supporters, who swarmed on to the pitch and surrounded the visitors' worst offender in an ugly mood.

Retribution from the FA soon followed — not only had we lost the match and the points to Southend but the Nest was to be closed for two weeks, including Palace's home game against Exeter at the end of November: we were in fact forced to play this match at Southampton, although actually the Palace won it 2-1. There was a touch of intended irony when the band played *Home, Sweet Home* upon the Palace's return to the Nest in mid-December, but we lost the match against Swansea (0-1) and our Northern Ireland international wing-half, Roy McCracken, with a broken leg, so that the last few weeks of 1920 were far from easy and there was still no real hint of what was to follow.

In the end the 3rd Division championship was won because of a magnificent run-in to the season. After losing at Grimsby on the first Saturday in February the Palace beat the Mariners in the midweek return, to begin an undefeated sequence of sixteen games, including eight consecutive victories before Easter, which took us to the brink of success. The vital pair of fixtures proved to be the ones against Southampton, who were our closest rivals for the title. On Easter Monday, back at the Dell, we fell behind in the 75th minute in front of a 21,000 crowd who broke the railings behind the Milton Road goal and tumbled out onto the pitch; fortunately nobody was hurt. Jack Alderson kept us alive with some brave saves before one of Palace's great unsung heroes secured the equaliser with the last kick of the game. Phil Bates was his name and his lob deceived the Southampton defence as it looped into the net.

Phil was one of the bravest men ever to play for our Club. He had suffered a nasty injury to his right arm while on active service and it became quite useless, hanging limp and withered at his side. He was a splendid attacking centre-half and played in all but the opening two matches of this 3rd Division championship season. He was unable to risk playing again after the end of the season because a blow on the injured limb would have had severe repercussions, though the esteem in which he was held by the Club and the fans of the time was demonstrated by two well-supported benefit matches willingly staged.

At the Nest the following afternoon Southampton again forged ahead, in the first half this time, but intense pressure in the second period brought Palace an equaliser, lashed home with a few minutes to go by our tough little inside left, Alf Wood.

Three more drawn games followed, but a 5-1 demolition of Northampton on a heavy, slippery pitch in the last home match made promotion all but certain, then a point from the return at the Cobblers' headquarters (2-2) left no doubt. The Palace were champions of Division 3 and had thereby secured a place among some of the great names in the game in Division Two!

Manager Edmund Goodman made several signings in the summer of 1921, though these were more to deepen the pool of talent available than to change the formation. Most significant of the new arrivals were goalkeeper George Irwin, who proved an able deputy for Jack Alderson, Harry Dreyer, a resolute half-back, and a pint-sized inside or centre-forward called Albert Harry — of whom much more will be heard.

Following some much-needed ground improvements, the Nest was made ready for 2nd Division football. The highly attractive visitors for the opening game, Nottingham Forest, pulled in an estimated attendance of some 20,000 — a new ground record — many of them eager to see at first hand the famous England goalkeeper Sam Hardy make his Forest debut.

But this was to be Palace's afternoon: the team played probably their best game in Division Two during 1921-25 and, once ahead, became quite invincible so that even the great goalkeeper was powerless to stem the tide. J. T. Jones, Palace's Welsh international centre-half, gave us the lead after 25 minutes with a powerful header that left Hardy grasping nothing but air and, even though Forest equalised, we had restored our lead through John Conner before the break with another headed effort. Then in the second half Ted Smith put us in full command following a clever move initiated by Roy McCracken, before winger John Whibley dribbled through from the halfway line, outpacing the Forest defence, drawing Hardy, then lashing the ball past him for a glorious goal.

Forest soon recovered from this opening day setback. Not only did they beat us (1-2) in the return match a week later, but they comfortably won the 2nd Division championship. For the Palace it was a marvellous victory, but it did not lead to any lasting success among the more illustrious company of Division Two, although we again reached the final of the London Challenge Cup, losing this time to Arsenal, by a single goal.

Without question, however, that 1921-22 season will always be remembered as the one in which the Palace secured their finest ever result in the FA Cup.

Drawn to meet 1st Division Everton at Goodison Park in the old 1st round in early January, the Palace cannot have contemplated the tie with much enthusiasm or confidence for, after all, the Toffees were a pedigree club, their side was enjoying a good run and we had been beaten twice before at Goodison in cup-ties in pretty comprehensive fashion.

The Palace not only won at Everton, they did so in riotous fashion — they won 6-0 against one of the leading clubs in the country! Just 18 months out of the Southern League and here they were sinking a 1st Division outfit without trace at their own distinguished headquarters. The impact of that result upon the footballing fraternity cannot be assimilated today — to merely say that it was a shock is to undervalue it. The contemporary press extolled us as a 'wonder-team' and that is roughly the modern-day equivalent of screaming headlines and excessive media hype. But it was, without question, a fabulous victory and is still, arguably, the Club's best result in any Cup-tie.

How did they do it? Unquestionably it was one of those days when everything went right for one side, but it is clear that the Palace were seldom on the defensive and actually had a couple more efforts disallowed for offside and another that hit the bar, so that Jack Alderson was able to calmly peel and eat an orange at one stage of the proceedings.

John Whibley started the rout, when he headed in Ben Bateman's corner in only the fourth minute and, when Croydon-born Bert Menlove's shot was deflected into the Everton net midway through the first half, an upset began to look a real possibility and Everton's original complacency was obviously wearing somewhat thin. The home side rallied in front of their own fans, but they proved quite unable to break through our sterling defence and it was left to the Palace to round matters off with four more goals in the last quarter. John Conner converted a Whibley centre, then Menlove headed home another cross. Alf Wood made it five and, after Everton had missed a penalty, John Conner completed matters five minutes from time.

The *Athletic News* regarded the result as a 'sensation' — but then felt that the Palace were 'likely to make good progress in the competition'. Regrettably, if that august journal was correct in its former assessment it was wrong in the latter: we were held 0-0 at the Nest by Millwall in the next round in front of a massed 25,000 crowd but went out 0-2 in the replay.

It was probably by virtue of his performance in the Everton Cup-tie and the publicity that surrounded it, that Bert Menlove was brought to the attentions of aspiring 1st Division Sheffield United, to whom he moved a couple of months later, to be replaced at the Nest by George Whitworth, who had 'guested' for us during the 1st World War and now joined us from Northampton Town, scoring a debut goal at Bury (2-1) on 18 March. Another goalscoring debut occurred a week later when little Albert Harry notched a brace in the return against the Shakers at the Nest from his original position of centre-forward. One of them was a header too! From that moment the Palace crowd had a new favourite whom they were to cheer for the next twelve years.

The summer of 1922 saw news circulate of the land the Palace were about to purchase for their new ground — later to be dubbed 'Selhurst Park' — while Mr Goodman negotiated probably the most complex transfer in the Club's history. No fewer than six players were involved in an exchange with 2nd Division rivals Coventry City. J. T. Jones, along with inside-forwards Tom Storey and Alf Wood, moved to the Midlands, while in return the Palace welcomed centre-half Bert Millard, full-back Charlie Cross and, later in the summer, inside-left Billy Morgan. The last two were typically inspired Goodman signings. Cross took over from 'Dusty' Rhodes at left-back early in the season and made a fine partner for Jack

Little, going on to play 221 League games for us, while Morgan made a more explosive contribution. He became a useful goalscorer in the ensuing two seasons, while fully justifying the £500 fee we had outlayed to acquire him in one match alone.

However, successes were few and far between for the Palace in 1922-23. George Whitworth scored 17 League goals from 36 games but the big centre-forward had little support from elsewhere. The few highlights of the term came towards its finish.

A heavy defeat at Leeds (1-4) was followed by a Good Friday reverse at the Nest by champions-elect Notts County (0-1) and very much worse occurred the next afternoon when West Ham, who pushed County all the way for the championship and finished as runners-up, administered a 1-5 hiding. And Easter Monday saw us led, so it would seem, like lambs to the slaughter, for the return against exuberant County up at Meadow Lane.

Well, we hung on in the first half and were pleased enough to reach the dressing room at half-time with the scoresheet still blank and dignity at least somewhat restored. But then we slammed in three goals in eight minutes in the second period and went on to win 4-0, appearing well-nigh invincible at times.

Four weeks later, in our last home game, we added further woe to relegated Wolves by scorching to a 5-0 victory, although in fairness it should be added that Wolves beat us by a single goal in the final match of the season at Molineux.

It had originally been hoped that the Palace could move into Selhurst Park for the 1923-24 season, but that had proved optimistic and Football League soccer continued at the Nest as before. The Nest had been a happy and successful arena for the Palace, and was to continue so in this season but, while the playing area was perfectly adequate in size, it was inclined to become heavy after wet weather and a lot of unkind things were said about it. The Nest was never an easy ground on which to see from the terraces and the press seats in the stand got drenched when it rained, thus reducing the correspondents' copy to pulp! An added hazard in winter was the smoke from the nearby shunting engines, which mingled with any fog or mist and caused loss of visibility. The Palace did well there but it is easy to see why the Club was eager to move to Selhurst Park.

A lot of interest was generated in the summer of 1923 by the Palace signing of Chelsea centre-forward Tom Hoddinott. Tom was a Welsh international, tall, slim and possessing pace and elegance. With 13 goals this season, he and George Whitworth (16) made a good striking pair, but this was to be the only season in which Tom showed his true ability for us.

Although the Palace finished up just one place better off in Division Two, 1923-24 was much more evenly balanced than its immediate predecessor. It only took the Palace three matches to gain their first victory this time (4-3 at Port Vale to avenge an opening day defeat (1-2) at the Nest), but our top 2nd Division performances this season were in the month or so before Christmas.

Tom Hoddinott's best game for the Palace occurred when title challengers Stoke City came to the Nest on 24 November. Tom put on a great display, hit a first half hat-trick himself, led his line with vision and verve in a fog-shrouded game and helped Palace to a morale-boosting 5-1 victory. Our next win came three weeks later against The Wednesday. This time George Whitworth scored our three goals in a convincing victory. True enough we lost 0-6 at Hillsborough a week later, but captain Albert Feebery was badly injured and never able to play again. Undoubtedly it was Whitworth's hat-trick in the first match which had so impressed the Wednesday officials that they eventually signed him at the end of the following season.

Able to step immediately into the strong, driving wing-half role held since pre-war days but now vacated by Albert Feebery, was young Bob Greener who had joined us from the north-east a couple of years before. Bob was to have a fabulous Palace career over the next decade as a player with 317 first-team appearances and then, subsequently, as club trainer and on the ground staff, eventually totalling 34 years' service.

However, the Palace reserved their finest performance of 1923-24 for an FA Cup-tie. Tottenham, from the higher reaches of Division One, were our illustrious visitors for a 1st round encounter at the Nest on 12 January 1924. The heavy pitch soon cut up and a typical Cup match ensued with plenty of excitement and drama for the 17,000 fans so that it became clear that either a piece of sheer brilliance from the sophisticated North Londoners, or some opportunist finishing by the Palace would settle the matter.

The breakthrough came just after half an hour. Roy McCracken won the ball and slipped a pass to Albert Harry, who had a marvellous match. The little winger was away. He beat 'Spurs' skipper, Arthur Grimsdell, tore past the left-back and cut in on goal before delivering a cross that was never more than a couple of feet off the ground. Several players went for it, but it was Billy Morgan, diving low among boots and studs, who got to it and glided a perfect header past the 'Spurs goalkeeper for an inspirational goal.

Ten minutes after the break it was all over, Billy Morgan finally netting from close range after shots from Hoddinott and Bill Hand had been blocked. Morgan was to do little more for the Palace in his career with us, but he had done enough in the 90 minutes against Tottenham to earn a permanent niche in any Palace chronicle. It also earned him possibly the most curious nickname ever accorded a Palace footballer — 'The Spurs Undertaker'. You don't have to be a parson to appreciate that one!

There was huge excitement at the Palace and in the wake of such a superb victory hopes were high of a run in the latter stages of the FA Cup competition. 1st Division Notts County were overcome (2-1) in a titanic struggle in the second round, after three goal-less draws and in the third replay of Palace's longest-ever Cup-tie. But disappointment was to follow for, when our old rivals from the 3rd Division, Swindon Town, came to the Nest for the 3rd round at the end of February, they also came from behind to dismiss us with a brilliant recovery initiated by the great Harold Fleming.

Although the Palace then also lost their next home game (against Oldham, 2-3) the season proceeded to its conclusion in positive enough style as we won four and drew the other two of the remaining matches at the Nest. The finale, a 3-1 success over Barnsley in the last fixture, was a fitting and appropriate farewell to that ground which had served the Club so well.

Selhurst Park was formerly a brickfield, with two chimney stacks on the site of the present-day playing pitch. It had cost the Palace £2,570 back in 1922. The ground was designed by Archibald Leitch, probably the leading authority on football stadia at that time, and built by Messrs Humphreys of Knightsbridge to a contract valued at something over £30,000. Unfortunately, however, an industrial dispute delayed work on the main stand so much, that some of the seats and other fittings were incomplete when it was opened prior to our first match of 1924-25 against The Wednesday on 30 August 1924.

The ceremonial opening took place a few minutes before the teams ran out on to the pitch. Sir Louis Newton, Lord Mayor of London, undertook that responsibility and was accompanied by Mr Sidney Bourne and Mr F. J. Nettlefold, Palace's Chairman and President respectively, and by the other directors. The ceremony itself consisted of the cutting of claret and blue ribbons across the entry to the original players' tunnel, followed by a brief speech from the Lord Mayor.

Although the 2nd Division of 1924-25 contained several other great clubs it is difficult to imagine more select opposition for the opening game at Selhurst Park, because The Wednesday line-up was packed with pedigree players, including six present or future internationals.

However, another international who might have been expected to appear was conspicuous by his absence, for Jack Alderson had refused to re-sign, because the Club would not allow him the Benefit match to which he believed he was entitled; it was a great pity that such a fine performer should leave in such acrimonious circumstances.

His replacement was Billy Harper, formerly with Manchester City and Sunderland, and no mean goalkeeper, but comparison with Alderson was not really possible until Billy Callender had taken over and grown to maturity a season or so later.

The match against The Wednesday attracted a crowd of some 25,000 to the new stadium, more than double the number to have seen the same fixture at the Nest in the previous two seasons, but most of them were in for a disappointing afternoon, because a goal conceded just four minutes after the start was sufficient to defeat us. It was scored by Wednesday's inside-right Joe Marsden, their close-season signing from Sunderland. To be honest, it appears that Wednesday controlled the game from that moment and were clearly in a class above our favourites, although the Palace did have opportunities to get on terms, only to spurn them all, and we hastened our own downfall by being much too elaborate in front of goal.

To their credit, the Palace quickly shrugged aside the disappointment of defeat against The Wednesday and soon strung together a series of creditable results. Only two days later they went to Coventry and secured an impressive 4-1 victory, while our next home game, against Hull City (1-0), saw us record our first success at our new headquarters. By early October we were in the top third of the table — by 1 November we were fifth after despatching Derby County (2-0).

High spot of the season was the return fixture against The Wednesday, in Sheffield, two days after Christmas, where we won a match played in pouring rain and on a quagmire of a pitch with a perfectly taken goal by George Whitworth two minutes before half time.

The Palace side had benefitted in those autumn and winter months from the inclusion at centre-half of ex-guardsman Jimmy Hamilton. Jimmy was a dominating figure at the heart of our defence and had a lot to do with our progress in the first half of 1924-25. He was to have a grand career with the Palace, totalling nearly 200 appearances, so that it can be clearly argued that the nasty eye injury he sustained when Blackpool were our visitors at the end of February, which rendered him unavailable for virtually the rest of the season, was a major reason for the disaster story which follows.

Palace's results in the second half of the season showed an alarming deterioration and we slipped down the table. The decline proved impossible to arrest and, by the time the season drew towards its climax, we were in grave danger after Good Friday and Easter Saturday defeats at Selhurst Park by Stoke and Barnsley (both 0-1). Palace bravely extracted a point at Stoke (1-1) in the Easter Monday return, but then crumbled badly at Wolves (1-3) in our last away game on Saturday 18 April.

Still, the Palace programme finished with two home matches and it seemed that a couple of points from these games would be sufficient to keep us in the 2nd Division. Thus, on 25 April 1925 Fulham came to Selhurst Park and Palace's hopes soared when Cecil Blakemore gave us a 20th minute lead. However, before half-time, Fulham were level and then they forged ahead. With little time remaining the Palace surged forward in a final onslaught and, when Albert Harry crossed the ball, it appeared to be handled by a Fulham defender. The referee pointed to the penalty spot, but was immediately engulfed by the visiting team. They persuaded him to consult a linesman (less well positioned than himself) and, having done so, the decision was reversed, a goal kick was signalled and Palace's hopes of salvaging a precious point were lost.

That weak decision by the official, allied to the fact that two of the other stragglers, Oldham and Barnsley, both won, meant that the scene was set for a climactic finale, for

Palace's last match of all was home to Oldham — and we had to win it to survive.

The atmosphere at Palace's opening match at Selhurst Park had been festive: for the dramatic show-down against Oldham on 2 May it was laden with tension, even before the teams appeared in front of a crowd variously estimated at between 15,000 and 20,000. Palace made four changes from the side beaten by Fulham, but the most significant one was the inclusion of the young Billy Callender in goal for his first senior appearance of the season.

For 75 minutes the battle raged without a goal and, it must be admitted, the demands of the occasion appeared to be too much for our men. We were tight enough in defence, but over-anxious in front of goal and neither side troubled the goalkeepers.

With a quarter of an hour, or fractionally less, remaining, there came the fatal blow. Oldham's outside-right had always been their most dangerous player and now he managed to get over a low centre in spite of the attentions of Charlie Cross and Joe Nixon. Oldham's centre-forward was ideally positioned and he turned the ball fiercely goalwards, though accounts vary as to whether it was a header or a shot. Callender rose in a valiant effort to try to tip it away — he managed to get a touch, but not enough to sufficiently deflect it. The death thrust had been administered and Selhurst Park was as quiet as any tomb as Palace's first season there ended in bitter disappointment.

Palace's programme writer of the day said that it would be a calamity if we were to be relegated, and who would argue that he had exaggerated, for it took the Palace 39 years to restore 2nd Division football to Selhurst Park.

If Palace's first season at Selhurst Park had ended in such disappointment the only way to describe the beginning of the next one is 'horrific'! With the 1925-26 term just three weeks old, relegated Palace had lost all five of their fixtures back among their old 3rd Division contemporaries, with an adverse goal aggregate of 5-16 and we appeared to be in real trouble. Certainly we lacked confidence and a reliable goalscorer, but Manager-secretary Edmund Goodman had weathered previous crises and he knew exactly the man he wanted.

His name was Percy Cherrett. He was a strong, bustling centre-forward with a proven goalscoring record and he was languishing in the Plymouth Argyle reserve team. He made his Palace debut at Brighton on 19 September (2-3), but the following Wednesday Percy made his first appearance at Selhurst Park and our fans warmed to him immediately as the big man scored a couple of goals and tore Bristol City's defence to ribbons while Palace ran out 5-2 winners. The next Saturday we romped to a 4-0 victory over Watford, three of them coming from Percy Cherrett headers, and in the end he finished that season with 26 strikes from 35 League appearances, having formed an exciting goal-scoring partnership with Cecil Blakemore, the pair thriving on the splendid service provided by wingers Albert Harry and the newly-signed flame-haired outside-left George Clarke.

Two particular matches at Selhurst Park in which Percy starred were of lasting interest to Palace fans. On Saturday 28 November 1925 Palace and Plymouth figured in an amazing 5-5 draw on a snow-covered pitch to record the highest scoring draw ever played on our ground in a first-class game, while one of the great occasions at our headquarters took place on Saturday 30 January 1926 when the Palace beat Chelsea 2-1 in a 4th round FA Cup-tie and set up an attendance record of 41,000, which was to last for nearly 40 years! I am sure readers can guess who it was put the Palace on the road to that superb result with a magnificent performance while also scoring a quality first goal!

Cherrett, in fact, was the last major signing made for the Palace by Mr Edmund Goodman, for that worthy gentleman retired from the post of manager at our Club in December 1925. Of course he continued as secretary, but he was succeeded as manager by Mr Alex Maley, who joined from Hibernian in Edinburgh and began a policy of recruiting men from north of the border. Probably Mr Maley's most successful signing was that of Scottish International full-back, Bobby Orr, from Greenock Morton, who joined us for 1926-27 and went on to make 70 League appearances for us over two seasons.

Another event of moment in the 1925-26 season at Selhurst Park remains unique in the Club annals as the only full England International match to be played here for, on St David's Day, 1 March 1926, England met Wales before a splendid Monday afternoon crowd of over 23,000. To the delight of a large Welsh contingent the visitors won 3-1 and were much the better side on the day.

Palace's second season at Selhurst Park coincided with the time when the offside law was altered. The earlier rule which required three men to be between the receiving player and the opponents' goal-line was amended so that now only two men were required. The immediate effect of the alteration was a great increase in the number of goals scored because it naturally took defences everywhere some while to adjust. Unfortunately, while the Palace were able to score goals as freely as most clubs — certainly after Percy Cherrett's arrival — we also found it impossible to stem the tide at the other end, and this was never better demonstrated than in the amazing 5th round FA Cup-tie in which we took part at Manchester City as the reward for having beaten Chelsea in the previous round.

Try to imagine how you would feel upon hearing that your side was losing 0-7 at half-time! Or what emotions you would display upon having travelled nearly 200 miles — yes, there were some loyal Palace fans at Maine Road who had taken advantage of a special train ticket — and then watched your favourites go seven goals in arrears within the opening 40 minutes! Thankfully, it does not happen often.

To their great credit the Palace rallied well after the break. Percy Cherrett got a couple. George Clarke notched a third and Roy McCracken netted from a melée following a Cecil Blakemore penalty which had hit the bar for 4-8, but City scored three more themselves to run out 11-4 winners and send a stunned Palace contingent back to the capital surely wondering what had happened.

The Palace team of 1926-27 was certainly more consistent than predecessors of recent seasons, and for the first time in five years we won the opening game of the season with a goal each from Percy Cherrett (a header) and Cecil Blakemore (overhead bicycle kick in the last minute), proving too much for Queens Park Rangers at Selhurst Park, although the visitors had netted within 30 seconds of the first whistle.

Even if we lost only once in the first eight games, that still left us two points and five places adrift of the leaders at the end of September — the old 3rd Division South was a hard taskmaster!

We eventually finished in sixth place, but it was nowhere really because we were no fewer than 17 points behind the champions, Bristol City. 1926-27 was aptly summed up in that the number of goals we scored — 84 of them — was only exceeded by four clubs, whereas just five defences conceded more goals than our own.

Coming to the fore at the Palace were two men who were to feature for many years and play major parts in the Selhurst Park story between the wars — Billy Turner and George Clarke.

Although Billy Turner was not a great goalscorer, everyone who saw him play for us is agreed that he helped to make hundreds. There was also no doubt that right-winger Albert Harry played much better with Billy there beside him at inside-right, or behind him at right-half and, under Turner's neat and shrewd direction, our forwards could become quite devastating.

Billy became known to Palace fans as 'Rubber', and certainly his resilience and adaptability were an unusual feature of those pre-war days, for later in his career he played both as a wing-half and as a full-back; indeed the only positions Billy never filled at the Palace were those of goalkeeper, centre-forward and centre-half! He was not a showman or a flamboyant character: he simply won the hearts of the Palace clientele with his whole-hearted and full-blooded displays in over 300 first team matches.

It is virtually certain that, if George Clarke had come to the Palace even a month before the end of the fateful 1924-25 season, we would never have been relegated. He was a magnificent winger: a ball player with plenty of craft and pace, clever and with a lethal shot — skills that have etched his name for all time into the Palace record books. He remains to this day among our leading League goalscorers, and few proven strikers have ever improved upon his 99 League goals. Of course, no winger has ever approached them.

George is best remembered as a provider of chances from which our centre-forwards could score. Big Percy Cherrett fed off him for two seasons but, as we shall see, it was Peter Simpson who benefitted most from the work of the talented left-winger, and it is no coincidence that Peter scored more goals in each of the three campaigns in which Clarke was his team-mate than in any succeeding season.

Palace's start to the 1927-28 season in Division 3 was poor and even if a run of misfortune in the matter of injuries was partly to blame, there was still no excuse for a pair of 1-6 defeats, at Southend in mid-September and at Luton a month later, so that when the Palace were knocked out of the London Challenge Cup by their old amateur rivals Leyton on 12 October there was nothing for it but for manager Mr Maley to resign.

Under Mr Goodman's temporary charge there was no immediate improvement, at least not until we dispensed a 5-0 hiding to visiting Charlton who had previously been undefeated on the afternoon of bonfire night, then followed up with a creditable point from a 3-3 thriller at Swindon and another home win, 2-0 this time, over Newport County.

Thus when Mr Fred Mavin, formerly the manager at Exeter City, took up his responsibilities at Selhurst Park in late November, the worst of the tide had been turned, but the new boss inspired the team to a much better all-round performance in the remainder of the season so that we were able to finish 1927-28 in fifth place.

The season was a huge success for George Clarke, who registered 22 League goals from his 40 appearances out on the left-wing — a record not only unsurpassed, but never even threatened by any Palace winger in the years since then. 1927-28 also saw the arrival of centre or inside forward Harry Havelock at the beginning of November. Strong and well built, Harry was a useful goalscorer for the Palace, but he was most unlucky with injuries upon his arrival. Having scored twice upon his debut against Charlton, he had to miss the next League game at Swindon; then, two weeks later, he sustained such a nasty leg injury in the FA Cup-tie at Dartford (3-1) that he did not re-appear for us for ten months. But Harry's 39 League goals for the Palace from 67 games tell of a striker of some ability and a valuable acquisition.

Manager Fred Mavin spent a busy summer in the transfer market on behalf of Crystal Palace during the 1928 close season.

It was from his former club, Exeter City, that he obtained the skipper of his restructured Palace side, full-back Stan Charlton, who had won the respect of Palace fans with his displays against us for the Grecians and was to go on to become a top-class defender for the Palace over the next four seasons. Alongside Stan was another new boy, Tom Crilly, who joined us with two more players from Derby County, inside-forward Jimmy Gill and veteran centre-half Harry Thoms, and became a lynch-pin in Palace defences for five years. The partnership betwen Crilly and Charlton grew into a most attractive feature of Palace line-ups and it was certainly significant, that during the period they were together at Selhurst Park, we were able to make two serious assaults on the divisional table.

From Torquay United came Lewis Griffiths, a suave little Welshman who possessed an instinct for goals. He netted on his Palace debut, our third match of the season, to help beat relegated Fulham 2-1 at Selhurst Park, then hit a brace to gain us a point from the return at Craven Cottage the following week (2-2), but an injury sustained in that game kept him out till nearly Christmas and, since Lewis scored 18 goals from his 27 Division 3 South matches, his three months absence proved crucial.

Another goalscorer, arrived from Chorley, was inside-left Hubert Butler. In this 1928-29 season Hubert was more of a provider for Lewis Griffiths and Harry Havelock, though he contributed ten goals himself, including a hat-trick at Brighton (5-1) on the Saturday before Christmas, but later in his Palace career he developed into a mainstream striker in his own right.

The side thus assembled by Mr Mavin soon showed that it was capable of at least holding its own in Division 3 South but, like many of its contemporaries, it was far more adept at scoring goals than preventing them, as witness the autumn run of five consecutive defeats, three of them at home and an awful 1-8 mauling at Northampton.

However, relief was at hand for there then joined us a tall, slim, elegant and totally dominating centre-half who was to become a household name in South London and Croydon, 'Jimmy' Wilde. Jimmy immediately cemented our defence and, even in this his first season, looked a most accomplished defender. He made his debut in a testing 1st round FA Cup-tie which brought Kettering Town, champions of the Southern League (Eastern section) to Selhurst Park with a centre-forward who had gained quite a reputation, one Peter Simpson no less! But Jimmy played Peter in immaculate style, the Palace went through 2-0 and Jimmy had earmarked that centre-half spot for his own. The Palace then embarked upon a 17 match unbeaten run in Division 3 South (never yet improved upon within a single season) and, from mid-table, began to look like possible champions, moving to within a point of the top after Easter.

The competition was fierce. With a month of the season remaining at least six clubs had serious aspirations, the Palace now clearly among them. None of them were able to sustain the run of good results which would have settled the issue and, come the last week, a 2-1 win down at Exeter and a 3-0 success over Gillingham at Selhurst Park put us level with Charlton at the head of the table, with everything resting on the outcome of the matches on the final Saturday, 4 May 1929. Unfortunately, that string of autumn defeats had taken such a severe toll of our goal-average that, while Charlton were playing away up at Walsall, it was necessary for us to gain a point over them from our home game against Brighton.

A crowd of over 22,000 flocked to Selhurst Park for the climax, but Brighton provided such tough opposition that we were only able to edge in front *via* a 70th minute penalty converted by skipper Stan Charlton. The tension was almost tangible, because in those days there was no means whereby the crowd could know what was evolving elsewhere and that narrow lead, which became a victory, would have proved sufficient to take us back to Division Two if Charlton, as it began to be rumoured, had dropped a point in the Black Country. But then their commendable 2-0 victory was announced and it was realised that, near to success as the Palace had come, all had been in vain and we were still rooted in the 3rd Division.

An interesting aspect of the closing stages of the 1928-29 season was the signing, and then the inclusion in our League side, of several men from the Kettering Town team that had come to Selhurst Park to meet the Palace in the 1st round FA Cup-tie. Goalkeeper Jim Imrie and inside-forward Andy Dunsire joined us in March and played several games, but winger or centre-forward George Charlesworth made a bigger impact. However, the most significant signing from Kettering, delayed until June 1929, was that of the man who is still Palace's most prolific striker, the great Peter Simpson himself.

Peter Simpson must rate as one of the best signings ever made for the Palace for, like Ian Wright something over half a century later, he came to us from a non-league set-up, quickly established himself as an exciting goalscorer who could turn and win matches, became an enormous favourite with the fans at Selhurst Park and went on to establish Club records almost, it seemed, at will.

Peter's Palace debut crystallised his capacity and remains unique in the Club annals to this day, because no-one else has ever scored a Football League hat-trick on their debut for us. Palace were trailing to a Norwich City opener in an early season, mid-week game at Selhurst Park, but Peter equalised with a hard low drive from an Albert Harry cross around the half hour, headed our second from George Clarke's centre six minutes into the second half, then pressurised the goalkeeper into mishandling another of his headed efforts to provide the Palace with a 3-2 victory.

A Scotsman from Leith, Peter became a famed and feared goalscorer with the Palace: within his first season he secured a new Club record of 36 League goals and became the target for the biggest clubs. Come 1930-31 he was in phenomenal form, hitting 46 goals in Division 3 South, still the Club record for an individual striker in a single season, including six in succession in a 7-2 defeat of Exeter. He went on to top our scoring charts for each of his first five seasons, eventually totalling 165 first-class goals for us, so that, even 30 years after his retirement Peter was still a popular local figure in his newsagent/tobacconists shop at West Croydon. Really, his efforts for the Palace are quite exceptional, and his name will always rank among the Palace immortals.

Yet even with the benefit of the talents of Peter Simpson the Palace were not able to climb out of Division 3 South in 1929-30. The reasons were twofold. Firstly, when Peter Simpson was not scoring goals hardly anyone else was able to do so either: Harry Havelock was second top League scorer with just 12 strikes, then came Billy Turner with 5! The second problem was that, once again, we were leaking far too many goals at the back, 74 in total, and there is no way you can hope for success with that sort of burden.

Our defensive frailty was embarrassingly exposed in the FA Cup where the Palace were drawn to meet 1st Division Leeds United at Elland Road. We lost 1-8, although some mitigating circumstances existed because right-back Tom Weatherby was crocked early on and spent most of the game as a passenger, out on the right wing.

Making one of his early appearances for the Palace in that disaster at Leeds was former England amateur international outside-left, Laurie Fishlock, who had joined us from Dulwich Hamlet. Laurie was no mean footballer, but he was also a magnificent cricketer. He quickly became Surrey's left-handed opening batsman and played at The Oval for more than 20 years.

The Palace were always near the top of the Division 3 South table in 1930-31 but, bearing in mind that only the winners were promoted from the regional Divisions, we were never really near enough, although up front we were in fabulous form. Peter Simpson was virtually unstoppable: he hit five hat-tricks and a four as well as the six goal spree already mentioned. George Clarke totted up 21 from the wing and Hubert Butler contributed 14 at inside-left. Altogether we scored 107 League goals, easily the best in the division and only once bettered at our Club and then in 1960-61 with the aid of a longer programme of matches.

There was no question that the forward line of 1930-31 was Palace's best in the first 40 years of our Football League career and for sheer effectiveness ranks among the finest we have ever had. Albert Harry at outside-right was fast and direct, while inside him was either powerful Harry Havelock or the ever-green Billy Turner. Peter Simpson and Hubert Butler developed a fine understanding together, with George Clarke absolutely devastating out on the left.

Unfortunately for the Palace there was also in Division 3 South that season the team with the best defence in the entire Football League in Notts County and it was soon apparent that, no matter how many goals all the other teams might score, County were going to concede so few that no-one was capable of preventing them from winning the title race. The Palace-County games were interesting as the best goalscorers met the best defence: a 2-2 draw ensued up at Meadow Lane in early December while matters also finished even at the Palace in April (1-1). After this we finished with a flurry of four consecutive victories, including a 5-0 victory over Torquay in the last game of the season to clinch the runners-up spot for the second time in three years — but in spite of all we were still a 3rd Division club.

Important events during the 1930-31 season were the death of Chairman Sidney Bourne in September and a change of manager in October. Mr Bourne had served the Club supremely well from its inception and, until nearly the end of his life, was to be seen at Selhurst Park with his inevitable cigar and Palace rosette. At the match against Newport County the day after his passing the teams wore black arm bands and the flag was flown at half-mast, while the Palace scored a resounding 7-1 victory to provide just the sort of farewell the Chairman would have wished.

Almost exactly a month later, after the 5-2 defeat of Fulham, manager Fred Mavin resigned because of the ill-health of his wife. This was regarded as a severe loss, but within 48 hours the directors were able to announce the appointment of Mr Jack Tresadern, formerly an international wing-half with West Ham and Burnley and the manager of Northampton Town.

Typical of affairs in the 1930-31 season were Palace's two extraordinary Christmas clashes against London rivals, Brentford. The Bees had two former Palace men in their line-up at Griffin Park on Christmas morning, one of them being our old favourite Cecil Blakemore, and they ran us absolutely ragged. It was 1-5 by half-time and 2-8 at the end. The following afternoon at Selhurst Park saw a different state of affairs! George Clarke and Peter Simpson had us two up in ninety seconds. A Jimmy Wilde free-kick made it 3-0 just after half an hour and if Jack Lane (soon to be playing for the Palace) reduced Brentford's deficit before half-time, Albert Harry and George Clarke extended our advantage after the break to leave the Yuletide honours even and everyone somewhat breathless after the Festivities.

There was also plenty of interest in the FA Cup-ties, and certainly no shortage of goals. Non-league Taunton and Newark were both dismissed by 6-0 victories at Selhurst Park with Peter Simpson netting three, then four goals respectively. Two drawn matches against Reading led to a second replay at Stamford Bridge with Palace emerging triumphant, thanks to George Clarke and Peter Simpson goals in the last five minutes of extra time. That gave us a home-tie against Everton in round four just five days later — and an exact reversal of the 6-0 victory of 1922. 'Dixie' Dean got four of them, but Palace were depleted by an early injury to Billy Turner while Billy Callender and Bob Greener were notable absentees due to injuries sustained in the Reading replay.

LEFT: Wing-half Roy McCracken missed the second half of 1920-21 with a broken leg after gaining international honours with Northern Ireland — the first Palace player to appear for the Province. CENTRE: The Palace team that met the Wolves at Molineux on 19 November 1921: back: Rhodes, McCracken, J. T. Jones, Alderson, Jones (trainer), Feebery; front: Bateman, Dryer, Menlove, Hand, Cartwright, Little. Palace won with a penalty from skipper Albert Feebery. RIGHT: Palace's Welsh international centre-half J. T. Jones, whose headed goal led to a splendid opening day victory over Nottingham Forest. MIDDLE: Selhurst Park in bygone days! Brickmakers from the works and their families in 1901. BELOW: The football ground takes shape, about 1923 — are those allotments behind the houses on Whitehorse Lane?

LEFT: Palace's former amateur outside right Ben Bateman provided the creative genius that opened up Everton's defence when Palace romped to their famous 6-0 FA Cup victory at Goodison Park on 7 January 1922. ABOVE: The opening day at Selhurst Park, Saturday 30 August 1924 and BELOW: action from the match against The Wednesday. Teddy Davison, Wednesday's goalkeeper breaks up a Palace raid in spite of the attentions of Billy Morgan (left) and George Whitworth. RIGHT: The great Albert Harry.

The Palace's FA Cup run of 1925-26.

ABOVE: Crystal Palace FC 1929-30; back: Jones (trainer), Charlesworth, Thayne, Hellyer, Simpson, Legg, Rivers, Fishlock, Cartwright (asst trainer); middle: Butler, Barrie, Wilde, Callender, Imrie, Greener, Weatherby, Crilly, Parry; front: Hamilton, Turner, Charlton, Clarke, Mr E. Goodman (secretary), Mr F. Maven (manager), Havelock, Griffiths, Duthie, Swan; on ground: Harry, Plunkett, Dunsire, McCarthy.

IT WAS ALWAYS CONTENDED THA
THE CENTRE-HALF POSITION WAS
MOST EFFECTIVE PLACE FOR A
TEAM CAPTAIN
AND NOBODY FULFILLED THAT CLAIM BETTER FOR CRYSTAL PALACE THAN "JIMMY" WILDE
DURING HIS TERM AT SELHURST PARK (1928-1937) WILDE PLAYED 278 GAMES
– ALTHOUGH "JIMMY" TO EVERYONE ACTUALLY HE WAS WILLIAM CHARLES!

GEORGE CLARKE, THE CRYSTAL PALACE OUTSIDE LEFT
WHERE'S GEORGE?
SO FAST IS GEORGE THAT I RATHER FANCY THE SLOGAN "WHERE'S GEORGE?" ORIGINATED FROM A BACK WHO WAS OPPOSED TO HIM!

"WHERE'S GEORGE

TOP RIGHT: Perhaps Palace's best captains between the two Wars were Jimmy Wilde and BELOW: Stan Charlton. LEFT: Palace's brilliant but tragic goalkeeper, Billy Callender.

CENTRE: George Clarke — Palace's flame-haired flying outside-left who scored 21 goals from the wing in 1930-31.

Ups and Downs

Although not without interest, the remaining pre-war years of the 1930s were somewhat lacklustre for Crystal Palace FC in the all-important area of playing success.

A highly commendable undefeated home record in 1931-32 might have provided a platform for a return to Division Two, but we were much less convincing away from home and were knocked out of the FA Cup for the first time by a non-league side, Bath City, on their glutinous Twerton Park pitch.

In the summer of 1932 a tragedy occurred at Selhurst Park when Palace's marvellous and highly rated goalkeeper, Billy Callender, committed suicide, depressed after the death of his beloved fiancée from polio. The shock affected many of Billy's colleagues and friends for long afterwards but at least Ronnie Dunn had the character and the ability to replace Billy in the Palace side and in the affections of our fans. He missed only one game in our 1932-33 season, because of a dose of 'flu and remained our number one 'keeper for four seasons.

On his way to becoming a Palace regular was full-back Oswald Parry, who had joined us from Wimbledon in 1931. Tall and strong, the big, blond Welshman made the left-back position his own during 1932-33 and eventually played precisely 150 first team matches for us, before moving to Ipswich Town in the summer of 1936.

Although 1932-33 saw the Palace finish fifth in Division 3 South it was, certainly in retrospect, a somewhat bland season with little of real moment besides the almost incredible 6-6 draw between the Palace and Portsmouth reserves at Selhurst Park on its opening day. One significant event occurred at the end of it with the retirement of secretary Edmund Goodman, thus severing the last link with the Club's formation almost 30 years before. Mr Goodman's comments were typically gracious: 'I have had very happy days with the club and wish it every success for the future' he said. 'No-one will be more delighted that I when the club regains a place in the 2nd Division and then I shall look forward to seeing them in the First'. It is a matter of regret that Mr Goodman did not live long enough to witness either event — but then, neither did thousands of loyal Palace people of that inter-war period, so long did the Club languish in the lower reaches of the Football League.

Manager Jack Tresadern took over the responsibilities of secretary and, prior to the 1933-34 season, went on record as saying that 'this year is going to be Crystal Palace's year'. However, although we began the season with three straight wins, the Palace of 1933-34 was simply an ordinary side in the League's regional 3rd division and finished in 12th place, twenty points adrift of the champions Norwich City, who had demonstrated all too clearly the gulf between the two clubs by winning the pair of Christmas matches and preventing us from scoring in either.

Palace did reach the fourth round of the FA Cup and met mighty Arsenal, then at the peak of their inter-war greatness, at Highbury, only to receive a 0-7 chastening for our impudence in front of a crowd of 56,000 — until the 1990 Cup Finals the biggest crowd ever to watch a Palace game.

1933-34 revolved around the story of three Palace strikers — Peter Simpson, Ronnie Rooke and Albert Dawes.

Ace scorer Peter Simpson was by now a marked man and the constant heavy attention he received from some of the 3rd Division defenders had reduced his pace a little and made him more injury-prone, so that while he contributed 20 goals from his 25 League appearances (including his last major haul for us, all four goals in our 4-0 victory at Aldershot in

November), to remain easily our top goalscorer, this was to be the last season in which he would claim that distinction.

However, in the Palace reserve side there was just the fellow to take over Peter's mantle — or so it seemed. Ronnie Rooke, big, powerful and strong, had been lashing goals for our second string at a stupendous rate for a year or so but, regrettably, whenever he was introduced to the first team he failed to reproduce such form. Altogether he hit 160 goals for our reserves in three and a half seasons, and he was to benefit greatly from a transfer to Fulham in 1936, before going on to gain a Wartime international honour and top the League goalscoring list with Arsenal in 1948 — but, prior to the War at least, he could not do it for us and, even when we come across him later in this history, when he becomes our manager in 1949, he will again cause frustration and disappointment.

A striker of superior calibre was Albert Dawes, who was scoring goals regularly for Northampton Town, the club where Palace boss Jack Tresadern had previously been in charge. In a brave (if vain) attempt to resurrect Palace's flagging challenge for the top place in the division, Mr Tresadern obtained the services of the cultured centre-forward or inside-left in January 1934. Albert responded with 16 goals from his 22 League outings with us in the remainder of 1933-34 but even this was not sufficient to rescue another lack-lustre season.

Albert quickly established himself both as a favourite among Palace fans and as a proven goalscorer. He was without question a brilliant marksman and his powerful shooting, sometimes from long range, was spectacular as well as effective. Early in 1934-35 he scored five goals in the match against Cardiff City (6-1); in 1935-36 he came within a single goal of topping the entire Football League list with his 38 strikes for the Palace and that same season saw him honoured by the FA when he was selected for the England squad for the international against Scotland at Wembley. Unfortunately for Albert, he was made 12th man and, with no substitutes allowed in those days, spent the match idle on the players' bench.

The typical Palace line-up for 1934-35 was by now considerably changed from the earlier years of that decade. Ronnie Dunn was playing at the peak of his form in goal, with Ted Owens and Oswald Parry in front of him. Ted joined us in the summer 1934 in a rare Palace deal with Preston North End and remained with the Club till after the War. He was as tough as teak, had a magnificent season for us in 1934-35, missing only a single match because of a Christmas Day injury down at Torquay (1-7) and was certainly one of manager Tresadern's best signings.

Jimmy Wilde was still our central pivot and made all 42 appearances, while sturdy, strong Nick Collins made his bow this term in the left-half berth he was to retain for over ten years. Billy Turner replaced injured Alf Haynes at right-half before Christmas, but there was a new face at outside-right following Albert Harry's departure, with Scotsman Jimmy Carson joining us from Bradford. Frank Manders was our regular inside-right and hit 14 3rd Division goals from his 36 appearances, the same number as the great man himself, Peter Simpson, who played in 28 games in what was to be his last season with the Palace. Top scorer was Albert Dawes — 19 goals from 31 matches, including the five against Cardiff City on 1 September. At outside-left was another newcomer in Bob Bigg, who was to prove our best left-winger since George Clarke and for a very long time to come. Bob was brought up in Thornton Heath and became immensely popular at Selhurst Park, while he started off in perfect fashion this season by scoring on his debut at Aldershot (2-2), going on to become second-top scorer with 16 goals.

Naturally, Palace fans hoped that the winning of the 1934 *Evening News* Cricket Cup for Footballers was to be a happy portent of success in the 3rd Division South, but in fact a better augury was to be found in Mr Tresadern's misfortune in breaking a leg during a training session! In the League we looked as if we might make a major issue of the divisional championship, but a 1st round FA Cup humiliation at Yeovil (0-3) coupled with heavy defeats at Reading and at Torquay on Christmas morning made nonsense of that. In the finish we were fifth — Charlton were promoted and had proved their superiority in mid-February, when they drew the season's best attendance of 25,250 to Selhurst Park then beat us with a late strike after Peter Simpson had put us on terms just before the interval.

There were major upheavals at Selhurst Park in the summer of 1935. First Peter Simpson left for West Ham, at a substantial fee, and then there was another managerial change. Palace fans were naturally sorry to see Peter go, but it had become inevitable that he would leave us for a better placed club at some stage and everyone wished him well, but it took most people connected with the Club by surprise when manager Jack Tresadern moved across London to take charge of Tottenham in July. History can make a harsh assessor, and so it is with Mr Tresadern at the Palace. We never seriously challenged for promotion under his stewardship and, with the quality of some of the players he had available in his five year tenure, that is a serious indictment. Even our second place in 1931 was gained largely with players he had inherited and the gap between us and the champions was huge.

The new manager was Tom Bromilow, who had won League championship medals with Liverpool in the early '20s and played five times at wing-half for England. He had previously been manager at Burnley but seemed more than pleased to come to Selhurst Park. 'This is my golden opportunity' he said upon arrival, and in fact Tom was to prove the best inter-war manager at Selhurst Park, second only to Mr Edmund Goodman.

'Golden opportunity' it may have been, but Mr Bromilow was unable to grasp it immediately either for himself or for the Club! Thus, although the Palace fared tolerably well and finished in a reasonable sixth place, our 1935-36 season will only be remembered for some interesting new signings, the infamous Pools War and the death of two chairmen.

Palace beat Cardiff City 3-2 in the first match of the season with Bob Bigg claiming a rare winger's hat-trick, but in mid-October 2nd Division Norwich City sparked a hectic flurry of transfer activity at Selhurst Park, when they came in with the generous offer of their record fee for Frank Manders. It would have been folly to have declined it, both for the sake of the Club and of the player, so Mr Bromilow wisely permitted the deal, then invested the proceeds shrewdly in Bob Birtley, a right side utility player from Coventry City and Jack Blackman, a vigorous, bustling centre-forward from Queens Park Rangers.

Both were first-rate signings. Both made useful contributions in the 1935-36 season and right up to the War, both scored on their Palace League debuts (a 5-0 rout of Millwall on 2 November) while Jack Blackman became a respected member of our training staff in the early post-war years. His 52 League goals from 99 outings is impressive by any standard and during the War seasons he was invaluable.

Scoring goals was not a problem for the Palace of 1935-36. We hit 96 of them in Division 3 South (Albert Dawes got 38, Jack Blackman 19), among our best-ever League tallies, but by conceding 74 we forfeited any hopes we might have had of climbing out of that section — and we were again embarrassed by a non-league club in the FA Cup when Margate put us out (1-3) in the second round.

Partly no doubt in reaction to that ignominious defeat, Mr Bromilow made his best signing when he secured Fred Dawes from Northampton Town in February 1936, with the expressed intent of strengthening our defence. Fred, brother of Albert and a composed full-back, was to become one of Palace's most faithful and reliable players and easily our longest serving captain right up to the days of Jim Cannon. Had the War not intervened it is possible, even likely, that Fred's career statistics with the Palace would have reached proportions which not even Jim or Terry Long could have attained — as it was he played 222 League games for us, with another 15 FA Cup ties. He was to become the only Palace man to make 100 appearances on each side of the War, he was always held in the highest esteem at Selhurst Park and it is difficult to think of a player who advanced the Club's reputation for integrity and fair play more than he did.

There had been growing acrimony between the Football League and the Pools giants over the use by the latter of the League's fixtures and matters boiled over in the early weeks of 1936. In an attempt to thwart the Pools companies from using the fixtures the League suspended the published programme of matches for 29 February at short notice and substituted other pairings, so that the Palace were host to table-toppers Coventry (3-1) instead of more humble Torquay, and the following Saturday we travelled to Newport County (5-2) instead of to Millwall. On 14 March Torquay fulfilled their fixture at Selhurst Park (1-0) but the opposition to the Pools companies had largely evaporated by this time because gates everywhere had been detrimentally affected by the uncertainties over fixtures and the League retreated from the issue in some considerable disarray.

It had been a blow to the Club early in October 1935 to lose the services of its highly regarded chairman, Mr Louis Bellatti, who died suddenly at his home in Purley. He had been a director since 1909 and chairman from 1930. At the Palace match the following Saturday, when Clapton Orient were our visitors (2-2), both teams wore black armbands and the crowd stood bareheaded while the band played *Abide with Me*.

Mr Bellatti was the Palace's second chairman in 30 years, but within six weeks it had become necessary to appoint the fourth, because poor Mr R. S. Flew, his successor, had also died, and Mr Carey Burnett was chosen.

There was astonishment in London's footballing circles when Palace manager Tom Bromilow tendered his resignation at the end of June 1936 after just twelve months in charge at Selhurst Park, at about the same time as director Mr C. H. Temple. Clearly all was far from well. Another director, Mr R. S. Moyes, took over as manager — but his stay was turbulent and brief.

Mr Moyes did perform one excellent piece of business on behalf of the Palace which was on the verge of being a masterstroke for it was he who obtained Scottish international centre-half George Walker from Notts County. Tall and well built, Walker made 41 appearances for us in his first season and took over the club captaincy from Fred Dawes, because he was recognised as a charismatic figure, a model professional and a great leader. For two and a half seasons he missed just three matches and his absence in the second half of 1938-39 could be said to have cost us the long sought promotion.

An intriguing signing made by Mr Moyes was that of centre-forward Jack Palethorpe from Aston Villa in October. Jack was an extraordinary fellow — he had gained the sobriquet 'Lucky' because wherever he went the Club won something! With him in their side first Stoke City, then Preston gained promotion. When he was at Sheffield Wednesday, the Owls won the Cup! In 1935-36 Jack was at Villa Park — and Aston Villa were relegated! But this only enhanced his reputation because he was out with appendicitis for all but the first six matches!

Palethorpe certainly lived up to his tag at the Palace — briefly. He scored a brace on his debut to help defeat Newport County (6-1) and netted at Southend (1-2) a week later. But his magic did not work for us and, while he added some finesse to our forward line, his meagre return of eight goals from 29 appearances tell of a man who found the rugged nature of Division 3 South not greatly to his liking.

In fairness to Mr Moyes his problems began before the season had even got under way. Albert Dawes fractured his jaw in a trial match and was unable to play in the opening games, then he aggravated it upon his return and was side-lined again. Fortunately, Jack Blackman, Bob Bigg and Bob Birtley were all in good form, but if we were not struggling we were certainly nowhere near the top of the table and went out of the FA Cup at the first hurdle in a replay at Southend (0-2). Mr Moyes attempted to re-structure matters somewhat. He sold Ronnie Rooke to Fulham in October and then signed goalkeeper Vincent Blore from West Ham for a substantial fee.

But then in early December chaos erupted at Selhurst Park. First, little over five months after his appointment, Mr Moyes resigned! It was later alleged that he disapproved of some payments made to Palethorpe and Blore — certainly in 1939 he was suspended by the FA for 12 months.

Then a week or so later the chairman also resigned! Amidst all this, Albert Dawes was permitted to leave the Club for Luton Town just before Christmas and it was also announced that Mr Temple would re-join the board while former manager Tom Bromilow would re-assume responsibility at Selhurst Park from 1 January.

Such happenings naturally devastated players and supporters. Our League position, never healthy, suffered further with morale far from improved when Albert Dawes returned to Selhurst Park in early January with his new team-mates and helped the Hatters administer a severe beating (0-4).

Tom Bromilow's task was difficult, but to his great credit he righted the Palace ship straight away. We were helped by a run of four home games in the next five fixtures — Swindon (2-0) and Bristol Rovers (3-0) were beaten; we earned draws at Cardiff (1-1) and against Gillingham (1-1) then restored some self-respect with an 8–0 rout of Exeter City. We finished the season in our poorest position (14th) since joining the League, but discerning fans of the period realised that it could all have been so very, very much worse.

The anger kindled by the departure of Albert Dawes was still smouldering as Palace fans considered the prospects for the 1937-38 season, but there was no doubt that there were, at last, some genuine grounds for hoping that the Club could make another sustained impact on the race for the single promotion place.

Right at the end of the previous season Manager Tom Bromilow had purchased one of the best wing-halves ever to play for our Club, Les Lievesley, from Torquay. Les was a powerful, dynamic fellow at all but 6 feet and over 12 stone and his acquisition was unquestionably a key reason for our enhanced showing in 1937-38 — and the best performance for a full decade the following term. He put in 53 consecutive appearances after joining us and, with George Walker and Nick Collins, helped to form an outstanding half-back line that is still spoken of with awe at Selhurst Park today. But, sadly, Les' life was to end in tragedy: after training paratroopers and commandos during the War, Les joined Turin of Italy, only to be killed with 29 other members of that club when the plane carrying them from a match against Benfica in Lisbon hit the cathedral at the top of Superga Hill on the edge of the city, before plunging into the courtyard in flames.

Also from the west country arrived a splendid goalkeeper, Arthur Chesters, from Exeter City, while a clever winger, Harvey Pritchard, came from Coventry to fill the gap caused by Bob Bigg's badly broken leg. Harvey was in great form for us on both flanks. He played in every game up to 5 March, netting six goals, then moved to Manchester City for Palace's highest transfer fee yet. Another useful new winger was Jackie 'Spider' Horton, who had previously played at Chelsea and Charlton.

Taken overall, the 1937-38 season represented a much better showing than the previous year and, but for some really bad luck with injuries, we might even have pushed the top clubs for the promotion bracket. Typical of our misfortune was the story of our two full-backs. Fred Dawes suffered a complicated knee injury in mid-December which kept him out for the rest of the season, while Ted Owens missed the middle three months after being carried from the field in the FA Cup-tie at Accrington (1-0). One result was that, when the Palace tackled Liverpool in our first appearance in the third round for four years, we had to do so with two reserves, Geoff Turton and Sam Booth, in those crucial positions. Nevertheless the Palace acquitted themselves well, took the Reds to a replay after a goal-less first match at Selhurst Park, and only went out after extra-time following a disputed strike, a penalty and an own-goal at Anfield.

Drafted in from Reading to help cover the key absences at full-back was Fred Gregory, a dependable enough defender but also an exciting occasional centre-forward. Fred possessed an immensely powerful kick, was hugely strong and, during 1938-39, scored five goals in two games when drafted in up front early in the season. Fred did not miss a single match in 1937-38 after joining us, and he lashed home a couple of penalties to aid the goalscoring cause.

But for Palace fans the best news of the entire season came in mid-February when it was announced that 'Our Albert', as our predecessors of that time dubbed Albert Dawes, was coming home to Selhurst Park after assisting Luton to promotion and playing in every position in their forward line.

By early April the Palace's considerably re-ordered team had forged their way from mid-table to sixth place, three points adrift of the leaders — but this was to be the peak of our efforts for 1937-38 and we closed the season in 7th position. For a change the plaudits this term must to go the Palace defence, which conceded fewer goals than at any time since the 1921 promotion. Up front we lacked a consistent goalscorer, although Jack Blackman bustled his way to 16 goals from his 29 games to show that, if he were given a decent service, he could produce what was wanted.

Certainly Tom Bromilow's Palace of 1938-39 was to come closer to winning promotion to Division Two than any other Palace team between 1929 and 1964.

There were but a few changes as the season progressed; Eric Steele was signed from Millwall in the autumn and Albert Wilson came from Mansfield in January to successfully increase our threat from the flanks; Bert Robson matured so well that he took over at centre-forward in mid-December and hit 11 goals from 20 appearances, while Bob Shanks deputised capably for George Walker after our popular captain's injury at the turn of the year.

On 1 October — the end of the week in which Neville Chamberlain returned from Munich to proclaim 'Peace In Our Time' — Palace chairman, Mr E. T. Truett, called for three cheers for the Premier before our match with Clapton Orient (4-2) and the band played the national anthem — by the time the proceedings were over, only goal average denied us top place in the table, with the Palace having a match in hand over the unlikely leaders, Aldershot.

However, this 1938-39 season was to prove the one season of glory for Newport County, and on 8 October Palace travelled down to Monmouthshire to lose 0-2. Newport leapfrogged over us to the top of the table and, while it was always close and exciting, Palace always lagged behind the Welshmen after that defeat.

During the close season of 1939 Mr Bromilow left Selhurst Park to manage Leicester City. He did so on the best of terms and with the knowledge that he had done his job well at the Palace. He had resurrected an ailing club and a fading team after returning to us in January 1937 and had been unfortunate not to gain promotion two years later.

Tom's natural successor was George Irwin, our former goalkeeper, who had served as club trainer under Mr Bromilow for a couple of seasons. As a former professional, George knew the game thoroughly and he was already well respected by players, officials and fans. He was a genial, humorous personality, though he had a streak of iron in his make-up that enabled him to drive himself and his players hard. Certainly, the coming War years were going to demand much from everyone in every walk of life and it was as well for Crystal Palace FC that our fortunes were in the hands of such a capable and well-equipped person.

LEFT: Ronnie Dunn. RIGHT: Peter Simpson poses for the camera. BELOW: The youthful Ronnie Rooke. RIGHT: Palace manager Jack Tresadern and goalscoring star Albert Dawes.

LEFT: The urbane Tom Bromilow, Palace's manager in the summer, 1935. RIGHT: Bustling centre-forward Jack Blackman joined Palace in October 1935 . . . here in portrait. BELOW: 'Lucky' Jack Palethorpe. Sadly, his magic seldom worked for us; Les Lievesley and Albert Wilson.

Liverpool's first visit to Selhurst Park! Palace goalkeeper Arthur Chesters and defenders (l-r) George Walker and Sam Booth, watch Geoff Turton rise for this header in the 1938 FA Cup tie. BELOW: Crystal Palace 1938-39: back: Birtley, Horton, Blackman, A. Dawes, Collins, F. Dawes, Owens, Hudgell, Jordan, Robson; second: Gregory, Lievesley, Daniels, Walker, Chesters, Tierney, Shanks, Brooks, Uren, Lewis; seated: Greener (trainer), Messrs Stanbury, Dr Wardill, Temple, Truett (chairman), Blaxill (directors), Burrell (secretary), Bromilow (manager), Irwin (trainer); on ground: Davis, Waldron, Smith, Bryson, Gillespie, Bigg, McLean.

World War II

The 1939-40 League season opened on schedule on 26 August 1939, with the Palace doing well to come back from a 1-3 deficit at half-time to win 5-4 at Mansfield. Following a 0-5 midweek defeat at Reading, Palace entertained Bristol Rovers on 2 September (3-0) and it was during the morning of the following day that War was declared and Prime Minister Neville Chamberlain made his famous broadcast.

The Football League tournament was immediately abandoned but, throughout the War years, the clubs were divided into various regional leagues and divisions for competitions which lasted anything from a few weeks to nine months, and sometimes overlapped!

Several excellent players turned out regularly for the Palace under the 'guest' system which again pertained, including R. C. Mountford, Huddersfield's quality right-back, Burnley's magnificent centre-half Harrold Spencer and the Oldham and former Manchester United striker, Bob Ferrier. The guest system proved of value to Crystal Palace in the longer term too, for Dick Graham, who was to become a successful post-war Palace manager, first came to Selhurst Park under this arrangement before signing for our Club, while Fred Kurz, an itinerant centre-forward from Grimsby, so won the hearts of Palace fans that they petitioned the Board to make funds available in order that the arrangement could become permanent.

Palace's first Wartime success was to head our Division of the 1939-40 South Regional League, although this was an attenuated competition of only eighteen matches, but in the following season Palace won a differently constituted league by the same title against opposition of the calibre of West Ham, Arsenal, Chelsea and 'Spurs. The 1940-41 competition was decided purely on goal-average and each club arranged as many or as few fixtures as circumstances dictated or opportunity allowed. Our success in 1940-41 owed much to the goalscoring efforts of Bert Robson, who hit 36 goals from 40 appearances and of old favourite Albert Dawes (27 goals from 23 games).

Palace's third Wartime honour was achieved by winning the southern section of the 3rd Division South in a tournament which ran from August 1945 to the end of the year, and this was the season in which Fred Kurz made such an impact at Selhurst Park, with 40 goals from his 38 appearances.

Strange, and to present day readers, unthinkable incidents took place in some Wartime matches: when Palace met Brentford on 22 March 1941 the Brentford side disputed a penalty award and the referee and all twenty two players left the field for some quarter of an hour, arguing the point! When they returned, Palace's Arthur Hudgell despatched the kick and Palace went on to beat the 1st Division side 5-0. Another time Palace were playing Southend and the Shrimpers' goalkeeper disputed a goal given to the Palace, then marched off the field. Play was held up for ten minutes or so while the referee retrieved the green jersey (and no doubt had a few timely words with the culprit!) and play resumed with the Southend centre-forward between the posts! Palace won that one 7-0. In contrast there was the occasion on 9 November 1940 when three hundred fans turned up at Selhurst Park for the match against Watford, but saw nothing at all because the 'alert' which heralded an air-raid and stopped or prevented play was in operation all afternoon.

Towards the end of the War and to the delight of football fans everywhere, the FA sanctioned a full competition for the FA Cup in 1945-46 and then added some extra spice, by ruling that ties were to be played on a home and away basis, the only season under which such an arrangement has pertained in that competition.

A Jim Mercer cartoon depicts wartime football at Selhurst Park.

Palace were drawn against Queens Park Rangers and the first leg was due at Shepherds Bush. Freddie Kurz had been in prolific scoring form and was hurriedly signed in order that he could play, although how much this was due to the supporters' petition simply is not known.

Two exciting but scoreless matches in front of big crowds took place, so a replay had to be staged at neutral Fulham, where the Palace went down to a goal scored after just a few minutes' play.

CRYSTAL PALACE
FOOTBALL CLUB

President :—Sir Adam Maitland, M.P.
Directors :—Messrs. P. S. Harper (Chairman), F. Broomfield (Vice-Chairman), E. T. Truett, F. J. Young.
Secretary-Manager :—G. W. Irwin.
NEAREST STATIONS : NORWOOD JUNCTION, SELHURST, and THORNTON HEATH.
Bus Services—133, 68, 75 ; 654 (Trolley).

OFFICIAL PROGRAMME

No. 16. Vol. XXXIX. SEASON 1943-44
Saturday, March 4th, 1944. Kick-off 3.0 p.m. Price : ONE PENNY

CRYSTAL PALACE 5

RIGHT WING. LEFT WING

1 TOOTILL, Goal

2 MOUNTFORD, Right Back — 3 YOUNG, Left Back

4 ~~DAWES, A.~~, Right Half — 5 BASSETT, Centre Half — 6 CABRELLI, Left Half

7 ROBSON 1, Outside Right — 8 ~~ROBINSON~~, Inside Right — 9 ~~PERRIER~~, Centre Forward 2 — 10 LEWIS (G.), Inside Left — 11 WILSON 1, Outside Left

Referee : E. PLINSTON (Beaulieu, Hants).

Linesmen :—
Blue Flag : A. C. GARWOOD.
Red Flag : F. B. TYRRELL

11 DUFFEY 1, Outside Left — 10 BROWN, Inside Left — 9 TURNER, Centre Forward — 8 ROBINSON, Inside Right — 7 REVILL, Outside Right

6 CHILTON, Left Half — 5 OAKES, Centre Half — 4 SMITH, Right Half

3 ~~JOBLING~~, Left Back — 2 SHREEVE, Right Back

1 HOBBINS (Goal)

LEFT WING RIGHT WING

CHARLTON 1

Next Saturday : **BRENTFORD** Kick-off 3.0 p.m.
(LEAGUE CUP SOUTH) (See Back

LEFT: Fred Dawes. RIGHT: Wing-half Nick Collins was a great favourite with Palace fans before and during the War. BELOW: An example of Palace's single-sheet programme issued throughout most of the hostilities. This match was an FA War Cup-tie against Charlton and Palace won 5-1. RIGHT: Bert Robson scored 36 goals from 40 appearances in 1940-41.

Part Two: Decline and Restoration 1946-69

THIRD DIVISION SOUTH

Fully competitive post-war soccer opened on the last day of August 1946 and at Selhurst Park there were sound reasons for optimism. Manager George Irwin had at his disposal a useful-looking squad and there seemed every reason to expect we could build on our wartime success.

There were five men available who had played for the Palace's pre-war League side: skipper and right-back Fred Dawes; Jack Lewis, a splendid and positive right-half; Tommy Reece on the opposite flank; Bert Robson, a clever centre-forward and Ernie Waldron, a dapper, tricky little inside-forward. During the War several astute signings had been made — Dick Graham and Fred Kurz have already been noted but there was also centre-half Bill Bassett from Cardiff City, who was to prove a tower of strength in Palace rearguards in the difficult years after the War. Bill was tall and almost completely bald, so that he would finish a midwinter match with his pate covered in mud and looking a pretty fearsome sight! But probably the best footballer on the Palace staff in August 1946 was young Arthur Hudgell, who had developed through the War years into a top quality, cultured full-back.

The portents then were excellent. Sad to say the actual performance was very much less so. Robson rarely produced his sparkling wartime form; Waldron was unsettled and soon signed for Aberdeen, but had to retire at the end of the season anyway through ill-health. It became difficult to field a settled side — only once could Manager Irwin put out the same team for more than two consecutive matches — and in our second match of the 1946-47 season Palace suffered their highest scoring League defeat. Having lost 1-3 at Mansfield on the opening day, when Ernie Waldron spent the afternoon in a local hospital rather than assisting his colleagues, because he had a fish bone stuck in his throat, we were at Reading the following Wednesday evening. Three goals in arrears after a quarter of an hour, Palace staged a creditable recovery to make the half-time score 2-3, but immediately after the interval Reading netted five times in a quarter of an hour and proceeded to reach double figures. However, for the record in the return fixture two weeks later Palace won 2-1: Fred Kurz hit the woodwork three times without the ball going into the net once and Reading's goal came right at the end of a match we dominated throughout. Truly, it is a strange game!

Certainly, when Palace did play to their full ability we were able to record some splendid victories. Two away wins in three days at Norwich and Leyton Orient in September and a 6-1 home victory over an admittedly depleted Torquay on Christmas morning provided convincing evidence that we could play attractive and effective football but, in all honesty, we were usually enigmatic and disappointing.

Palace were excused the early rounds of the FA Cup but, when the 3rd round draw was made, we were the only London club required to travel and it was to Tyneside to face mighty Newcastle United on 11 January. There was to be no repitition of the 1907 giant-killing: we lost 2-6 in a brave performance, with Bill Naylor netting our two goals. High up in the Gallowgate stand that afternoon was a scout from neighbouring Sunderland. He was so impressed with Arthur Hudgell's distinguished performance that Roker Park officials were constantly at Selhurst and, at the end of January, Arthur left us for Wearside at a then record fee of £10,000 for a 3rd Division player.

Other players were also soon on the move to 1st Division clubs as left-winger Howard Girling and Bill Naylor travelled across to West London to join Brentford. In February bitter winter weather closed in. Palace were only able to play a home match against Leyton Orient on 1 February because eighteen German prisoners-of-war had cleared the snow from the pitch that morning, while the game at Swindon on 15 March was played in a blizzard. We beat the O's 2-0 but lost at Swindon to a fiercely disputed penalty five minutes from time. In the end postponements inevitably occurred and the season was prolonged until the Whitsun weekend to accomodate the re-arrangements. Not untypical of the whole season, Palace drew 0-0 at home with Bristol City on the Saturday, but lost 2-4 at Port Vale on the Bank Holiday Monday.

By this time, though, the Palace had a new manager in the person of Jack Butler, formerly a player with Arsenal and an England international. If his pedigree on the pitch was impressive it was equalled as coach and manager. He had been in charge of the Belgian national side and the Denmark FA, had coached at Leicester and managed Torquay United. Bob John, another former Arsenal defender and regular Welsh international was the new Palace trainer and the two men had been contemporaries at Highbury.

These appointments were ambitious ones by the Palace board. Unfortunately they failed — dismally. Butler and John discovered, as many 1st Division players before and since have found, at the Palace and elsewhere, that running a 3rd Division outfit is a very different matter from, and far more demanding than, playing in the top flight.

In 1947-48 Palace were always a middle-of-the-table side and goals were hard to come by. The defence could rarely be faulted but Jack Butler sought to improve our striking power by signing Jimmy Clough, a raiding winger from Southport, and Alf Somerfield, an inside-forward who had guested for Palace during the War, from Wolves. Things did improve: Palace scored a splendid and remarkable 5-0 win at Watford on 14 February (easily our best victory there) and had two 4-0 home wins over Swansea and Bristol City in March and April. But we could still only finish in 13th place, with goal aggregates of just 49 for and the same number against. Dick Graham made full appearances and Fred Dawes had another solid season, while Fred Kurz scored a creditable 18 League goals with precious little support elsewhere.

The FA Cup brought at least some excitement to a rather drab season, but even here Palace flattered only to deceive. We defeated Port Vale at Selhurst Park and Bristol City at Ashton Gate after extra time, to reach the 3rd round, in which the draw brought Chester to the Palace for their first-ever visit. An eager crowd of some twenty-two thousand turned up hoping to see us dismiss the men from the Northern section, but Chester scored eight minutes before half-time against the play and were then able to resist all Palace's efforts to redress the situation.

If 'disappointing' sums up Jack Butler's first full season of 1947-48 then only 'disastrous' will do to describe 1948-49. The Palace had reverted to the Club's former and original colours of claret and blue shirts and white shorts which had been dispensed with for a decade, but the change brought us no luck whatever.

The Palace had a lamentable record this season. We leaked goals but could score few ourselves in spite of the noble efforts of Fred Kurz who scored virtually one third of our total. The defence toiled earnestly but was alway suspect under pressure and prone to mistakes, so that we let in five goals on no fewer than four occasions and could rarely prevent opponents from scoring. Jack Butler put out a total of thirty-three players throughout the season. Yet we were always in the lower reaches of the 3rd Division South table, hit rock-bottom after Christmas and never recovered sufficiently to get off it, finishing six points behind the club in twenty-first place. In the Cup we were dismissed in the 1st round, Bristol City gaining speedy revenge for our success in 1947-48 with a single goal victory at Selhurst Park.

It was a tale of one woe after another. Jack Butler was bitterly upset by it all and insisted that his letter of resignation be accepted by the Club. He left with dignity, but that was little or no consolation to the Palace supporters (who remained loyal in spite of it all), for their Club had suffered its worst season since joining the Football League and now faced the indignity of having to apply for re-election for the first time.

Immediately upon Jack Butler's departure the Palace appointed another former Arsenal personality as our player-manager — Ronnie Rooke. Rooke was no stranger to Selhurst Park even if his success was limited. But now he came to us as one of the leading lights of London football and the League top scorer in 1947-48 with 33 strikes.

Rooke's appointment at the Palace was in line with progressive thinking among some of the ambitious clubs in the lower divisions. Hull City and Notts County had pioneered the way by signing 'big-name' men of the day in Raich Carter and Tommy Lawton respectively: drawing phenomenal crowds Hull won the 3rd Division North title in 1948-49 and County were to do so in the South section in this 1949-50 season. Rooke, it was hoped, would duly lead the Palace the same way before long.

The new manager made several interesting signings, the best of which turned out to be Jock Watson, a strong centre-half who had been with Rooke at Fulham and then played for Real Madrid, and little Wally Hanlon, formerly of Brighton and Bournemouth, a tricky winger who became a firm Palace favourite.

In a pulsating game at Selhurst Park on 10 September against star-studded Notts County in front of a thirty thousand crowd, Jack Lewis scored his last goal for us as Palace ran County close but were unlucky to lose 1-2. Lewis was a grand player, one of our best half-backs to be sure. The London FA called upon him for their fixture with the Belgian FA in Brussels and Palace's first post-war representative honour, but a few weeks later Bournemouth bought him for the substantial fee for those days of £7,500. He had played 124 League games for us and most of the fans were really sorry to see him go. Then Fred Dawes came to the end of his playing career at Bournemouth on 1 October when he sustained a nasty head injury. He was to continue to serve the Club faithfully in administrative and managerial capacities but it was a sad end to an illustrious Palace career.

Jack Edwards (destined to become another great Palace favourite and club skipper) deputised for Fred in the next match — a real roughhouse at Millwall in which Ronnie Rooke eluded some tight marking to score his 101st League goal and was subsequently sent off. Palace won 3-2.

For much more salutary reasons Rooke certainly gained Palace some welcome if unaccustomed publicity. After his return from suspension we slammed five past Exeter on 17 December to win 5-3, then drew 4-4 at Ipswich on Christmas Eve with the player-manager scoring twice. The first two months of 1950 saw an excellent playing record of six victories and two draws (both away), including a really fine 1-0 win at Notts County, where Fred Kurz's goal wrecked their unbeaten home record, and a 6-0 thrashing of Brighton at Selhurst Park when Rooke himself grabbed a hat-trick. The papers dubbed Palace 'The Rooke Regiment' and there were some big crowds to see them play. Inevitably Rooke was our leading scorer with 21 League goals.

Palace were knocked out of the FA Cup at the first hurdle at Newport, but in an historical context the most important feature of 1949-50 was the approach by a group of businessmen to Percy Harper, then the club Chairman, with a view to joining the Board and adding to its financial resources. Three of the existing directors resigned immediately; the other two, including Harper, went soon afterwards. The new board, under Chairman David Harris, included Arthur Wait, who was to become a key figure in Palace's climb through the divisions and exhilarating rise to Division One.

The summer of 1950 was a busy one at Selhurst Park. First Ronnie Rooke announced his decision to hang up his boots, in order to concentrate upon his managerial role; then, with the encouragement of the new Board of Directors, he went out and spent nearly £30,000 on new players — an enormous outlay. The most expensive import was wing-half Bill Whittaker from Huddersfield, who cost us £10,000; Les Stevens, a winger came from Bradford for £7,000; Morris Jones, a proven goal-scoring inside-forward at Swindon, cost £4,000 as did Charlie Rundle, a centre-forward from Tottenham, while wing-half George Smith from Southampton cost £2,500.

The massive outlay was to no avail when Palace opened the season at home to Aldershot. We lost 0-2 and Rundle spent most of the game as a passenger after an early ankle injury. Everything continued to go wrong. We lost five of the first six matches, using seventeen players in the process, including Rooke himself, who returned to the side in a vain attempt to stem the tide, and it was obvious that Palace were going to have a difficult season. By mid-November Palace were at the foot of the table with just four wins from eighteen League matches and nine points, and Millwall had knocked us out of the Cup in the 1st round at Selhurst Park. The Board decided that Rooke would have to leave — unfortunately the wreckage could not be dismissed so easily.

The directors also decided to put two men into the Manager's office: Fred Dawes, that great Palace favourite, and Charlie Slade, who had done some good work for the Club on the scouting side and was a respected coach. But frankly, in spite of the obvious qualities of the two men, the appointments were naive. Both men were in an impossible situation: the task they had inherited was thankless. The financial position which Dawes and Slade took on precluded any positive remedial action and morale was low. Then things deteriorated from bad to worse when it was announced in mid-February that Dick Graham's recurring back injury would prevent him from playing again, and Morris Jones' jaw was badly smashed in the home game with Millwall to put *him* out for the season.

Palace never even looked like getting off the bottom of the table. Dawes and Slade managed to infuse some spirit into the side but our playing record was appalling. We had just two victories in a total of 22 outings in 1951 and finished with just one win in the final twenty games. Palace fans did not see a single home win in the last ten matches, and our leading scorer was Rooke himself with just five goals!

No club had started 1950-51 with greater optimism than Crystal Palace but no club had suffered keener disappointment. Our playing record of just eight successes and eleven draws, with a paltry 33 League goals, was our worst of all time, and it would require several years to remedy. The outlook was gloomy indeed.

August 1951 therefore saw an air of unease at Selhurst Park and a greatly reduced playing staff as the directors sought to recoup some of the massive outlay they had encouraged twelve months earlier. Two useful new signings were those of George McGeachie, a wing-half from Rochdale who skippered Palace for the first third of the season, and Les Devonshire, a winger from Chester, as Fred Dawes and Charlie Slade sought to steer the Club into more settled waters. But it was not to be: all too soon Palace were in dire trouble again.

By mid-October we were just two points away from the foot of the table and the directors, implicitly admitting that their choice had been a mistake, decided that another change of management was necessary. Charlie Slade reverted to the job he did best, as chief scout, while Fred Dawes' services were dispensed with completely. This was shabby treatment to as loyal a club servant as could be found anywhere and was needlessly harsh. The main responsibility for the acute situation in which the Palace club now found itself lay with the directors themselves, who had given Ronnie Rooke carte-blanche in the spending spree of summer 1950.

The man who took up the challenge was Laurie Scott who, like Rooke and Butler before him, was a former Arsenal star. Scott was a polished, intelligent right full-back and had represented England in seventeen consecutive internationals in the late 1940s. It had taken a five-figure fee to prise him away from Highbury, but he made his Palace debut before a crowd of around twenty-one thousand for our home game with Ipswich on 20 October. Palace played really well and won more convincingly than the 3-1 scoreline suggests, with goals from Cam Burgess (2) and Fred Price. Burgess had arrived a month beforehand from Chester upon the recommendation of his former clubmate, Les Devonshire, and was to score some useful goals for Palace. In this season of 1951-52 he equalled Rooke's (then) post-war scoring record of 21 League goals and he did it in just 22 matches!

Things stabilised under Scott's control — the team became more settled and results improved slightly. Certainly, with young Johnny Rainford blossoming at inside-right and Burgess' explosive finishing, Palace gained in confidence and became an attractive side to watch. Thus, when April 1952 arrived Palace had risen to a mid-table position, but then, with only one victory and two home draws in our last nine matches we faded away to fall among the stragglers again.

The 1952-53 season eventually turned out a much happier one than its immediate predecessors. Bill Simpson at inside-left from Aston Villa was the only new face in the team for the opening match at Brighton (1-4), but another summer signing who would render the Club valuable service was Cecil 'Archie' Andrews from Portsmouth, a wing-half. Soon to arrive were Bob Thomas from Fulham, able to play at centre or inside-forward, Les Fell, a right-winger from Charlton who had appeared in the Valiants' 1946 FA Cup Final side, and Colin Grimshaw, an inside-forward or wing-half from Arsenal.

However, in the early part of this season Palace had another bad time, although after Fell, Thomas and Grimshaw had joined we began to improve considerably and Cam Burgess embarked upon a terrific run of goalscoring. Cam hit three hat-tricks in four matches and twelve goals in six games in October and November to pull Palace away from the bottom of the table with a sequence unparalleled in terms of goals scored since the War, but Palace had another lean period between December and mid-March and this included the disastrous defeat in the FA Cup by non-league Finchley.

The original fixture was abandoned because of fog, with Finchley leading 3-1, but poor Palace could take no advantage of this reprieve and were unable to prevent the amateurs from repeating the dose when the match was replayed four days later. It was all highly embarrassing, for Palace's troubles began before the first match ever started. Bob Thomas and Les Devonshire got lost in the north London fog and had to phone the Finchley ground to admit that they were stranded over at Park Royal! Palace fans who were at Finchley were thus startled to hear a broadcast appeal for any of our players who were there to report to our dressing room, and Bob Bishop thus deputised for Thomas because he was able to wear Devonshire's boots.

If that event was farcical so was the game itself, after visibility deteriorated so badly that the linesman had to stand ten yards or more inside the pitch in an attempt to follow the play; the referee had no alternative but to abandon proceedings after 62 minutes. Palace and their fans were highly relieved, but poor Bob Bishop never had another chance to play in our first team (though he was subsequently to become a director of the Club!). Then came the final awful twist when the amateurs piled on the agony in the second game, took their chances and despatched us by the same scoreline.

These were tough times in which to support Crystal Palace and the spectre of a third application for re-election in five years began to loom at Selhurst Park, but hopes of a revival were kindled in mid-February with a fine 4-3 victory over second placed and highly fancied Northampton, on a snow-covered pitch upon which Cam Burgess netted a 29-minute hat-trick, and our optimism was subsequently confirmed in the last two months of the season.

Bill Simpson and Bob Thomas began to score regularly, with Simpson now playing at centre-forward and relishing the service provided by Les Fell. Another regular in the side over these last two exciting months of 1952-53 who earnt himself a permanent niche in the Palace annals was goalkeeper Roy Bailey. By the end of the season Palace feared nobody and were a match for anyone: in the last game of the season, played on the Friday evening before the FA Cup Final, we beat the champions of the Southern Section, Bristol Rovers, in the most terrible conditions, after twenty-four hours of continuous rain.

Palace carried this excellent form over into the first part of the next season, 1953-54, which remains unique to this day because we began our fixtures on a Thursday! We drew 2-2 at home to Northampton. Without ever causing the least anxiety to the division's pacesetter, Palace had a modestly successful first half of the season, although we had our occasional falls from grace, like the 0-6 defeat at Northampton at the end of October and the humiliation of another FA Cup exit on a non-league ground, this time at Great Yarmouth.

But in 1954 we deteriorated beyond recognition and finished the season only one place above the re-election positions. An important new signing for 1953-54 had been Jess Willard, from Brighton, a wing-half who occasionally played at centre-forward and who became a great servant of the Palace club as coach and scout once his playing days were over. Ernie Randall, a useful centre-forward from Chelsea, scored regularly for Palace early in the season but his career was blighted by a broken leg in the Christmas morning encounter against Norwich Ciy (1-0), and in his absence our decline really set in.

In retrospect the most interesting feature of the 1953-54 season was the installation of floodlighting at Selhurst Park. A series of entertaining friendly matches against leading English, Scottish and foreign clubs was arranged, the inaugural match being against Chelsea on 28 September, which resulted in a 1-1 draw and a rare goal scored by two players! Both Ernie Randall and Albert Foulds got a simultaneous touch to Palace's headed equaliser.

Laurie Scott remained our manager for just over a month of the following season, during which time Palace played eleven matches, won but one of them, gained just seven points and were on the receiving end of several high scores, the worst of which was the 1-7 defeat at Watford on 7 September. After the goal-less home draw with Swindon on Saturday 25 September the Board decided to remedy the situation: Mr Scott was relieved of his post and a statement was inserted into the programme for the next match, against Bournemouth, on Wednesday 29 September, when Palace recorded their second win of the season (2-1).

The managerial vacancy was filled some two weeks later and the new incumbent, Mr Cyril Spiers, was introduced to the supporters via the programme for the floodlit friendly match against Clyde on 13 October (1-1). Spiers had been a fine goalkeeper in his day for Aston Villa, 'Spurs and Wolves, and had a distinguished managerial record at Cardiff City and, briefly, Norwich. He was a quiet, hardworking, fatherly sort of man and his speciality was his ability to spot a likely youngster, induce him to sign for a League club and then groom him, perhaps over several years, for the limelight. This was a complete shift in the policy of the Palace, for since the War, and long before it, we had imported most of our players from other clubs.

Obviously, such a policy could not be expected to pay immediate dividends. Nor did it at Selhurst Park. Palace seldom appeared likely to have to apply for re-election, but we finished only four points clear of those who did. There were a few bright spots to the season to enliven the supporters' hopes for the future and most praiseworthy among these was the 2-2 draw at highly placed Southampton on Saturday 23 April. Conversely, no Palace fan who was there will ever forget the slough of despair into which we were thrown two weeks before Christmas when, having won at Swindon in the 1st round of the FA Cup for our first away success in twelve months, we were despatched from the competition by the Northern League amateurs, Bishop Auckland, by four goals to two in front of our own supporters.

The shift in policy continued in 1955-56 but this season was a most trying one for Palace and their fans for, while the youngsters in our colours could play most attractively at times — and never better than in a 3-0 win over Queens Park Rangers at Loftus Road on Monday 5 September — the Club finished the season next to bottom and we had to seek re-election for the third time. Equally, Southampton put us out of the Cup straight away in a replay at the Dell after holding us at Selhurst Park.

The frustrations were extremely hard to bear, but in retrospect it is possible to see that Mr Spiers' efforts were beginning to come to fruition, even if there was no tangible evidence there and then. By the conclusion of the 1955-56 season Spiers had produced useful strikers in Mike Deakin, Barry Pierce, George Cooper, flame-haired Jimmy Murray and the ill-fated Ron Brett; had moulded Jimmy Belcher into a mature and cultured wing-half alongside another fabulous discovery in Terry Long, and had found two promising wingers who really should have made more of their careers, Bernard Harrison and Harry Gunning. Best of all, Johnny Byrne, one of the finest players produced at the Palace, was already on the Club books and appearing for the reserves.

There were further disappointments in 1956-57. It took us eight games before our first win of the season and we were always in the bottom third of the division although, as in the previous term, the young Palace side proved its potential on isolated occasions, like the 4-1 victory secured at Watford on 3 November. Another hint of the profitable outworking of Cyril Spiers' long-term policy was seen when two noteworthy debuts were made on the same afternoon by youthful players who were to have important roles in Palaces' future destiny: Vic Rouse in goal and Johnny Byrne at centre-forward, lined up in a Palace League side for the first time on 13 October, when we were at home to Swindon Town (0-0).

Palace's biggest gate for a League game (22,627) was at the final match of the season. This brought Torquay to Selhurst Park on Wednesday 1 May with a large contingent of their own fans for, if they could win, they would gain promotion to Division 2. The outcome was a splendid game with a draw a fair result. Barry Pierce put us ahead seven minutes after half-time but the men from Devon equalised eight minutes later.

As this season progressed Palace utilised an interesting attacking policy that might well have been years ahead of its time, by deploying Pierce and Mike Deakin as twin centre-forwards. It was probably seen at its most effective when Barry notched a hat-trick in a Selhurst Park FA Cup replay against Brentford, to take us to the third round for the first time in nine years.

There had been initiatives since the early 1950s for the formation of national 3rd and 4th Divisions from the then existing Northern and Southern sections of the 3rd Division and it was eventually decided to implement this at the end of 1957-58. The Palace had been to the fore in these initiatives and our Chairman in 1956, Mr John Dunster, had put the case on behalf of the lower division sides to the Football League.

Palace faced this prospect with high hopes of finishing in the top half of the table, but it was an all too familiar tale that evolved. In spite of occasional excellent results — none better than the 3-0 whipping of Plymouth who were complete with expensive Jimmy Gauld from Everton (himself later jailed for four years as a ringleader of a match-fixing betting syndicate in 1964) on 26 October and which took us into the upper half for the first and only time. We could never string together more than two consecutive victories in the whole season. Similarly in the FA Cup: two meritorious wins, at Margate (3-2) and at home over Southampton (1-0), put us all in good humour for the 3rd round tie at home to Ipswich, but our poor finishing and a superb display by our former goalkeeper Roy Bailey nullified our chances of further progress; we lost 0-1.

By the middle of March 1958 the situation confronting the Palace was starkly clear: there were six weeks of the season remaining and we had a dozen games left to play, but we were

LEFT: Arthur Hudgell had developed into a fine full-back at Crystal Palace, CENTRE: and leading goalscorer in the early post-war years, Fred Kurz. RIGHT: George Irwin, former Palace goalkeeper and manager from 1939 to 1947.

down in 16th place with considerable lee-way to be made up if we were to avoid becoming founder-members of the new League basement. Manager Spiers had brought some additional experience to leaven his young players when he acquired winger Tony Collins from Watford, but it was now obvious that something else was needed. Mr Spiers sought to supply that elusive ingredient with one more signing, his last for the Club.

He obtained the distinguished, cultured expertise of Johnny McNichol, the Scottish inside-left from Chelsea's championship winning side of three years earlier. Johnny's arrival was a master stroke: he scored on his debut against Port Vale on 13 March to secure our first win in six games and altogether he found the net on seven occasions in those last twelve matches. It seemed as if we might still manage to creep into the top half of the final table — but Johnny had arrived that little bit too late. We lost the next two fixtures, at Brighton (one of Johnny's former clubs) and at Watford, only to win the next home game against Exeter City. But two Easter draws against Colchester followed by home and away defeats by Queens Park Rangers within the space of rather less than seventy two hours — and that in spite of being in the lead on each occasion — made it certain we were doomed.

Time had run out for Manager Cyril Spiers. It was his misfortune that the time at his disposal was foreshortened by the coming of the make or break season of 1957-58, for perhaps another twelve months would have produced a different outcome. However, the hard fact was that yet another post-war manager had failed to bring the Palace any success and we were in the new 4th Division. Mr Spiers saw the situation for what it was and left soon after the season ended.

Now, if the Palace were ever going to make any progress, it was going to have to be from very humble beginnings indeed.

LEFT: A rare picture of Charlie Slade. CENTRE: Arthur Wait was a member of the new administration early in1950. He became a key figure in the Club's advance over the next twenty years. RIGHT: New manager Laurie Scott took over in October 1951. BELOW: This team represented Crystal Palace against Cardiff City on 23 November 1946 (1-2); the picture was given to fans with their Christmas programmes; back: Kurz, Guthrie, J. Lewis, Graham, Hudgell, Bassett; front: Girling, G. Lewis, Dawes, Naylor, Robson.

LEFT: Ernie Randall. BELOW: The scene from the top corner of the Holmesdale Road terracing at Palace's inaugural floodlit match against Chelsea (1-1). RIGHT: Winger Les Devonshire, who joined Palace from Chester in the summer, 1951 CENTRE: and Albert Foulds.

ABOVE: Palace's Tommy Tilston (far left), Ken Bennett (centre) and Wally Hanlon (far right) cannot break down Aldershot's defence on Tilston's debut, 4 February 1954; these were the original Selhurst Park floodlights and cables. BELOW: A Palace squad pose during a break in training during 1955-56; back: R. Greenwood, Andrews, Saunders, Bailey, Edwards, Moss; front: Berry, Belcher, Deakin, Tilston, Gunning. LEFT: Len Choules and RIGHT: Jack Edwards.

AS JIM MERCER SAW IT
HERE THEY ARE ↗ ALL THE NINE GOALS SCORED BY CRYSTAL PALACE ON SATURDAY — AND WE ARE PREPARED TO SWEAR AFFIDAVITS OR ANYTHING ELSE AS TO THE ACCURACY OF THE TOTAL
JOHNNY BYRNE HAD THE DISTINCTION OF SCORING THE VERY FIRST GOAL OF THE SEASON (IN 50 SECONDS)
AND HALF OF THE 15,653 ATTENDANCE HAD THE DISTINCTION OF CHEERING THIS Number 1 GOAL
Did you see what I saw?
No- Neither did you!
THE REMAINING HALF JUST COULDN'T BELIEVE IT
The 9th
EXCLUDING THE OPINION OF ACCRINGTON'S GOALKEEPER, THE PALACE DID A FINE JOB OF WORK
JOHNNY BYRNE FINISHED WITH FOUR GOALS
ALAN WOAN HAD THREE
AND RON HECKMAN SCORED TWO
RECENTLY Manager ARTHUR ROWE SAID TO US THAT THE SEASON WOULD BE ONE OF "EXPECTATION"
SATURDAY'S GAME ALSO INCLUDED APPROBATION
Accrington's equalised!
CONSTERNATION - EXHORTATION
and another makes nine...
ANTICIPATION - CALCULATION / AND EXHILARATION
WE HAVEN'T MENTIONED WEDNESDAY'S GAME WITH DARLINGTON — NINE PALACE GOALS ARE ENOUGH TO GO ROUND IN ONE SESSION OF CARTOONING.
Jim Mercer '60

TOP: Disciplinarian George Smith, Palace's manager, 1958-60. CENTRE: Arthur Rowe began the restoration of Palace's fortunes immediately upon appointment as manager. BOTTOM: New signing, Ron Heckman. RIGHT: Here's the celebrated Jim Mercer cartoon depicting Palace's 9-2 rout of Accrington Stanley on the opening day of the 1960-61 season.

Humble Beginnings

The appearance of Crystal Palace FC in the new, national 4th Division for 1958-59 was admittedly a disappointment to everyone who had the Club's well-being at heart, but it was not without its interest too, for the Club and the fans were meeting new opponents, visiting new grounds and renewing old rivalries.

Crystal Palace met nine clubs for the first time under League auspices in the new 4th Division in 1958-59: Barrow, Carlisle, Chester, Crewe, Darlington, Hartlepool, Southport, Workington and York. We renewed acquaintance with Port Vale, who had left the Southern Section of the 3rd Division back in 1951 to play in the north; Oldham and Gateshead, whom we had last met in 1924-25 in Division 2 (the latter as South Shields) and, longest of all, Bradford Park Avenue, whom we had played in just one Football League season in 1921-22.

George Smith, Palace's new manager, and a tough disciplinarian, vowed before the season began that, if he did not gain promotion for the Club within two years, he would resign. It soon became apparent that it was not going to happen at the first try! Palace won the first fixture handsomely enough, 6-2 against Crewe at Selhurst Park on Saturday 23 August 1958, but we never threatened the best teams and were, at times, down in the middle of the table. We finished seventh, six points adrift of Shrewsbury Town, the club in the fourth promotion place.

Palace's best performances were reserved for Cup competitions. In the FA Cup we again reached the 3rd round but lost bravely to 2nd Division promotion candidates Sheffield United at Bramall Lane, while in the Southern Floodlight Cup (a sort of southern precursor of the Football League Cup) Palace victories over Reading, Millwall and FA Cup Finalists Luton brought us a stirring Final tie at home to Arsenal on Monday 27 April 1959. A crowd of 32,384 saw Mel Charles score a fine winning goal after Johnny Byrne had hit a marvellous equaliser with ten minutes to go on an unforgettable evening.

However, there was honour and distinction for one Palace player towards the end of the 1958-59 season, when goalkeeper Vic Rouse was selected to play for the full Welsh national side in their home international championship match against Northern Ireland in Belfast on 22 April 1959. He thus became the first international player from the 4th Division. Wales lost 1-4, but Vic performed creditably, producing several fine saves and preventing his side from taking a really heavy beating.

George Smith could do no better at the Palace helm in 1959-60, although he was unfortunate that potentially his best close-season signing, Dave Sexton, formerly of West Ham and Brighton, was prevented by injury from appearing in little more than half the games. The only truly memorable feature of the season was the 9-0 annihilation of hapless Barrow here at Selhurst Park on 10 October in which Roy Summersby, probably Smith's best signing, scored four times, the first occasion since the War on which a Palace striker hit more than three goals. But that result, witnessed by just 9,566, must be seen in its context, for Palace had lost the previous four matches and they lost the next one too. Accordingly, we spent most of the season hovering around the middle of the table. True, we showed some improvement in the early spring; that is, until we went to Rochdale on 26 March and lost 0-4 to a side which included former Palace skipper Jack Edwards and our former winger Tony Collins. Frank Lord, later to be Palace's coach under Malcolm Allison, was at centre-forward for the 'Dale and scored two of the goals.

Palace gained some credit for a spirited display in a 3rd round FA Cup-tie at Scunthorpe, who were then a strong 2nd Division side, in a 0-1 defeat upon the only occasion at which we played at the Old Show Ground but, as the season progressed and it became apparent that we were doomed to at least one more season in the 4th Division, George Smith kept his word and left.

The Palace directors did not have far to search for a successor. Smith's assistant since 1958 had been Arthur Rowe, the former and famous Tottenham and England centre-half and one of the top thinkers in the game. He was an experienced manager too. In the 1940s and early 1950s he had transformed 'Spurs from 2nd Division mediocrity to champions of the division and followed that by immediately winning the Football League title in 1950-51, with cultured, flowing football.

The Palace Board had sought Rowe's services in 1958, but he had not been physically fit enough to accept full responsibility then. Now, on 15 April 1960, he decided to take up the challenge — and how thankful all of us at Crystal Palace are that he did so, for he took Palace to promotion for the first time in forty years with attractive, polished play and set the Club on the road to glory.

The only close-season signing was Ron Heckman, a blond, fast-raiding winger from Millwall, well known to London soccer fans. Palace's 110 League goals in 1960-61 were due in no small part to the efforts of this man, whose 14 goals from 42 matches set up a post-war scoring record for a winger at our Club (which only Peter Taylor has equalled), and those of Johnny Gavin over at outside-right.

However, Mr Rowe also made an astute signing early in October when, with several Palace forwards injured, he secured his former 'Spur, Dennis Uphill, from Watford. Uphill was a strong, burly centre-forward, well suited to life in the lower divisions, and took a lot of the physical pressure off Johnny Byrne to play a laudable part in Palace success.

Our first match of the 1960-61 season had the Palace patrons positively purring with satisfaction as the side, adopting Rowe's 'push and run' tactics, put on a fabulous display to smash the now defunct Accrington Stanley 9-2. This was quickly followed by a 'double' over Darlington and a 5-1 win from a rain-interrupted match at Doncaster. Palace thus had a superb base from which to launch a promotion bid, but lowly Hartlepool surprised us by holding us 2-2 at Selhurst Park and then we came up against Peterborough United, in their first season in the League, home and away inside five days. They trimmed us to size 0-2 at Selhurst to push us off the top of the table and at London Road we were well beaten 1-4 in a terrific match, which left us outside the top four promotion places altogether.

Palace, steadied by Rowe's experienced hand, came back well, climbed to the top of the table again by the end of October and stayed there till the spring. Then, having lost only two League games out of twenty one, we suddenly faltered and Peterborough, who had always been at our heels, were able to topple us from the leadership. Even though we finished with four consecutive victories we could not catch them, but there was no great worry on that score because, at last, the Palace had gained promotion. Not that it was simply a promotion season; it was a record breaking one too: Palace hit 110 League goals (albeit in 46 matches) to break the previous record of 107 set up by Peter Simpson and company in 1930-31, while Johnny Byrne, with 30 League goals, established a post-war scoring record that remains unbeaten. Roy Summersby, our second highest scorer with 25 League goals, also broke the previous best of 23 held by Mike Deakin.

Other heroes from the 1960-61 promotion team were skipper Johnny McNichol, who began at half-back but finished the season as full-back, Vic Rouse in goal, towering Gwyn Evans and Len Choules who sewed up the centre of our defence most effectively and wing-halves George Petchey and Terry Long, who both rendered the Club grand service after their playing days were over.

1960-61 was also the inaugural season of the Football League Cup. Palace's exploits do not take long to relate, for we lost our first match in it, 0-2 to Darlington. Laurie Scott, the former Palace manager, returned to Selhurst Park with Hitchin Town in the 1st round of the FA Cup, but Palace saw off the amateurs 6-2, only to lose to Watford in a thrilling replay in the next round to a very late goal indeed, in injury time at the end of the extra half hour.

ABOVE: Palace's Roy Summersby, Johnny Byrne and George Petchey cannot find a way through Hartlepool's defence at Selhurst Park on 3 September 1960 (2-2). BELOW: Crystal Palace 1960-61; back: Brolly (trainer), Petchey, Byrne, Truett, Barnett, Evans, Rouse, Choules, Kerrins, Lunnis, Long, Mr A. Rowe (manager); front: Uphill, Summersby, Noakes, McNichol, Easton, Colfar, Gavin, Heckman.

LEFT: Stalwart captain of the 1960-61 promotion side was Johnny McNichol. RIGHT: Terry Long and George Petchey were versatile defenders while ... BELOW: ... the glamour was provided by internationals Johnny Byrne and Vic Rouse.

Successful Sixties

There were three new players in the Palace side when we began our first season in the 3rd Division in August 1961: full-back Roy Little from Brighton, who had appeared in the 1955 and 1956 FA Cup Finals with Manchester City; Ronnie Allen, the famous West Bromwich Albion and England centre-forward or winger, who had been linked at the Hawthorns with Dick Graham, and Andy Smillie, a talented little fellow from West Ham, who based his game upon that of the immortal Hungarian master Ferenc Puskas.

Palace started well. Continuing to play the stylish 'push and run' game, we won 2-1 at Torquay on the opening Saturday, then beat Notts County 4-1 and Swindon 3-1 at Selhurst Park. We topped the table in September and remained in the top six throughout the autumn. Further honours came the Club's way when Johnny Byrne became our first English international since May 1923, lining up against Northern Ireland at Wembley on 22 November.

However, Palace's impetus faded: we had slipped back to tenth place after the 3 March defeat at Peterborough (1-4), in which Byrne played his last game for us before signing for West Ham at the then record fee between two British clubs of £60,000, plus the return of Ron Brett, and we ultimately concluded affairs down in 15th place. Probably our best performance of the campaign was when we revived memories of our former glories in the FA Cup in a third round tie at Aston Villa. Byrne and Ronnie Allen were magnificent and we appeared to have held the highly placed 1st Division outfit to a splendid 3-3 draw as the seconds ticked away in injury time. But, to the dismay of all the Palace fans at Villa Park and of the neutrals who had been greatly impressed by our display, we conceded a killer goal in the last minute, when a drifting cross-cum-centre from Villa's outside-left, Harry Burrows, eluded Vic Rouse's groping hands and ended up in the corner of the net.

Another supremely important event in the annals of the Club was the visit to Selhurst Park on the night of 10 April 1962 of the crack Spanish and European side, Real Madrid, to mark the new floodlighting system. This occasion was masterminded by the then Palace Chairman, Arthur Wait, and it is to his eternal credit that he inspired such a momentous evening. It was cold, wet and raw, but we forgot all about the weather as Real paraded their fabulous skills and will always remember Puskas, Di Stefano and Ghento . . . as well as Palace's fabulous fight back from two down in eight minutes, to 3-4 with a wonderful goal from Terry Long and the Spanish senors clearly apprehensive as to the outcome right to the end.

Between March and September 1962 the Palace played twenty consecutive League games without recording a victory — our worst-ever sequence in the entire history of the Club, and one we do not want to see challenged! By Christmas 1962 we were next to bottom and in acute danger of dropping back to the oblivion of Division Four. The Club's decline could not be solely attributed to the absence of Johnny Byrne — that was merely one factor in a thoroughly depressing time. The Club and the players, but particularly Arthur Rowe, were badly affected by the tragic death of Ron Brett in a traffic accident at the end of August, and then, with problems enough besides, Arthur Rowe was struck down by illness and forced to drop his responsibilities.

Dick Graham, our former goalkeeper and assistant to Mr Rowe since January 1961, took over. He immediately changed the style of play and made two masterly signings. Palace began to adopt a much more direct game, which involved less close passing and greater use of the long ball, and it paid immediate dividends. Graham's first signings were those of

Cliff Holton, a striker of vast experience with Arsenal, Northampton and Watford, and 'Dickie' Dowsett, another proven goalscorer, from Bournemouth. Big Cliff added power to a diminutive if skilful forward line, while Dowsett provided the ideal foil and was a clever header of the ball. In their first match together they helped Palace romp to a first class 3-0 success at home over Millwall on Boxing Day on a freezing surface.

The transformation was amazing to see. Palace's forwards became a real striking force and the second half of the season, protracted till nearly the end of May because of the long winter freeze-up, was a much healthier one. It included 6-0 and 5-0 routs of Bradford Park Avenue and Wrexham here at Selhurst Park and a fine 4-1 victory at Watford, where Holton scored a hat-trick against his former club and the Watford patrons rose at the finish to acclaim their erstwhile hero.

We ended the season on 23 May with a 4-0 win up at Barnsley to finish in eleventh place: in view of the disastrous start to the season that was an achievement of high merit of which Dick Graham could be justly proud. Our involvement in the Cup competitions came before the improvement in our performances and so was brief and embarrassing. We lost 1-2 at Leeds in the League Cup after being in front for most of the match while in the FA Cup we succumbed 2-7 at Mansfield in a 2nd round replay — our worst Cup result since the War.

Dick Graham made only one close-season addition to the existing staff, which had played its way so confidently out of serious trouble in the second half of 1962-63, and that was of tough little midfielder or winger, Bobby Kellard, from Southend. Then later in the season, the manager made two most astute signings which probably made all the difference between success and failure, for in 1963-64 Dick achieved what all but one of his predecessors had failed to do — he gained Palace promotion to Division Two, thus emulating the feat of Edmund Goodman way back in 1921.

Graham knew precisely the players he wanted and, without prevarication or delay, he went out and got them. First of these was John Sewell. Graham signed this immaculate full-back from Charlton on 25 October, to stiffen our normally redoubtable but occasionally erratic defence after we had lost two consecutive matches. Sewell's contribution to our promotion campaign was restricted to just eighteen matches by a nasty injury at Millwall, which put him out for the remainder of the season. Sewell was later to lead the Palace to much greater heights, but he had already proved a successful signing. The other player drafted in mid-season was Brian Whitehouse. Cliff Holton, Dickie Dowsett and Peter Burridge were a forceful striking trio but, just as Palace were beginning to find goals a little too precious for a side with serious promotion ambitions, Graham bought the former West Bromwich Albion man from Wrexham. Whitehouse scored on his debut, at Selhurst Park against Hull on 23 November (2-2), and in the last, tense, agonising run-in to the season, he hit six goals in the final nine games.

Palace were a strong 3rd Division outfit, of that there was not doubt. We played an aggressive, abrasive style, but we played with discipline and there were quality performances in the side, especially from Bill Glazier and Ronnie Allen. Bill Glazier in goal was a formidable opponent and, though he reached his prime after he left Palace, he was always safe and dependable. Like his predecessor, Jack Alderson, in the 1920-21 promotion-winning side, Bill made full appearances. The rest of the defence was notoriously tight: this was never better shown than in four consecutive matches in January and February, when the forwards netted just a single goal per game but the defence only conceded one, to enable us to take seven points out of eight. Again, it was only in the eighth home match of 1964 that the defence was eventually breached.

Skipper of the side was Ronnie Allen, the former Albion and England winger or centre-forward. His experience and guile ideally qualified him to marshall Palace on the field although we were denied his presence in the last nine matches because of a dislocated knee.

The season started with a dreadful 1-5 beating at Coventry, but wholesale team changes gained a scoreless draw at Reading and further re-arrangements produced a 3-1 win over Mansfield. Nine matches without defeat in the early autumn took us into second place but then we lost twice, both by 1-3 margins at Watford and Oldham. However, by the end of the year we had regained the number two position. We lost an unforgettable match at Bournemouth 3-4, but then put together fourteen undefeated matches, including ten victories, so that by Easter we were on top of the table. In spite of massive support Palace could only finish with five draws and two defeats but the fifth of those draws, at Wrexham on Wednesday 22 April, was enough to ensure we won promotion.

There was every chance that Palace would take the 3rd Division championship too. We needed only a draw at home to Oldham (who had themselves been in contention with us for most of the season) in the final game but, although we led at half-time with a Cliff Holton penalty, Oldham's balding outside-right, Bob Ledger, hit an 11 minute hat-trick in the first quarter of an hour of the second period to deny our hopes of such glory, for Coventry beat Colchester and snatched the title on goal average.

Nonetheless, Palace were back in Division 2 and it was a jubilant scene when, after the match and the season were over, the players who had made the triumph possible came to the 27,967 crowd and threw floral bouquets to the fans who had supported them and their predecessors, some from the last time Palace played a 2nd Division match back in 1925.

It may seem surprising to modern day readers, but some people complained about Dick Graham! Some supporters and some parts of the press decided that Dick's tactics were dour and dull, while his habit of announcing his team as late as possible and making several positional changes was allegedly annoying and confusing. Palace fans would defend Dick on both charges, although perhaps with more justification on the first than on the second.

Our defence *was* easily the best in the Division, and was adept at soaking up pressure. Dick was deploying Alan Stephenson and Brian Wood in an early but highly effective dual centre-half role and Bert Howe, Don Townsend and John Sewell were all at their best at the time — but with forwards of such proven goalscoring skill as Cliff Holton, Ronnie Allen and Peter Burridge in the side Palace could not fairly be described as 'dull' and, by the time we were finding scoring difficult, we had become one of the sides all the other clubs in the division wanted, planned and strove (but, usually, failed) to beat, and perhaps their frustrations led to outbursts of unreasoned criticism.

One must admit however, that Dick Graham's 'numbers game' could be rather perplexing — it certainly raised the ire of plenty of opponents, though whether it confused any of them or actually assisted the Palace is debatable. But it is worth remembering that in those days most programmes (not the Palace one, I hasten to add!) still persisted in laying out the team in the formation of full-backs, half-backs and forwards, so Dick was also chipping away at the old thinking of the game, which decreed that a player with a certain number had a pre-ordained role to fulfil on-field.

In contrast to success in the League our Cup hopes were extinguished early in both competitions in the West Country. Bristol Rovers put us out of the League Cup (0-2) at the first hurdle, leaving us still without a victory in the new competition. In the FA Cup Palace had no trouble disposing of Harwich and Parkestone in the first round at Selhurst Park, notching our highest-ever score in the tournament with an 8-2 win. Alas, the tables were swiftly turned in round two for, on 7 December 1963, Palace fell where many more distinguished clubs had fallen before them, on 'The Slopes of Huish' at Yeovil (1-3).

Before the Palace could open their 1964-65 Football League season they accepted an invitation to play in the inaugural match at the new Crystal Palace Sports Centre, up at their original home, on 19 August 1964. Our opponents for this showpiece were West Ham, the FA Cup holders, but Palace romped to a gritty 4-1 victory to provide a fine augury for the season ahead, which was to develop into the most successful one in the Club's history to that date in each competition.

However, at the start, there were one or two setbacks! For example, our first match in the 2nd Division since May 1925 was against Derby County here at Selhurst Park on Saturday 22 August 1964. Dick Graham was content to rely entirely upon men who had been closely involved in gaining promotion the previous April and most of the 22,935 crowd were delighted when Peter Burridge gave us an early lead. But, with Bill Glazier and his colleagues clearly out of touch, Derby equalised before the half hour and then applied great pressure after the break, scoring twice in five minutes just after the hour. Cliff Holton did bring some respectability to the proceedings with a late reply, but there was no doubt that Palace had been given a nasty lesson.

Mr Graham decided that no fewer than six changes were required for the midweek visit to Swindon, including the debut of John Jackson in the Palace goal. But it was to prove no story book debut for 'Jacko' and Palace were well beaten by Bert Head's team, which included Don Rogers at number eleven; then we went down again in the third match of the season, with Bill Glazier back in goal, at Swansea.

But Palace recovered quickly and well: we recorded our first victory when Swindon came up for the return match on Wednesday 2 September, and then proceeded to win no fewer than five consecutive matches: indeed, during the month of September we played eight League games and won seven. Alan Stephenson was outstanding in the centre of our defence as Palace came to terms with the 2nd Division and, for the middle months of the term, we were actually on the edge of the promotion bracket. We finished seventh; a highly creditable achievement for a newly promoted club and all the more so in this instance, because we had played the second half of the season with the injured Brian Wood absent from our defence. At that time it was the best season's performance in the Club's sixty-year history.

Dick Graham retained Palace's high work-rate of the previous season and a half, in order to secure this achievement, but he gradually adjusted his tactics to include greater skill, through the signings of Keith Smith from Peterborough in November and David Burnside from Southampton just before Christmas. This duo certainly added class to our attack, which now had a well-balanced mixture of craft and punch. Burnside was a great ball artist and scored twice on his Boxing Day debut, to enable Palace to come from behind to defeat Portsmouth 4-2 here at Selhurst Park. Keith Smith was the scorer of one of the fastest-ever goals in the history of football, and certainly the fastest in the annals of our Club, when he netted in just six seconds in the reverse fixture of the opening match of the season, at Derby, on 12 December, where Palace gained a 3-3 draw.

Another indication of Dick Graham's skilful manipulation of the transfer market was shown when Bill Glazier moved to Coventry City in October for the then record fee for a goalkeeper of £35,000. Graham immediately purchased Welsh international Tony Millington from West Bromwich Albion to make Palace a handsome profit of some £30,000 in the week! However, it was the emergence of John Jackson shortly after this that was to become one of the features of the 1965-65 season for, by the end of the year, 'Jacko' was earning high praise for his goalkeeping performances and, by the season's end, he was in undisputed possession of the Palace goalkeeper's jersey.

In March Ronnie Allen left the Palace to return to the Midlands as senior coach at Wolves, after playing exactly 100 League games for us, and it was at this time too that there began to emerge a new wing-half/midfield player named David Payne, who was to become a great Palace favourite and a quality player for us in the 1st Division.

Palace's FA Cup progress illustrates most effectively the fine balance Dick Graham and his team had attained. To overcome Bury (then a vigorous 2nd Division club) in the 3rd round to the tune of 5-1, with only ten men after Brian Wood had been stretchered off with a badly broken leg, was a triumph for the Palace stormtroopers. Southampton were dismissed at the Dell in much the same style, but Palace then outplayed the renowned footballers from 1st Division Nottingham Forest, at their own game, to win by a convincing 3-1 margin and reach the last eight for the first time since 1907. This superb performance on a heavy snow-flecked ground was the peak of Palace finesse and achievement under Dick Graham: I had travelled down overnight from Durham University to see this match and was amply rewarded. In fact a new record crowd of 41,667 turned up on that cold February afternoon — but within three weeks that record had itself been eclipsed, for 45,384 people came to see the 6th round tie against mighty Leeds United. The match itself was something of an anti-climax and Palace were never able to equal the tough Yorkshiremen, going down 0-3 in a bruising encounter.

In the Football League Cup the Palace at last gained their first victory, beating Tranmere 2-0 on our initial visit to Prenton Park. We then went on to beat Southampton but bowed out in a Selhurst Park replay to eventual finalists, Leicester City.

Dick Graham's first move towards improving the squad available for the 1965-66 season was, to say the least, a bitter disappointment for most Palace fans, because he allowed Cliff Holton to leave Selhurst Park. Cliff had undoubtedly been Dick Graham's best signing and had done a terrific job since the bleak midwinter days of 1962-63. He had gained a huge following at the Palace and, even if he was beginning to slow up a little and spend more time in defence than formerly, his sheer presence in our side added power and experience, while his arrival in opponents' penalty areas for set pieces still caused chaos. Cliff moved to Watford from the Palace and then on to Charlton in February 1966.

Dick's objective was to replace Cliff with big Derek Kevan, the former West Bromwich Albion and Chelsea centre-forward and ex-England international. Alongside Kevan was another new striker, Ian Lawson, an England Youth international who joined us from Leeds, having previously been with Burnley. On paper it should have worked out well enough, but unfortunately neither Kevan or Lawson proved at all successful for Palace, and inevitably both the two players and the manager came in for strident criticism from the fans.

In fairness to Dick Graham it must be pointed out that, even if his flair in the transfer market had deserted him, he was still capable of making useful signings on the Palace club's behalf. During the summer of 1965 Dick also brought in two experienced players who were to serve the Club most usefully — Ernie Yard, a versatile player who came from Bury but was the only Scotsman on the Palace books, and Jack Bannister, a strong, competitive midfield man, who arrived from Scunthorpe but was well known to Mr Graham from their days together at West Bromwich and who made over 100 League appearances for the Palace.

Leaving at this stage were Peter Burridge, who added yet another London club to his career list by joining Charlton in November, while Bobby Kellard went to Ipswich. Later in the term, Brian Whitehouse joined Burridge and Holton at the Valley, but by then Stewart Imlach had returned to Selhurst Park as player-coach — and there had been a managerial change as well.

Just three days into the New Year it was announced that Dick Graham himself was leaving Selhurst Park — sacked, with two years of his contract still to run — and that Arthur Rowe would take temporary charge. Within a few hours of the news breaking Graham was handed a letter signed by his twenty-one senior professionals, regretting his departure and thanking him for what he had done for the Club. This was perhaps a little surprising, because Graham had had his disagreements with many of the players and several of them were on the transfer list, although Arthur Rowe immediately vetoed all outgoing transfers. The most publicised tiff between the tough, uncompromising Graham and his players had been on Euston Station as the team prepared to journey to Carlisle for the 2nd Division fixture on 11 December. It culminated in the 21-year-old Alan Stephenson being sent home. The incident appeared to blow over, but the tensions obviously continued and three weeks later Graham was dismissed.

Dick's contribution to the Palace between December 1962 and January 1966 can scarcely be over-estimated. He took Palace from an almost certain return to the 4th Division to a respectable position in Division Two. He left with his head high, the gratitude of the fans and sharing their sorrow that he and they could not have gone on to even better things together.

However, in the light of later Palace history, even the dismissal of Dick Graham was not the most significant event in the 1965-66 season at Selhurst Park. Rather it was the League debut, first goal and early career of a man who was to have the unique distinction of playing in both Palace teams that were to gain promotion to Division One in 1969 and 1979, of captaining our 1st Division side in 1971 and then, in 1981, of becoming Palace's manager . . . Steve Kember.

Steve Kember was a local lad who joined the Palace as an apprentice in December 1963, having already played for Croydon and Surrey Schools. He played regularly for the Junior teams and signed as a full professional in December 1965. He was a gifted player, a great forager in midfield, a splendid passer of the ball; he possessed surprising reserves of energy for a player of his size and his driving, resilient skills served Palace faithfully and pleasingly in nearly three hundred matches.

Palace were a mid-table 2nd Division side throughout this 1965-66 season and Dick Graham's departure had little or no effect upon the playing record. Perhaps the most interesting occurrences were the highly competitive pre-season friendly at the Crystal Palace Centre, in which West Ham avenged their defeat of twelve months earlier with a 2-1 victory gained by a penalty just before the end, and the first match of the season at Birmingham.

Birmingham had been relegated from the 1st Division the previous April, so this was a testing start to Palace's season. Birmingham took a 13th minute lead but, just before the interval, Ian Lawson volleyed a surprise Palace equaliser on his debut. Birmingham restored their advantage late on in the 84th minute but, in the last moments, Palace gained a corner and Alan Stephenson leapt high at the far post to nod the ball home. However, while the ball was still in flight, and before it had crossed the goal-line, the referee began to blow his whistle for the end of the match and, although the ball hit the back of the net while he was still blowing, the 'goal' could not stand, for it is the first note of the final whistle that signals the close of the game.

It was towards the end of the season, on 18 April 1966, that the appointment of Palace's new manager was confirmed. Largely due to the persistence of the Palace Chairman, Mr Arthur Wait, Mr Bert Head was installed as Palace boss.

Mr Head had gained a great reputation while manager of Swindon Town from 1957 to 1965 but it was from Bury that he joined Crystal Palace and the Shakers' chairman was heard to remark, 'We've lost and you've got the best manager in the business'.

The 1966-67 League season opened on Saturday 20 August, an afternoon of tropical heat. Palace's opponents were Carlisle United at Selhurst Park and Palace played extremely well in the torrid conditions (the temperature did not fall below 80 degrees for the first hour of the game!) to win 4–2. Two new Palace men each scored a brace of goals on their club debuts that afternoon: Tom White and Bobby Woodruff.

Tom White was a stocky, robust but extremely talented centre-forward who had joined us from Aberdeen. He did not have the best of luck with injuries while he was with us, but his presence early in the season helped Palace ease to within a point of the top of the table by the second week of September. Bobby Woodruff was well known to Bert Head, for the manager had discovered him at Swindon. Woodruff had moved on to Wolves but gladly rejoined his former boss at Selhurst Park. He was renowned in football for his phenomenal long throw-in, which gave his side the equivalent of a corner whenever they gained a throw-in within twenty yards of the corner flag; he could reach the penalty spot from the touch-line without any difficulty. However, Bobby was very much more than an exponent of the art of the long throw — he was a fine header of the ball and his accurate passing and skilful dribbling were greatly appreciated by Palace fans. Bobby was a goalscorer too: his 18 League goals for us in this 1966-67 season, which he equalled in 1967-68, was easily our best in the higher divisions of the League until the days of Mark Bright and Ian Wright so, although injury and illness prevented him from playing a full part in the promotion season of 1968-69, he was a major factor in bringing Palace that success.

Two other important signings by Bert Head were those of John McCormick, who joined us in the close season with Tom White from Aberdeen and Cliff Jackson from Plymouth. It would be another fifteen months before Palace fans would catch more than a glimpse of McCormick, for the injury jinx hit him too, and he could only appear twice in our League side this season, but what service he was later to render.

Cliff Jackson joined Palace in September 1966 and was another of Bert Head's 'Swindon Old Boys', although he had been down at Plymouth since 1963. Cliff could play successfully as a winger or as a striker and was a useful member of our side, reaching his peak for us in 1968-69 to help us gain 1st Division status.

There were departures too, of course, and a most unusual one took place early in September 1966. Palace were due at Molineux for our 2nd Division match on Wednesday 7 September and in the team line-ups in the match programme we had David Burnside listed at number eight. However, during the very day of the match Burnside was transferred to Wolves and actually played against us and to cap it all he scored Wolves' goal! Steve Kember neatly tucked away our equaliser.

Later in the season three fine servants left the Palace for other clubs: Stewart Imlach went to Notts County in March 1967 as assistant manager, while defenders Brian Wood and Bert Howe moved across London to join Orient in December and January respectively. Palace's former manager Dick Graham was now the chief at Brisbane Road and began a trend, continued when George Petchey became their boss, of taking Palace players to the East London side.

As the season progressed Bert Head made several signings. In September he added Barry Dyson of Tranmere to our staff — the only member of the Prenton Park club ever to sign for Palace. Barry came to us with a fine scoring record in the lower divisions but he found life in Division Two rather too demanding, and he moved back to the 3rd Division with Watford in January 1968. Eddie Presland came to us as a tall and sturdy full-back from West Ham in January 1967. He played every match for us in 1966-67 after his signing and missed only two in 1967-68.

The most popular signing took place on 15 February 1967 when Mr Head persuaded Johnny Byrne to return to us from West Ham. By co-incidence a friendly match with Leicester City (1-1) had been arranged for the following evening and the Palace fans welcomed their former favourite back to the Selhurst Park fold by singing 'Hello Johnny, Welcome home, Johnny', to the theme tune of the hit musical of the period, *Hello Dolly*. It was an emotional night and Johnny hit our goal to demonstrate the wisdom of Bert Head's judgement.

Potentially this signing could have made an enormous difference to Palace but sadly, it never worked out that way and he moved on to Fulham on the day of the transfer deadline in the following season, 16 March 1968. Negotiations for this move took place almost entirely on the Manchester-London train on which the Palace team were returning from a 1-2 defeat at Blackburn and the Fulham boys from a 1-5 drubbing at Manchester City. Byrne's Palace career embraced 259 League and Cup games, he scored 101 goals for us and was the first post-war player to net over a century of goals for the Club, while his 30 League goals in 1960-61 remain the post-war record for a single season.

In spite of a run of misfortune with injuries, Palace had a really good season in Mr Head's first full term. Although Tom White and John Sewell broke their collar bones in consecutive matches in early September we were second in the table in mid-November, after an excellent 2-1 win at Coventry (the eventual champions). The other promoted side were Wolves and we took three points from them and from Coventry — actually saving our best performance of the whole season for Wolves and the final game. They came to Selhurst Park on 13 May with Ronnie Allen as their manager and former Palace men David Burnside and John Holsgrove in their side. They knew they would be promoted but, if they could gain a draw at our expense, they would go up as champions. A splendid crowd of 26,930 saw Palace sweep the visitors imperiously aside with a powerful and confident display: we were three up after little more than an hour, finished 4-1 and could have had another two or three goals!

Palace paraded a new strip for the 1967-68 season — the all-white one favoured since 1964 was replaced by claret jerseys with a thin light-blue stripe, white shorts and light-blue socks with a claret turnover.

We began the season without any significant additons to the staff and made a brilliant start to the new campaign by winning 3-0 at Rotherham on the opening day, easily our best result there. Our first home game was against Derby County, who had just appointed a new manager who would soon lead them to great success, Brian Clough. However, on this occasion Palace won 1-0 with a 29th minute header from Bobby Woodruff.

Apart from a disappointing defeat at Barrow in the Football League Cup, Palace continued to progress and, by the evening of Saturday 30 September, after our 1-0 defeat of Queens Park Rangers at Selhurst Park, we were sitting, for the first time in our history, on the top of the 2nd Division table. A record crowd for a Football League fixture of 38,006 saw Terry Long strike the 38th minute goal that put Palace there.

Terry Long had joined the Palace club in May 1955 from Wycombe Wanderers and he played most of his games for us as a wing half-back or full-back. He made his debut against Walsall at Selhurst Park on 28 September 1955 when another Palace debutant, Jimmy Murray, scored both our goals, to secure a 2-0 victory. Terry missed just four matches in the 1956-57 season, then made full appearances in each of the next three League seasons, so that between 5 September 1956 and 4 March 1961 he made 214 consecutive League appearances — a figure only improved upon by John Jackson (222).

Terry was a model professional and a great club-man and he received a richly deserved testimonial on 11 October 1966. He was a steady defender, though he could play as an inside-forward too, and a clever footballer. He did not often score goals but, when he did, they were often important or spectacular affairs, like the one against Rangers or the one that brought the crowd to its feet against Real Madrid. Like Johnny Byrne, Terry played for the Club in four divisions of the League (Third (South), Fourth, Third and Second) and his 442 League appearances plus 38 Cup-ties for us have only been exceeded by the great Jim Cannon.

With Palace still riding high in the 2nd Division, this was an ideal time for another great servant of the club, George Petchey, to play his testimonial and on 15 November 1967 the Palace side faced a team of stars, largely from the bigger London clubs, called an 'International XI', before 10,243 loyal fans for George's benefit. Palace won 6-3 and our last three, from Bobby Woodruff, Cliff Jackson and Tom White, were all scored in a cracking blitz in the last five minutes.

George Petchey had come to the Palace in the summer of 1960 to play under Arthur Rowe. He helped Palace to gain promotion the following April and he continued as a regular first team man with Dick Graham, making 24 appearances in the side that won its way into Division Two in 1963-64. Unfortunately, George's career was brought to a premature end by a troublesome eye complaint and his final match for us was the 6th round FA Cup-tie against Leeds (0-3) on 10 March 1965. After Dick Graham left the Palace in January 1966, George assisted Arthur Rowe as team coach and retained the post when Bert Head arrived. He helped to mould the Palace side that gained the Club its entry to the 1st Division and was an integral part of our set-up in the top flight from 1969 to 1971 before he became manager of Orient.

Palace remained at the head of the 2nd Division for just two weeks. A 0-2 defeat at Blackpool in pouring rain on 14 October toppled us and we never regained the premier place. After the Christmas-New Year fixtures against Portsmouth (both 2-2 draws) we were sixth; at the conclusion of the Easter games, which included a 6-0 rout of Norwich, we were down to twelfth and we finished the season eleventh. During this period of relative decline Palace were knocked out of the FA Cup in a Selhurst Park replay by Walsall. The Saddlers' goal at Fellows Park was a thunderous free-kick from Colin Taylor but Bert Head was so impressed with Taylor's striking power that he bought him in May 1968 and Colin's eight League goals for us in 1968-69 were of great value in our surge to Division One.

Starring for Palace by this time was Mark Lazarus, who had joined us from Queens Park Rangers for £11,000. His experience on the right wing and ability to score goals from the flank were in no small part to assist Palace to promotion in 1968-69 and he became a huge favourite with the fans, who loved his ecstatic celebrations after he had found the net.

Coming to the fore too was Phil Hoadley. Phil was the one member of the 1967-68 FA Youth Cup side that reached the semi-finals of that competition for the first time, who was to go on to make an impact in the Football League. He made his senior Palace debut as a substitute some three weeks after Coventry Juniors had put us out of the Youth Cup on 27 April 1968 — in Palace's 2-2 draw at Bolton — and remains the youngest player ever to appear in a Palace shirt at 16 years and 3 months of age. Well built, strong in the air, Phil played exceptionally well in Palace's overpressed defence in the 1st Division and made a total of 73 League appearances for us, before he became George Petchey's first signing as the manager of Orient in October 1971 and went on to make over 250 appearances for the East London club.

Palace received three big fees around the time of the spring transfer deadline. As well as Johnny Byrne's departure, Tom White left us for Blackpool and Alan Stephenson got his wish for 1st Division football by joining West Ham, for a club record fee in the region of £75,000. Upon Alan's departure the club captaincy was awarded to John Sewell and now the scene was set for an epic season.

Mel Blyth arrived from Scunthorpe United towards the end of June 1968 to provide another key component in the Palace side. Tall, strong, and fair-haired, Mel began as a wing-half-cum-inside-forward but he developed into a magnificent back-four man, where his stature made him a natural central defender. His partnership with John McCormick became a feature of this promotion season and of Palace's stay in the 1st Division between 1969 and 1973, while over that period only John Jackson appeared more times than Mel.

Three autumn signings completed Mr Head's assembly of the team which was to crown his leadership with success. The first of these was in September, when tough Roger Hoy joined us from 'Spurs to add defensive and midfield strength. Then in October Mr Head made the first of a series of highly successful sorties across the border for players from the Scottish League. On this occasion be brought back John Loughlan, a talented left back, and Tony Taylor, a winger at the time, but soon to become a mighty midfield man for us, from Greenock Morton.

Thus Mr Head's team was complete. Each member of it was a gifted footballer and under Bert's expert guidance they were blended into a formidable unit. The magnificent John Jackson was in goal with the immaculate John Sewell at number two and John Loughlan at left back. Our central defensive pillars were John McCormick and Mel Blyth. In front of them were the talented local boys David Payne and Steve Kember with midfield dynamo Tony Taylor. Roger Hoy filled in at full-back or in midfield. The front runners were Mark Lazarus, Cliff Jackson and Colin Taylor, and Bobby Woodruff, who played either as a striker or in midfield, but had the misfortune to break his collarbone as the season approached its climax.

Palace gave early notice of their intentions, by winning the first three matches of the League season and going to the top of the division, but we lost 0-4 at Middlesbrough, another aspiring side, and we forfeited the leadership to them. Palace never fell far away — although there were at least half a dozen clubs seriously involved in the promotion race until late on. By the end of October we were in eighth place, four points behind the leaders; at the turn of the year we were fifth with the same margin. At the end of January, with Palace still in contention, if trailing the pacemakers somewhat, a four week gap was torn in the fixture list by ice and snow. When Palace resumed they were in inspired form!

Palace's first match upon the resumption was on 22 February at home to Hull: we came through 2-0 and never lost another match in the League until we were in the 1st Division. Including that Hull victory, Palace played sixteen matches and won ten of them. The game that told Palace supporters that there was a real chance of the almost unbelievable coming true was when Palace went to table-toppers and promotion favourites, Derby County on Wednesday 5 March, and won a sparkling encounter with a goal from Bobby Woodruff. Palace followed this up three days later with another majestic performance at Birmingham, who were also well to the fore in the promotion stakes. Steve Kember slid in our goal from an acute angle to win the match for Palace.

Palace beat Millwall 4-2 on 19 March to slip neatly into second place, although Middlesbrough pushed us back at the end of the week by pasting Hull 5-3, while we only drew with Charlton, another promotion-seeking side. We regained that second position with a 2-1 win at Carlisle a week later and then Middlesbrough came down to the Palace on Good Friday and played out a 0-0 draw in front of a 41,381 crowd. Palace had a superior goal average, so we remained in front of them, beat Portsmouth the next day and then secured two confident 0-0 draws at Huddersfield and Preston. The second of these gave Palace promotion in everything but name, because 'Boro unaccountably lost at home to Bury and were now unable to catch us, while Charlton were four points behind, with both clubs having two matches left to play.

36,126 fans turned up for Palace's last home match, against Fulham, to acclaim the side. Palace made statistically certain with a 3-2 win, after Fulham had led 2-0 and George Petchey had had a few meaningful words with the Palace side at the interval — but Charlton lost at home anyway! The scenes of jubilation at Selhurst Park almost defy description. It was wonderful! Although since repeated, this was the occasion upon which the Palace first reached Division One, so perhaps the emotions that accompany such a success were felt most sharply then.

There was one match left to play, a re-arranged game at Blackburn. Our hosts applauded us onto the field, Palace won 2-1 more comfortably than the scoreline suggests, but John McCormick and Rovers' Frank Kopel were sent off in some tense exchanges near the end.

LEFT: England international Ronnie Allen came to the Palace summer 1961. ABOVE: An improved floodlighting system for Palace's home game against Notts County (4-1) on Wednesday 23 August 1962. BELOW: Dick Graham adopted a more direct style as Palace's manager in December 1962 and later challenged the football establishment with his 'numbers-game'. RIGHT: Immaculate John Sewell came in October 1963 from Charlton Athletic.

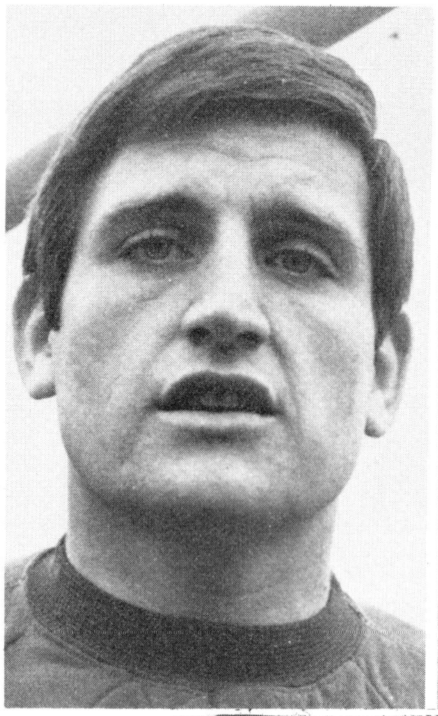

LEFT: John Jackson made his debut at Swindon (0-2) in the second game of 1964-65 and became our undisputed first-choice goalkeeper by the end of the season. CENTRE: FA Cup fever hit Palace after the Forest success; the queue for tickets for the 6th round tie against Leeds stretches down Holmesdale Road. RIGHT: Bert Head was installed as manager in April 1966. BELOW: The Crystal Palace team which appeared in the final match of the 1963-64 season, against Oldham (1-3) on 25 April 1964: back: Howe, Long, Petchey, Glazier, Wood, Stephenson; front: Kellard, Whitehouse, Holton, Burridge, Werge.

LEFT: (l-r) The signings Bert Head made for Palace in the summer of 1966: John McCormick, Bobby Woodruff, Tommy White, Brian O'Connell and Hugh Brophy. TOP: Talented local boy David Payne. RIGHT: John McCormick was the lynch–pin of Palace's defence in the 1968-69 promotion side. CENTRE: Crystal Palace 1967-68; back: Mr B. Head (manager), Andrew, Long, White, McCormick, Presland, Payne, Dyson, Bannister, G. Petchey (coach); front: Sewell, Light, Byrne, Stephenson, Woodruff, C. Jackson, Brophy, Kember; on ground: J. Jackson, Parsons. BELOW: Action from Palace v QPR on 30 September 1967 sees (left) Danny Light and Tom White foiled by keeper Ron Springett and defender Hunt, and Terry Long scoring the decisive goal after fine work by Bobby Woodruff and Tom White. This took Palace to the top of the old 2nd Division for the first time. RIGHT: Something of a mix-up between Cliff Jackson and Bill Wigham during the tense Good Friday morning promotion clash involving Palace and Middlesbrough on 4 April 1969. The Arthur Wait Stand is going up.

ABOVE: Crowd scenes as the Palace players parade in the Directors' Box after beating Fulham 3-2 on 19 April 1969 to make statistically certain of a place in the 1st Division. BELOW: Crystal Crystal Palace FC 1969-70; back (l-r) Thorup, Blyth, J. Jackson, Hynd, Parsons, McCormick, Woodruff; middle: Petchey (coach), C. Jackson, C. Taylor, Kember, T. Taylor, Payne, Hoy, Mr B. Head (manager); front: Queen, Sewell, Lazarus.

Part Three: Status and Set-back 1969-95

THE TURBULENT YEARS

Having taken Crystal Palace into Division One for the first time, Bert Head's immediate task was to keep them there. He was assisted by two former Palace wing-halves — trainer Jess Willard, with the Club since 1953, and George Petchey, who had appeared regularly in the 1960-61 and 1963-64 promotion winning sides — while the assistant manager was the great Arthur Rowe who, in 1961, had taken Palace to their first promotion in forty years in his first season in charge.

There was extensive activity in the form of ground improvements at Selhurst Park — the most significant since its opening in 1924 — during the summer of 1969, primarily in the erection of a new, handsome Arthur Wait Stand. Work had begun during the spring of 1969 and the last half dozen or so matches of 1968-69 had been played against the backdrop of earth movement and newly driven piles, but it continued apace during the close season under the personal direction (and with the personal involvement) of the Chairman himself, who was quite determined it should be ready in time for Palace's 1st Division debut. The Stand is 270 feet long, 33 feet high and has a depth of 137 feet so that, at the time of its erection at least, its roof had the largest span of any stand at any Football League ground. Until 1990 only its upper two tiers were seated accommodation, the rest a popular standing enclosure. It was officially opened on Wednesday evening, 26 November 1969 by Sir Alf Ramsey, prior to Arthur Rowe's Testimonial match and remains a fine memorial to a devoted Palace servant and a remarkable man.

As he had done most successfully in the Second Division, Bert Head looked largely to Scotland, where the transfer fees were less inflated, to augment his playing strength for the challenge of the First Division. Roger Hynd, a tall, dark, strong central defender came from Rangers for £22,000 to play alongside evergreen John McCormick; Per Bartram, a Danish international forward, also arrived from north of the border, joining Palace from Greenock Morton, the club from which Mr Head had obtained full-back John Loughlan and winger Tony Taylor, and there was Gerry Queen, a stylish £45,000 striker from Kilmarnock, probably Mr Head's most effective signing for Palace over our four years among the elite between 1969 and 1973. Not only did Gerry top our goalscoring chart in this 1969-70 season but on his day he was as good as any of his contemporaries and would almost certainly have won a string of Scottish international caps if he had been appearing for a more fashionable or more successful outfit. He possessed considerable skills, had grace and power and was strong in the air, yet was always willing to battle for his side to the final whistle. His value to the Palace is best measured by the fact that he was easily our leading scorer in Division One between 1969 and 1973 with 24 top flight goals, while his tally of 18 in the first two seasons represented precisely one quarter of our total.

Conversely, it was not long before the promotion-winning side began to break up: Colin 'Cannonball' Taylor returned to Walsall in mid-September without playing in the top flight, and by Christmas, those two great favourites, Mark Lazarus, our ebullient outside-right, and Bobby Woodruff, he of the prodigious long throw-in, had gone to Orient and Cardiff respectively.

Palace's first match in the First Division could not have created greater interest if we had been able to choose our opponents: it was at Selhurst Park and against Manchester United! A record crowd of 48,610 paid record receipts of £16,250 for that unique occasion on 9 August 1969 and was certainly treated to an exciting afternoon's entertainment even if the match fell some way short of being a classic. It was surprising for some fans to see a team of United's calibre fall for Palace's long throw-in routine, which had reaped such high dividends in the lower division, when Mel Blyth's header from Roger Hoy's delivery dipped over Jimmy Rimmer to give Palace the lead and secure our first-ever goal in the top flight. Mel was undoubtedly Palace's man of the match. As well as netting that important goal he coped superbly with the great Bobby Charlton, and this upon his own Division One debut.

Charlton managed a United equaliser but Palace went ahead again when Gerry Queen opened his account, evading David Sadler, then firing past Rimmer and for a little while it looked as if Palace might achieve an outstanding result but Willy Morgan popped up to equalise again for United. Frankly, Palace fans were quite content that afternoon with the draw their favourites had gained in competition with one of the leading clubs.

After the excitement and glamour of the opening match Palace always played with enthusiasm. We beat Sunderland four days later with an early goal from Tony Taylor and another after 66 minutes from Cliff Jackson, to extend our unbeaten run to 18 matches — still the Club record — then led at Everton on the second Saturday of the season with a goal after only six minutes, fired home in spectacular fashion from some twenty yards by Mel Blyth, only to go down 1-2 in unfortunate circumstances to a fluke equaliser and a controversial penalty. As the season progressed the gulf between the First and Second Divisions proved wider than we had thought, Palace began to struggle and sustained some particularly heavy home defeats. Arsenal won 1-5 at Selhurst Park and Chelsea repeated the lesson in a match on 27 December 1969, at which our new attendance record of 49,498 was established.

By that Chelsea defeat the team had scored a bare 22 goals from 26 League matches and it was clear that additional firing power was needed. To add experience and quality Bert Head borrowed Bobby Tambling, who had been deposed from Chelsea's first team, for three matches, under the new 'loan transfer' scheme and in early February he also signed Jim Scott, a tall, dark, ball-playing Scottish international winger or centre-forward from Newcastle, for £20,000.

Palace managed just one solitary away victory this term, but they gained it in inspired fashion and in highly demanding circumstances at Maine Road, Manchester in mid-March in a re-arranged midweek encounter. Manchester City had won the League Cup the previous weekend and this was the night of their gala celebration. But with John Jackson in magnificent form, the defence weathered the early and emotional surge of City pressure, Palace gained control of midfield, and then Gerry Queen scored from close range. The second half was pretty hectic, but Jackson's confidence spread to the entire team and the star-studded City line-up grew more and more frustrated as their celebration night went wrong.

In fact Palace did the 'double' over City by winning the Selhurst Park return. This was our final match of the season even though it was played as early as Monday 6 April and, urged on by a 27,704 crowd (which was a couple of thousand *below* the season's average!), Palace gained both points with a 21st minute goal by Roger Hoy. Our fans stormed on to the pitch at the final whistle to acclaim their heroes, confident that our top-class status had been ensured by this success, but it actually depended upon whether either Sunderland or Sheffield Wedneday could gain three points from their remaining two games, now that our own programme had been completed. Thankfully, they both failed and Palace were safe.

By early June 1970 manager Bert Head had signed three players with considerable top-flight experience to strengthen his back four and striking line. The first summer signing was that of stylish, intelligent, left-back Peter Wall for £25,000 from Liverpool. Peter joined us on 5 May 1970 and served the Club honourably and well for eight years, making a major contribution to our cause in the two 1st Division seasons after he joined. Then, just as England were beginning their unsuccessful defence of the World Cup in Mexico, Mr Head obtained the services of two accomplished strikers from Chelsea. Bobby Tambling now joined Palace on a permanent basis along with blond, six-footer Alan Birchenall, for a Club record fee of £140,000.

Later in the summer Palace again hit the headlines when an impressive new bonus scheme was announced which, it was reported, could earn players a weekly pay packet of up to £300; the close season also saw the departures of Cliff Jackson and Roger Hoy from the 1968-69 promotion team to Torquay and Luton Town respectively. Roger Hynd left for Birmingham City for £25,000 at the end of July.

Although Palace managed only a single point from their opening pair of matches, *and* we lost our first home game of the season 0-1 to Manchester City on Wednesday 19 August, for the rest of the first half of the season and a little beyond, we gave every appearance of having learned the necessary lessons from the previous season's narrow escape. Gerry Queen and Alan Birchenall quickly came to an understanding of each other's play and abilities and some good, even impressive results were secured. Newcastle and Blackpool were both beaten 1-0 at Selhurst Park and an outstanding 1-1 draw was gained at Anfield, when a Gerry Queen header stunned the Kop and Liverpool only managed to stutter to a second half equaliser on Tuesday 25 August, while the single goal victory earned by Bobby Tambling's 'special' over Manchester United at Old Trafford on 10 October certainly turned Bobby Charlton's five hundredth appearance for United sour, and provided huge cause for celebration among Palace fans who had made the trip.

Indeed, at one stage Palace were actually third place in the First Division table! This followed a 2-0 win at Huddersfield on 12 September, brought about by goals from Gerry Queen (his fourth in eight outings) and man of the match Steve Kember (his first of the season) in quick succession around the hour. Palace were behind Leeds United and Manchester City, but ahead of Arsenal on goal average.

Perhaps the most memorable 1st Division match during the autumn of 1970 was the visit of Leeds United on 7 November. As strong as any outfit at the time under Don Revie, Leeds drew a crowd of 37,963 to Selhurst Park and these enthusiasts were treated to an emotional and exciting afternoon. Leeds scored a fine opener in the 52nd minute when an Allan Clarke back heel and Paul Madeley cross unlocked our defence, for Paul Lorimer to head past John Jackson, but Palace responded in great style and put the northerners under terrific pressure. But the breakthrough would not come so that, when we were denied a clear penalty with some seven minutes left, as the otherwise immaculate Terry Cooper impeded Jim Scott then bundled him over, it looked ominous for Bert Head's team. However, with just three minutes to go, John Sewell hoisted another cross into Leeds' packed goalmouth. Lazily it arched up, over and down towards the big Leeds 'keeper, Gary Sprake, who stretched upward to collect it. But . . . pandemonium erupted when the ball slipped from his fingers, over his shoulder and into the net in front of the Holmesdale Road fans. Jack Charlton pounded the wet turf in fury, but Palace and their fans were jubilant and justice had been seen to be done.

At Christmas, Palace were still among the top ten and a splendid home victory over Liverpool on 16 January (when a certain humble curate, born in Croydon, but then serving his time in the northwestern diocese, was featured in the programme as 'fan of the week'!) secured by Gerry Queen on the hour from the closest possible range, then by an excellent rearguard action in which John Jackson was outstanding. Another three weeks later over Ipswich, courtesy of a rare but welcome goal by Peter Wall (his first for the Club), kept us there, but there followed a miserable run of eight matches with only one point and a rapid slide down the table to the fringes of the relegation zone. Palace finished in eighteenth place after losing the last match of the season 0-6 in a shock rout at Southampton, our worst defeat for over a decade.

However, in the Football League Cup, Palace equalled the Club's then best performance by reaching the fifth round before an injury-depleted side went out 2-4 to Manchester United at Old Trafford. This was a match that was hollow after Alan Birchenall was hurt and substituted after only a few minutes' play. To be honest, Palace had not exactly had to excel in order to reach this stage and might even have suffered the embarrassment of an early exit when lowly if likeable Rochdale had come to Selhurst Park on 9 September in round two and astonished us, by coming back from 1-3 down to snatch a draw in the last four minutes before Palace's astonished fans and, believe me, so full of confidence were the visitors that it was we who were thankful when the final whistle came! Surely, Palace made no mistake at Spotland, winning 3-1 after 'Dale had missed some good early chances, but after sending Lincoln packing 4-0, we were drawn against Arsenal. Over forty thousand Londoners watched a rousing if goalless encounter in which 'Jacko', John McCormick, David Payne and Mel Blyth were superb, and Alan Birchenall and Bobby Tambling posed endless problems for Arsenal at the other end.

So — to the replay at Highbury on 9 November, regarded by most of the pundits and certainly by the massed supporters of the north London outfit if not by that club itself as almost a formality, but this was unquestionably Palace's best performance of the season as well as our best-ever at that difficult and demanding venue. Arsenal squandered several openings before Gerry Queen put us ahead after goalkeeper Bob Wilson had failed to hold a shot from Jim Scott and, with a quarter of an hour to go, the hoped-for upset became more than a possibility when the Gunners' big, ungainly centre half John Roberts felled Gerry Queen with a judo throw. Thankfully, the referee awarded the obvious penalty and Bobby Tambling stepped up to rifle it home to the delight of all Palace fans in the big crowd, which had otherwise fallen still. Arsenal put us under intense pressure after this but John Jackson was absolutely commanding and inspired his defence, in which substitute John Loughlan was deputising for the injured skipper John Sewell, to keep the Gunners at bay and record an historic Palace victory. The context of this success was significant too. It was Arsenal's only home defeat of the entire season as they powered their way to their famous 'double', but Palace returned to Highbury the following Saturday for the 1st Division fixture and gained a point from a 1-1 draw, so that, while Arsenal rightly gained high praise for their 'double', we certainly felt that, at that time at least, *we* were the top team in London!

On 17 March 1971 John Jackson was at last rewarded with the representative recognition he so thoroughly deserved. He was selected to play for the Football League against the Scottish League at Hampden Park. He provided his usual splendid game and a Ralph Coates goal gave the English League victory, but Palace fans of the period will for ever believe that 'Jacko' was worthy of even higher honours and that he should have been given the opportunity to parade his brilliance in the full England side.

The end of the 1970-71 season saw Selhurst Park chosen by the FA as the venue for the FA Cup third-place play-off between Everton and Stoke City (2-3) on Friday evening 7 May. This was only the second occasion upon which such a fixture had been played.

On 12 May Palace marked the retirement of club skipper John Sewell with a testimonial match against FC Bruges from the Belgian League. John had played 258 games for us after joining in October 1963 from Charlton. He had assisted the Club (sometimes as captain) into Division Two in 1964 and captained the promotion side of 1968-69. He made 70 top-flight appearances over our first two seasons in Division One and this record was only bettered over the period by John McCormick, John Jackson and the much younger Mel Blyth, so that John's is a name which will forever be honoured in Palace annals.

After the domestic season had ended Palace made their first competitive sortie into Europe, in the Anglo-Italian Tournament. Their best effort was to beat the Italian champions, Inter

Milan, on Inter's ground, with two Bobby Tambling goals. Unfortunately, our other results failed to keep us in the competition, which was eventually won by Blackpool, assisted by a certain goalkeeper whose name would become highly familiar to Palace fans — John Burridge!

The only change in the staff at Selhurst Park for the beginning of the 1971-72 season was chief coach: popular George Petchey left on 12 July to become manager of Orient and was replaced by the former Manchester City centre-half, Dave Ewing. There were no additions to the playing squad but David Payne was deputed to slot in at right-back in place of John Sewell.

Now parading in white shirts with a broad claret and blue stripe, Palace won their opening match of the season at home to Newcastle 2-0, with goals from Bobby Tambling and Tony Taylor, for the first time in Division One when 1971-72 began on 14 August. With seven defeats in the next eight matches the season was barely five weeks old when it was already evident we were in dire trouble. We had lost all but two of our nine League games and were firmly anchored at the foot of the table with just three points and five goals to our credit. It was a perilous position; one which called for drastic action. Bert Head unhesitatingly took that action in breathtaking style.

Within a week in mid-September Alan Birchenall had gone to Leicester City for £100,000 and Steve Kember, Palace's captain, had left the Selhurst Park he had graced since 1966 for Chelsea, at a fee variously reported between £150,000 and £170,000. Bobby Kellard (£50,000) arrived back at the Palace from Leicester, striker John Craven (£35,000) joined from Blackpool, Bobby Bell, a central defender, came from Blackburn for £60,000 and Sammy Goodwin (£40,000) moved in from Airdrie. Palace fans were extremely sorry to see Steve Kember leave for he was recognised as a high-calibre player who had been instrumental in gaining Palace their place among the elite and was a great favourite with us all.

Much to Mr Head's credit, the upheaval seemed to work and immediately Palace beat Everton at Selhurst Park and gained away points at Leicester (0-0), Newcastle (2-1) and Coventry (1-1). By early December the team had moved out of the bottom two places. John Craven's arrival was to prove significant. He scored seven vital goals to finish as second-top scorer behind Bobby Tambling, but the return of 28-year-old Kellard was considered by many to be one of the two major factors in the praiseworthy Palace revival.

To replace the gifted and popular Steve Kember was no easy task, but Kellard was always a man for a tough job and he was no mean footballer. Although Palace fans of the mid-'60s had seen him play successfully as a winger in our 1963-64 promotion side and then in Division Two, Bobby was now firmly deployed in midfield. His industry and skill were amply demonstrated again and he soon became team captain. He missed only one match in the remainder of that tense season and contributed three goals from the penalty spot at a crucial stage. Palace recouped £12,000 of their investment in him when he moved to Portsmouth just after Christmas 1972, having fulfilled in the most testing circumstances all the hopes that had been pinned upon him by Mr Head and the Palace fans.

The other major factor in Palace's recovery had been two further Scottish signings by Bert Head. Taking advantage of a virtual media blackout caused by a strike in the newspaper industry in October, Bert persuaded Celtic to part with international forwards Willie Wallace and John Hughes for a bargain fee of £55,000. Wallace was a clever player, a great user of the ball. Hughes might have become a prolific scorer but he was badly injured in the game against Sheffield United at Selhurst Park on 4 December, when he was the inspiration behind a convincing 5-1 victory. In what proved to be the turning point of the season for Palace, he scored twice himself, ran riot in the Sheffield defence, but was never the same player after the injury.

That was an afternoon to be remembered with relish by every Palace fan present. Our favourites were rooted at the foot of the table in contrast to the Blades, who were in a highly meritorious fourth position, but Palace rampaged past the United challenge, outplaying their opponents in every department, scoring spectacular, even brilliant goals that had our fans leaping from their seats in frenzied delight. Bobby Kellard was the mainspring of the triumph: his drive and will to win were already well known but his industry, courage, sheer refusal to be beaten in any confrontation and his shrewd passing enabled him, on this and several subsequent occasions, to compete with and even better the highest regarded players in the land.

But the game belonged to John Hughes, a big bear of a man, christened 'Yogi' by the fans at Celtic after the cartoon character. The name followed him to Palace and this match was the occasion upon which he endeared himself to our supporters. More of an individualist than a team player, he was always awkward to mark, troublesome to check. By the end the Blades had resorted to dubious, highly physical tactics to cut him down to size and he ended up after one amazing run crunched to the ground.

In only the fifth minute a swiftly taken free kick by Gerry Queen sent Tony Taylor clear to clip a left foot shot past John Hope. Two minutes later Queen put Hughes in possession. He flicked the ball up and over Len Badger, charged into the penalty area, then hammered a fulminating left footer inside the near post! Gerry Queen himself got the third after twenty-five minutes, with the help of a deflection and it was already apparent that we were watching something quite out of the ordinary and a team transformed. The last two, scored in the second half were, quite simply, magnificent. First, Hughes moved past a couple of defenders out near the left touchline, then lashed a wickedly curving thirty yarder that swung late away from Hope and into the top right-hand corner of the net, and then John McCormick strode through some weak challenges to record only his second Palace goal with another shot from long range. The result took Palace up two places and out of the relegation spots and we continued to play ourselves clear of the danger zone with a side that had again become a team with fight, determination, character and skill.

It was those qualities which saw us to eventual safety with a four point margin over the relegated clubs, although at one or two stages matters still looked ominous and as if the outcome might be a decidedly close-run thing, particularly after a 1-4 defeat at Liverpool in January and a run of seven games for just two points in March-April. With four games left and Palace 0-2 down after only four minutes at home to Arsenal, there was still considerable room for anxiety in Palace hearts but Bobby Kellard struck a nineteenth minute penalty and, in a fiercely competitive encounter, John Craven headed a deserved equaliser on the hour. We then lost 0-1 at Sheffield United, but overcame Stoke City 2-0 in the penultimate match while Nottingham Forest were losing to Wolves and thus ensured our safety. Bobby Kellard scored his third penalty in the month of April only seconds into the second half, to settle our nerves and Gerry Queen headed the second after seventy minutes to bring evident relief to everyone.

During the bout of intense transfer activity in the autumn, George Petchey had quietly returned to his old club to snap up central defender Phil Hoadley for a bargain £30,000.

One of the most contentious matches ever played at Selhurst Park was in January 1972. Palace were drawn to meet Everton in a third round FA Cup-tie on Saturday 15 January and the trouble began early with a spiteful foul by Joe Royle on 'keeper John Jackson. Matters on the field soon got out of hand and ill-disciplined players and a weak referee brought something approaching a riot to our ground. Twice the crowd invaded the pitch and there was a real threat to the safety of certain culprits and the referee, who threatened to abandon the match. The result was a 2-2 draw, but fortunately Bert Head and Harry Catterick and their players, aided by a different official, produced a splendid replay at Goodison Park which ended 2-3 to Everton and with handshakes and smiles all round.

Among the young players with the Palace at this time was one Jim Cannon, then aged just seventeen and already scoring goals for the Club from defence. His effort knocked 'Spurs out of the Youth Cup in a third round tie while Nick Chatterton, Paul Hinshelwood and Dave Swindlehurst were all featuring in the Under 17 junior side.

Although the 1972-73 season was to end in disaster it started optimistically enough for Crystal Palace in September when Raymond Bloye became Club Chairman, with Arthur Wait Life President, while on the playing side there was a well-deserved promotion when long-serving Terry Long became assistant manager, a just reward for this likeable man, who had joined the Palace from Wycombe Wanderers back in May 1955.

However, as early as only the third match of the season, against Liverpool at Selhurst Park on 19 August, there was a stern warning of the difficulties ahead when Peter Wall broke his leg in a tackle with his former team-mate, Tommy Smith — the 'Anfield Iron'. This necessiated a re-shuffle in Palace's defence and, after young Bill Roffey had deputised for a while, the position fell to hardworking and selfless Tony Taylor. Taylor, who had joined us in October 1968 from Morton, had paired up successfully with Steve Kember in midfield and played, as occasion demanded, in a variety of roles. He could function splendidly as an attacking winger but now began to operate most effectively as a full-back. Tony became known as the 'Play-me-anywhere-as-long-as-you-play-me' man, and over four seasons in Division One only John Jackson and Mel Blyth bettered his 150 appearances.

Martin Hinshelwood made a successful debut at Southampton (0-2) in September, but Palace had already been ousted from the League Cup by 4th Division Stockport County in front of our own fans and things were clearly deteriorating, so another re-organisation via the transfer market was set in motion. Regrettably though, this time the desperate moves by manager Bert Head were doomed to failure. Within a week over a quarter of a million pounds was paid to secure midfielder Charlie Cooke (£85,000) and full-back Paddy Mulligan (£75,000) from Chelsea, as well as Iain Philip, a strong midfield or back four man, from Dundee for £105,000. To partially offset this, Gerry Queen joined the Palace 'old boys' at Orient for £70,000 and Willie Wallace moved back north of the border to Dumbarton.

By mid-October, Palace were bottom of the 1st Division table with only two wins and eight goals from their opening thirteen fixtures, and it was on 14 October 1972 at Wolverhampton that John Jackson's remarkable sequence of 138 consecutive 1st Division appearances and 222 consecutive League appearances, going right back to the first match of the 1967-68 season, was finally broken through sickness. Beyond any measure of doubt, 'Jacko' was the main reason for Palace's survival in Division One. Time and again it was his superb displays that salvaged precious points for Palace against the odds. Points which, at the end of the seasons, made all the difference between survival and relegation. It was his misfortune to be a great goalkeeper in an age of great goalkeepers — Banks, Shilton, Clemence, to name but three. Undoubtedly, in a different generation, John Jackson would have gained many more honours than his single representative appearance for the Football League.

On 4 November Palace at last gained their third win of the season and moved off the foot of the table. That victory was over Everton at Selhurst Park and was the stage for the story-book debut of Don Rogers, who joined his old manager from Swindon and scored the single goal of the game. £150,000 Rogers of the cultivated, lethal left foot, phenomenal acceleration and supreme control revitalised Palace for a while and the next victory was an amazing 5-0 rout of Manchester United on 16 December which was also the occasion of £100,000 Alan Whittle's debut. Incredibly, it was Palace's right-back, Paddy Mulligan, who began the downfall of the Old Trafford sophisticates, hitting a ninth minute opener from Don Rogers' pass and another three minutes before the break, cutting in onto an opening made by Rogers' magical acceleration. Alan Whittle paved the way for Rogers to net the third a minute after the interval and a grandstand finale provided by a Whittle rocket and Rogers rounding Stepney to calmly net the fifth left Palace fans almost delirious with joy.

But while this victory lifted us to nineteenth place, Palace never improved sufficiently to climb clear of the relegation struggle even though there was another signing, in January 1973, that of diminutive Derek Possee from Millwall for £115,000. In February Palace won 4-0 at West Bromwich Albion, then beat Stoke City 3-2, but we had an appalling March, gaining just two points from six games so that we became locked in a titanic battle for survival. Thus, on Friday 30 March the board of directors took the bold step of appointing the ebullient Malcolm Allison as our team-manager, with Bert Head moving upstairs as general manager.

The following afternoon, Saturday 31 March, Allison strode onto the centre-spot like a matador before the match, flanked by Ray Bloye and Bert Head to be hailed by the Palace fans, and Palace went on to beat Chelsea 2-0, to record our first victory over London opponents in 32 Division one matches. Iain Philip cracked a beautiful opener from twenty five yards after half an hour and Jim Cannon had a great day too, making his senior debut and scoring Palace's second goal just before the hour had elapsed.

Seven matches left to play then — but Palace gained only one point in the first five of them! Our only hope was to win against fellow-strugglers Norwich City on Easter Tuesday at Carrow Road. The tension was almost unbearable, but deep into injury time Palace were holding on to a 1-1 draw thanks to a Don Rogers goal. Then Norwich were awarded a free kick out on the right — it seared into our goalmouth and in the ensuing mêlée the Canaries scored. Heartbreak! The final whistle went ninety seconds later and Palace's efforts to remain in Division One were over.

Ironically, we won our final match of the season at Malcolm Allison's former club, Manchester City, 3-2, but it was a lost cause and Crystal Palace FC was about to embark upon some of the most testing years in its history.

The summer of 1973 was a time of substantial change at Selhurst Park and not without controversy. Bert Head resigned quietly and with typical dignity and left on 3 May after seven years. It was farewell to 'The Glaziers' and all hail to the proud 'Eagles' as Malcolm Allison sought a more aggressive, assertive image at Crystal Palace FC. The Club itself was re-organised with new faces in virtually every department. Alan Leather had been appointed Club Secretary in January 1973 — now Frank Lord joined as Coach with Dave Horn as Trainer. The scouting responsibilities were revamped too and now fell to Derek Healey (who left after two seasons) and Arnie Warren to whom great credit must be given for Palace's eventual success at the end of the decade. Charlie Simpson became physiotherapist towards the end of the year while an immediately obvious change was the introduction of a new strip of red and blue stripes.

On the playing side, John Craven joined Coventry for £60,000 and manager Allison made it clear that several other players might well be on the move. Terry Long severed his lengthy connections with Palace and teamed up with George Petchey at Orient. David Payne also made the move across to east London for a fee of £20,000.

With high hopes of a quick return to the top flight, Palace began 1973-74 with a home match against Notts County, who had just come up from the third division. A crushing 1-4 defeat clearly showed that the swift return to Division One was not going to be a mere formality. Far from it! There was more, much more to come! In fact the 1973-74 season turned out to be the most traumatic in the history of the Club and a miserable one from the playing point of view. Many fans were deeply disappointed when the invincible John Jackson left in mid-October for Orient, at a bargain fee of £30,000, thus concluding a career with us that dated back to August 1964 and embraced 388 first class matches; his testimonial match against Chelsea later in the year was a highly emotional occasion. Meanwhile Charlie Cooke and Don Rogers lost their lustre, Stockport County knocked us out of the League Cup for the second year running and Bobby Tambling departed for a post in Cork.

Poor Palace got just one point from the first six matches and went the first fifteen games without a win. It was our worst-ever start to a season. Eventually we beat Bristol City 1-0 at Ashton Gate on 19 November with an Alan Whittle goal but by then confidence had totally evaporated and it was more a question of survival for the second term running rather than of glory.

In the autumn and early winter another drastic rebuilding programme was put in hand. Sweeper-cum-midfield man Derek Jeffries (£100,000) arrived from Manchester City and central defender Roy Barry (£50,000) from Coventry at the end of September. In mid-October Peter Taylor, arguably Malcolm Allison's best signing for Palace, joined us from Southend for £100,000, but by the end of the year Palace were still eight points from safety.

Malcolm Allison provided League debuts for Dave Swindlehurst, Paul Hinshelwood and Nick Chatterton, preferring them to the more established players, and then bolstered his defence further with Ben Anderson from Cape Town, South Africa, and stylish full-back or sweeper Stewart Jump (£60,000) from Stoke City. Jeff Johnson (£12,000) was signed from Manchester City and just before Christmas, Mick Hill, a tall striker, came from Ipswich for £36,000. Meantime, two players left the Palace — Iain Philip went back to Dundee for £50,000 and Charlie Cooke returned to Chelsea for £17,000. The outlay on players over the past sixteen months or so had been an enormous drain on the Club's resources, putting us deep into the red, and this had coincided with a period of remarkably high interest rates.

However, as the new year of 1974 came in, Palace, already dismissed from the FA Cup by third division Wrexham, found new heart and new form. They beat West Bromwich Albion on New Year's Day (1-0), drew at home to fancied Bolton 0-0 then, in their first-ever Sunday fixture (brought about by the power crisis and the three day working week), won at Notts County, 3-1 on 20 January. In fact Palace lost only twice between then and Easter and two fine away victories, 2-1 at Nottingham Forest where Mel Blyth completely shackled Duncan McKenzie and Derek Possee and Don Rogers netted either side of half-time at the end of March, plus a great 3-1 win at Fulham on Good Friday before massed Palace support really did give solid ground for hope of escape from the predicament in which we found ourselves.

On Easter Saturday however, we lost 2-3 at Millwall and then allowed Fulham sweet revenge on the Tuesday to leave Palace third from bottom. Of course, 1973-74 had to be the season when the Football League introduced 'three up and three down', and when Palace lost 0-2 to Hull for the second defeat at Selhurst Park in five days, the signs were distinctly ominous.

In front of a massive Palace contingent, the Eagles won their penultimate match, 1-0 on a hard, dusty pitch at Swindon, who were already doomed to relegation. The issue now was starkly, painfully simple: Palace had to beat Cardiff on 30 April in the last match of the season at Ninian Park. For Cardiff a draw would be sufficient for safety.

What a night it was! Around four to five thousand Palace fans in a 26,781 crowd saw the away side take a deserved lead in the 29th minute when Stewart Jump touched home Peter Taylor's corner, only for elation to become frustration when Cardiff equalised five minutes before half-time. There was only one team in it after the interval: Peter Taylor hit the base of a post, a Mel Blyth drive from 35 yards was hit with such ferocious power and accuracy that it threatened to take the 'keeper into the net with it, and so it went on. Ten minutes remained and the home crowd were already whistling for time! Whittle, Possee and Mulligan all went close, but to no avail. And then the final whistle: Cardiff jubilant at yet another narrow escape,

Palace despondent, but cheered from the arena by their loyal fans . . . but the question now to be pondered was whether that loyalty would stretch into the third division?

So rapid had been the fall from the top division that many Palace players were still being paid 1st Division wages when the 1974-75 season opened. With the inevitable drop in income and an over-large playing squad, an urgent re-appraisal was needed by Allison. Before the season started two men were on their way: Derek Possee left in July for Orient at a fee of £55,000, less than half the figure paid eighteen months earlier, and on 14 August Tony Taylor went to Southend for £20,000 to give Palace a £7,500 profit. Incidentally, someone worked out that Taylor was the twenty-eighth professional player to leave Selhurst Park in just seventeen months!

It was perhaps understandable that Palace should open the season with diffidence and in the early matches there were several disappointing performances, particularly away from home. However, these were balanced by some excellent play at Selhurst Park, notably in the 5-1 defeat of Watford in a League Cup replay and when Swindon Town were trounced 6-2. When Palace's away form improved we climbed the table and moved into second place on 6 November after a well-earned point from an evening game at Blackburn.

There was an early season opportunity for Palace fans to show appreciation for a Palace warrior, whose career had come to an end, when the Club awarded John McCormick a richly deserved testimonial on 3 September 1974. Queens Park Rangers provided the opposition and 12,461 Palace people came along to pay tribute to this craggy defender, whose performances for us, particularly in Division One, had been nothing short of heroic.

There was an important flurry of activity in the transfer market in September too when Mel Blyth (the final link with the 1968-69 promotion squad) and Don Rogers left for Southampton and Queens Park Rangers respectively. Mel went on to great things with Saints, including an FA Cup-winners' medal but Rogers career was now sadly in decline. On his day he had been everything any fan could ever ask from a goalscoring winger or striker. His glorious goal on his debut against Everton in November 1972 was an absolute delight and he netted 13 goals from his 26 League games that season. But not even his mercurial skills were sufficient to save us from relegation and, like a number of Palace players at the time, his form deserted him badly in division two. As part of the Rogers transfer deal Terry Venables and Ian Evans arrived from Rangers and both made their Palace debuts at Hereford on 18 September, but Palace lost 0-2.

Another departure, later in the season, was that of captain Roy Barry, who moved to Hibernian for family reasons, while a new arrival was Phil Holder, a tough little midfield player from 'Spurs.

On 29 October Crystal Palace FC were hosts to the England Under-23 side who were playing Czechoslovakia in the UEFA competition. Palace winger Peter Taylor, now rapidly becoming the darling of Selhurst Park, was selected for his first international honour by England manager Don Revie and had a marvellous opening half hour. He scored England's first goal in only the third minute, then flighted the 19th minute free kick from which Mick Mills put England two up and firmly on the way to a 3-1 victory.

By Boxing Day Palace were again in second place in spite of having won only two League games in two months, but then three consecutive away defeats at Gillingham, Charlton and Aldershot suggested the side was a spent force. But Malcolm Allison drove his men forward again and the Eagles responded with a commendable run of twelve matches without defeat which brought us back to the brink of the promotion pool. The run ended with two 1-2 away defeats, at Grimsby (an ill-tempered battle this, with three players sent off) and Chesterfield, which virtually extinguished Palace's hopes. Promotion rivals Charlton faltered however on the run-in, and Palace were not doomed to a further season in the lower reaches until after our penultimate match. We beat Gillingham 4-0 at Selhurst Park in a re-arranged game but Charlton beat Preston 3-1 on the same evening and finally clinched promotion.

In retrospect the most important features of the 1974-75 season at the Palace were Terry Venables' decision to retire from playing to become the Club coach, and Kenny Sansom's debut at Tranmere (0-2) in the last game of the term on 7 May, but other items of interest included the colossal 44,701 crowd for the FA Cup 4th round replay between Wimbledon and Leeds, staged at Selhurst Park on 28 January; Palace's first-ever League fixtures with Hereford, Tranmere and Chesterfield, and the appearance of a pair of brothers on opposing sides when Palace met Wrexham. In both the games Graham Whittle played for the Welsh club while Alan Whittle appeared for Palace.

Once the persistent rumours that were circulating in the summer of 1975 that Malcolm Allison was going back north to manage Stockport County had all come to nothing, the 1975-76 season got under way. It fell into two distinct parts. From August until January Palace set a scorching pace in the League, including the creation of a Club record as we won the first five matches, opening up a lead of seven points at one stage while remaining unbeaten away from home until 20 December.

Leading scorer at this time was a determined, tousle-haired young striker named David Kemp. Small he was in physical stature but he could certainly tuck away the goals and in this, his first season as a League footballer after joining us from Slough Town, he was something of a sensation. Ian Evans too was among the goals — he scored Palace's first hat-trick since October 1966 when he netted all three in our 3-2 victory over Colchester on 30 August. Meanwhile, Eire international Paddy Mulligan (who commanded a regular place in the Republic line-up, yet only featured in the Palace reserves!) went on a free transfer to West Bromwich Albion.

After January it was in the FA Cup that Palace excelled but at the same time we fell away badly in the League so that, after looking favourites for promotion and the divisional championship, we only finished in a disappointing fifth place, although we retained a slim chance of slipping into the third promotion place right up to our final match at Chester (1-2) on 4 May.

But in the FA Cup at least Palace set a new Club record and became only the fifth 3rd Division side to reach the semi-finals. We knocked out Walton and Hersham and Millwall before Christmas and non-league Scarborough in the third round in early January, before gaining a terrific success by beating Leeds United at Elland Road through a Dave Swindlehurst header. Do not let the single goal scoreline fool you though — Palace outplayed mighty Leeds that afternoon, confounding them with our sweeper system, with Stewart Jump playing as our extra man at the back; a four goal margin would not have flattered us but the Peacock's goalkeeper, David Harvey, was absolutely outstanding and kept his side in the game. Palace then beat Chelsea 3-2 at Stamford Bridge in round five and Sunderland 1-0 at Roker Park in round six with fabulous performances to enter the last four, but then lost to Southampton 0-2 in a dour, lack-lustre encounter in which we failed entirely to do ourselves justice.

Of course this was Palace's first long Cup run in years and it was now that the world saw Malcolm Allison at his flamboyant best, with his 'lucky' fedora (which became an instant south London fashion!) as well as the champagne and outsize cigars. The younger fans in particular relished every moment of it all and at least there was a substantial success to cheer even if we did fail to reach the final itself. Malcolm Allison's Eagles, born three years before and bruised and battered by two relegations, could preen their feathers at long last!

However, Big Mal took the failure to reach Wembley really hard and, when Palace threw away the promotion that had appeared so certain, it became too much for him. He resigned and left Selhurst Park on 19 May 1976.

Any evaluation of Malcolm's contribution to Crystal Palace FC must take into account two factors which will never appear to his credit in any book of football records. First it was Allison who brought Ian Evans and Terry Venables to Selhurst Park and, though injury was to reduce Ian's input to our cause, he was a fine skipper and a mighty asset in defence. Terry Venables' own contribution was to prove highly valuable even if it was eventually to turn sour. Secondly, it was under Malcolm that a revitalised Palace scouting team was able to spot and attract to the Club young men of such outstanding ability that they would win the FA Youth Cup two years in succession (a feat no club had achieved since 1961), many of them going on to become household names in the game, although, regrettably, usually with other clubs. But, even though the mid '70s will always be remembered by Palace fans for the famous FA Cup run he inspired, it is difficult to regard his main period in control of Crystal Palace FC as a successful one, even though the seeds of later progress were sown.

Peter Taylor was Palace's on-field inspiration in the Cup run. It was his free kick (for a foul on himself) from which Dave Swindlehurst headed the decisive goal at Leeds: Peter scored two in the demolition of Chelsea and it was from his fine run and perfect cross that Alan Whittle struck the winner at Roker Park. This, combined with his continued progress with the England Under-23 side, made Taylor a much marked and a much wanted man and, after Palace's failure to reach Wembley or win promotion, it was obvious that he would not remain with us much longer. On 30 September 1976 amiable Peter moved across London to Tottenham (who, like Palace, had turned him down after schoolboy trials!) for a fee of £200,000.

Palace's Youth side also played in a Cup semi-final in this 1975-76 season. They reached the last four of the Youth Cup before going out in the two-legged tie to the competition winners, West Bromwich Albion. Already the appointment of coaches John Cartwright and Alan Harris was bearing fruit for it was these men, along with Arnie Warren, now chief scout, who were the architects of that Youth team.

Finally, in 1975-76 both Peter Taylor and Ian Evans made their full international debuts, and at the same venue; Evans for Wales against Austria (1-0) at Wrexham on 19 November and Taylor for England versus Wales at Wrexham (2-1) on 24 March. He came on as a second-half substitute and scored a goal. This was Palace's first full England 'cap' since Johnny Byrne's international debut in 1961, Palace's first-ever England goal and, with Evans in the Welsh team, it was the first time since 1 April 1922 that the Club had provided players for opposing sides in a full international.

It was on 1 June 1976 that Terry Venables was appointed manager at Crystal Palace FC: the next three or four years were to prove dramatic and successful. With Terry at the helm Palace were seldom headline news and gone were the breathtaking ventures into the transfer market. Instead he ushered in an era of steady, positive hard work in fashioning first a team that could battle its way with skill and style out of the 3rd Division and then another one from the young, aspiring stars in the Youth squad which would, it was hoped and expected, be capable of bringing even greater success.

The extraordinary feature of Palace's 1976-77 promotion campaign was that we never actually moved into the promotion bracket until after the final match of the season! That said, such an outcome appeared highly unlikely early in the term when Terry Venables had plenty of problems. The playing side was unsettled and in the first couple of months he called upon no fewer than twenty different players, and his dilemma, whether to use the unsettled Peter Taylor or not, was only resolved when Taylor moved to 'Spurs at the end of September.

A rising star appearing on the Palace scene was striker Rachid Harkouk. Chelsea born of an Algerian father and a Yorkshire mother, Rachid was our leading scorer with 11 goals. Tall, pale and slim, his gaunt frame appearing all arms and legs when he was at speed, Rachid was quickly nicknamed 'Spider' by the fans and he carried a shot like a bullet.

Palace held three trump cards which eventually brought us success. We had a core of players who knew each other's play by instinct in Jim Cannon, Paul Hinshelwood, David Swindlehurst, Ian Evans and Nick Chatterton who all made their hundredth Palace League appearances during this season, and Terry Venables' expertise created a new, perhaps unlikely but superbly effective full-back partnership between former midfielder and striker Paul Hinshelwood and the brilliant Kenny Sansom. Then George Graham arrived from Portsmouth on 8 November in an exchange deal with David Kemp, who moved to Fratton Park, and once George had settled down he became Palace's midfield director.

Promotion was eventually won for two reasons: a superb defence, where Jim Cannon, Ian Evans and Kenny Sansom all made full appearances, conceded only 40 goals all season — at the time a post-war Palace record and still bettered only by the Championship sides of 1920-21 and 1978-79. Secondly, Terry Venables was able to sign the goal-getting striker he needed to boost the Club's goal ratio. Terry had wanted Jeff Bourne of Derby County for a long while, but the asking price was much too high. Then Chesterfield showed interest in a left-side midfield player, Ricky Heppolette (who had only arrived from Orient in October), and goalkeeper Paul Hammond decided in February to move across the Atlantic to Tampa Bay Rowdies.

Hammond had played regularly for the reserve side and probably only came to the attention of most Palace fans when deputising for John Jackson three times in the autumn of 1972, but he had justified manager Malcolm Allison's faith in him to replace the legendary Jackson (even if such a move was unnecessary), and Paul had been an ever-present member of the side which took Palace to the 1976 FA Cup semi-finals and of the promotion team of 1976-77 until he chose to leave us. Tony Burns was re-instated as first-choice goalkeeper and this seasoned professional added his experience to the defence as Palace gained promotion in a thrilling climax to the season, then played a further 29 matches for us in Division Two.

Jeff Bourne joined the Eagles in early March 1976 and soon settled down at Selhurst Park. He scored his first goals in the 3-1 defeat of Gillingham on 5 April then, as Easter approached, really began to make his presence felt. Palace, who had formerly found goals so hard to come by, suddenly began to score. After the three against Gillingham we ran up five in the next home match against Swindon with Jeff again getting a couple, then hit four more against Sheffield Wednesday. Then came a set-back which would have killed off the challenge of a lesser club as Palace were sunk 1-4 at struggling Port Vale in a highly physical encounter.

However, we recovered well by winning at Chesterfield and then beat Wrexham 2-1 at Selhurst Park. Wrexham, with a game in hand, were still favourites to go up but Palace, undaunted, hammered rugged Lincoln City, managed by Graham Taylor, by 4-1 in the last home match to creep within a point of the Welshmen. And so to the final match of the season — a re-arranged fixture at Wrexham!.

George Graham was suspended for this one, having been sent off at Port Vale, and Tony Burns was not sufficiently recovered from an injury he had sustained against Lincoln, so Nick Chatterton filled the vacated midfield berth and twenty-year-old goalkeeper, Peter Caswell was brought in for his debut. Although he was patently nervous, and his kicking was considerably affected, Peter did well in this crucial match and made several fine saves in a creditable individual performance.

Palace had enormous support for a midweek game at such a distant venue and were delighted as two well-taken goals by Dave Swindlehurst and former schoolteacher Steve Perrin put us in control after fifty minutes, but Wrexham surged back with two quick replies and the golden chance seemed to have slipped away as the minutes ticked by, for a draw was all Wrexham needed to earn promotion at our expense.

There were only ninety seconds left when Kenny Sansom launched one of his enormous throw-ins from the far right corner; in the goalmouth mêlée, Rachid Harkouk hooked the ball home with precise accuracy just under the bar, but above the groping fingers of Brian Lloyd, the goalkeeper. Wrexham were stunned and Palace came again: Harkouk slipped a perfect ball through to Jeff Bourne and the number nine rammed it into the corner of the net with Wrexham in disarray. There was just time for the ball to be re-centred and kicked off before the final whistle went! Palace were now in third place, above Wrexham, but the Racecourse men could still reclaim it if they could beat the divisional champions, powerful Mansfield Town, in their home game the following Saturday. They hit a post once, but seldom looked like scoring and indeed Mansfield snatched a winner near the end to wrap everything up. The bunch of Palace fans, who had returned to Wrexham for this match, can never have cheered a goal for another club so loud and for so long!

The 1976-77 season also produced some fine Cup performances. The League side played two splendid matches with mighty Liverpool, holding them 0-0 at Anfield, where Palace were unquestionably the better side and the Kop was hushed, before going out 2-3 in the replay. The Palace Youth side reached the final of the FA Youth Cup for the first time in the Club's history beating Everton by a Terry Fenwick goal two minutes from the end of the second leg at Selhurst Park.

In 1976-77 then, Terry Venables, like Arthur Rowe a former 'Spurs player before becoming Palace's manager, had emulated the achievement of that great man and taken Palace to promotion when it was so desperately needed, and in his first season in charge of the Club too.

Back in the 2nd Division, Palace's attainments in 1977-78 were encouragingly high. The newly promoted Club finished the season in ninth place with a side that, by the end of the campaign, regularly included six members of the FA Youth Cup-winning squad, while the Youth team won that competition again by beating 1st Division opponents, Aston Villa, in the one-off final at Highbury, for the second successive year.

But 1977-78 also had its disappointments. First of these was the complete inability of striker Jeff Bourne to recover his goal-scoring touch after the summer recess, and he left Palace in February 1978 for Dallas, USA, after playing 17 2nd Division matches for us, which produced just one goal for him. Then there was never a more sickening occurrence than the serious break sustained by club captain and central defender Ian Evans to his right leg, in a tackle with George Best in the home match with Fulham on 1 October. That injury threw Palace right out of gear and the loss of the accomplished Welsh international could scarcely be over-estimated.

Evans had captained the 1975-76 Palace side that had done so well to reach the FA Cup semi-finals as a third division outfit, but his best season was undoubtedly 1976-77, when he skippered Palace to promotion to Division Two, making full appearances, while his international career blossomed. He became the regular central defender for Wales and was part of their most successful side for many years. They gained some impressive results against continental opposition but probably their finest achievement, during Ian's time, was the 1-0 win they secured at Wembley on 31 May 1977. This was the Principality's first victory over England since 1955 and their first on English soil for over forty years! Altogether, Ian had gained 13 full caps for Wales and of course he had made an invaluable, unique contribution to Crystal Palace as a player.

1977-78 saw the League debut of Peter Nicholas, Billy Gilbert and Terry Fenwick, powerful defenders in the Youth Cup-winning side of the previous term. These three, plus Ian Walsh and Jerry Murphy (who had each made a single League appearance in 1976-77) and Vince Hilaire (a real veteran with three previous appearances!) became regular and impressive members of the first team while David Fry, the goalkeeper, also made his debut, in the final match of the season.

Meanwhile, Peter Wall had taken a contract in Los Angeles with California Surfs after making 177 League appearances for Palace and acting as captain on occasions, both in the 1st Division and after Ian Evans' injury.

It was one of those 'beat the transfer deadline' moves that brought the ebullient John Burridge to Selhurst Park from Aston Villa for a £40,000 fee on 9 March 1978 and it came twenty four hours after Steve Perrin, that useful striker, had gone to Plymouth for £30,000. Burridge was already an experienced goalkeeper with an extrovert personality who had played for Workington and Blackpool before his spell at Villa Park. He came straight into the Palace side and became a huge favourite with Palace fans, whom he would delight with his energetic pre-match warm-ups out on the pitch. Tony Burns went to Memphis Rogues on loan after Easter and then signed for Plymouth in August 1978.

As the season progressed the Palace defence tightened its ranks. Kenny Sansom, mature beyond his years; Paul Hinshelwood, unsung but improving all the time; Billy Gilbert, settling in at number six, learning restraint and developing into a top quality defender, and big Jim Cannon, now the captain. Jim was spotted for Palace in Glasgow and to most supporters at Selhurst Park it was simply incredible that the Scottish selectors could not recognise his potential value to their national side.

There was an important move into the transfer market in mid-summer 1978 in which one player left Selhurst Park and another joined the Palace squad. Queens Park Rangers had shown interest all through the previous season in Rachid Harkouk and at the end of June he took his scoring talents to Loftus Road, Palace receiving a £90,000 cheque. A few days later, after Terry Venables had sought him out on the beaches of southern Spain, Palace paid a Club record fee of £200,000 to Preston North End for their skipper, Mike Elwiss — and now the scene was set for an historic season.

The early results of 1978-79, notably the 3-1 defeat of fancied Luton at Selhurst Park in our first home game, with Vince Hilaire demonstrating his immaculate skills so effectively, gave promise that Palace were going to be a force in the promotion stakes, and a stunning 3-0 win at Millwall in great heat on 16 September — Kenny Sansom's hundredth League appearance — took Palace to the top of the table.

The Eagles had a profitable encounter with Aston Villa in the League Cup, taking the 1st Division club to a second replay, staged at Coventry, before, in the absence of Jim Cannon, going out to the power of Andy Gray who scored twice in a 0-3 Palace defeat. It was with the proceeds from that third round tie that Palace brought Steve Kember back to his old home on 24 October 1978. Kember had played 130 League games for Chelsea before moving on to Leicester City and now the Filberts required a £40,000 fee to release him. But this was a gilt-edged investment for Palace, who undoubtedly benefitted from the experience and skill of their old favourite, clearly himself pleased to return.

Three weeks after Kember's arrival, hardworking midfield man, Nicky Chatterton, the fair-haired son of Palace's groundsman, Len, was transferred to Millwall for £75,000 plus defender Tony Hazell. Nicky had served Palace well for more than five seasons, scoring 31 goals in 151 League appearances and he became a grand servant for the Lions too. Another player to leave Palace in the autumn of 1978 was winger Barry Silkman. Terry Venables had brought him to Palace in the summer of 1976 on a free transfer from Hereford United as a replacement for the unsettled Peter Taylor. Now Malcolm Allison took Barry to Plymouth for £30,000 then later in the season, to Manchester City, when Big Mal teamed up again with Tony Book at his old club.

At the halfway stage, just before Christmas, Palace were two points clear of Stoke at the top of the second division table, with Brighton and West Ham another two points behind but, in a goal-less draw on our first-ever visit to Cambridge United, Palace suffered a cruel loss when Mike Elwiss limped off with cartilage trouble and was unable to play another first team match for us, his career in ruins. It took Palace a long while to adjust to Mike's absence and we scored only two goals in the next six League games.

However, just when it became absolutely essential, Palace's young defence began to break the hearts of opposition strikers. In the first half of the season they had not been exactly generous with the goals conceded, but in the second half they conceded only eight! True, Palace were knocked off their proud perch at the top of the table, but in the last third of the season they came back to snatch the honours, beginning with a crucial and magnificent 2-1 victory over promotion rivals Sunderland in a midweek game on 14 March. Early goals from Vince Hilaire (eight minutes) and Jim Cannon (ten) silenced the big Roker Park crowd and sealed the Wearsiders' fate.

It was a tense run-in for all the promotion aspirants. Despite their youth, Palace lived with the tension better than the others and lost but once — at Newcastle (0-1). This was our only defeat in twenty matches after Boxing Day, and over the last nerve-wracking six games from Easter Saturday (14 April, when we won at Bristol Rovers with a late strike by Ian Walsh), the Eagles dropped just one point, at Leicester City in a Friday night game.

In the end, because of fixture re-arrangements brought about by the appalling winter, Palace came from behind to clinch promotion and the 2nd Division championship. The point dropped at Leicester left us in fourth place, but the victory over Notts County (2-0) on 28 April was gained while Stoke were held 0-0 by Newcastle and Sunderland went down at home. All four promotion contenders won away on the last Saturday of the season: Brighton and Stoke thus assuring themselves of success, Sunderland after going behind at Wrexham, and Palace, with a stunning header from Dave Swindlehurst at Orient, whose side included former Palace favourites John Jackson and Alan Whittle.

Palace were still fourth but had a game left to play — at home to Burnley; the others had all completed their programme. The issue was clear enough: Palace needed a single point from the Clarets to gain promotion, but a first-ever victory over their Lancashire opponents would gain us the coveted championship.

On the night, somewhat fortuitously at times Burnley resisted intense Palace pressure. Led by Steve Kindon and Leighton James, they were just beginning to pose a threat themselves in the last quarter of the game when, with 14 minutes remaining, Vince Hilaire sent over a perfect cross for young Ian Walsh to rise above his tiring marker and head the ball like an arrow for the top right hand corner of the net. It was a picture goal; one fit to win a battle, and there was an enormous explosion of noise from Palace's massed fans to greet it. Dave Swindlehurst, game to the last, clinched matters with a low, right-footed drive with only a few minutes left. At the final whistle the players fled to the safety of the tunnel as pandemonium broke out. The astonishing record crowd of 51,482 poured on to the pitch and, amid scenes of immense joy and jubilation, the Palace team came into the Directors' box to receive and acknowledge the riotous cheers of their fans; the old ground has never witnessed scenes quite like those as that vast throng engulfed the arena and acclaimed their heroes.

ABOVE: Manager Bert Head parades his new signings for 1970-71: (l-r) David Provan, Peter Wall, Alan Birchenall, trialist Pat Ferry, Bobby Tambling and Gerry Humphreys. LEFT: The fateful moment from Palace v Leeds (1-1) on 7 November 1970. Gary Sprake had apparently caught John Sewell's cross safely . . . but it is about to squirm from his grasp for a deserved equaliser. RIGHT: Palace's first-ever victory over Liverpool was secured at Selhurst Park on 16 January 1971 and here's the goal that earned it! Gerry Queen (left) has just touched the ball over the line and he and the Reds' Larry Lloyd are entangled in the rigging as Tony Taylor throws up his arms in delight. This picture also shows the former standing enclosure at the front of the main stand.

ABOVE: Crystal Palace FC 1971-72; back (l-r) Mc Cormick, Birchenall, Hardie, J. Jackson, Blyth, Queen; middle: Pinkney, Payne, Wall, Kember, Hoadley, Tambling, Wharton; front: Long (coach), T. Taylor, Humphreys, Loughlan, Scott, Mr B. Head (manager). BELOW: Crystal Palace FC 1972-73; back (l-r) Queen, Goodwin, Blyth, McCormick, Jenkins, Craven, Bell; middle: Mr B. Head (manager), Brown, Goldthorpe, J. Jackson, Hammond, Pinkney, Wall, Long (coach); front: Wallace, Tambling, Mann, T. Taylor, Kellard, Payne.

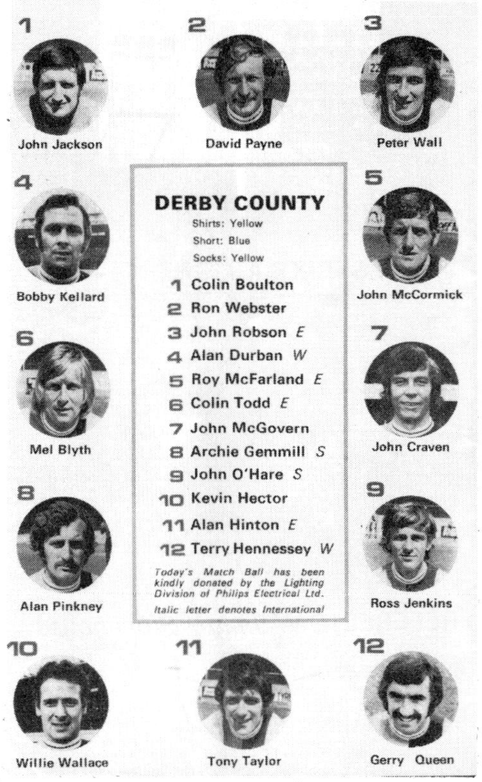

1 John Jackson
2 David Payne
3 Peter Wall
4 Bobby Kellard
5 John McCormick
6 Mel Blyth
7 John Craven
8 Alan Pinkney
9 Ross Jenkins
10 Willie Wallace
11 Tony Taylor
12 Gerry Queen

DERBY COUNTY

Shirts: Yellow
Short: Blue
Socks: Yellow

1 Colin Boulton
2 Ron Webster
3 John Robson *E*
4 Alan Durban *W*
5 Roy McFarland *E*
6 Colin Todd *E*
7 John McGovern
8 Archie Gemmill *S*
9 John O'Hare *S*
10 Kevin Hector
11 Alan Hinton *E*
12 Terry Hennessey *W*

Today's Match Ball has been kindly donated by the Lighting Division of Philips Electrical Ltd.
Italic letter denotes International

LEFT: The innovative line-up page which Palace introduced for their programme in season 1972-73 with the opposition in the centre surrounded by the names and pictures of our players; against Derby County, opening home fixture on Tuesday 15 August, 0-0. RIGHT: John Jackson played 138 consecutive 1st Division games between 1969 and 1972 and was the main reason for Palace's survival. BELOW: Stuart Jump was an immaculate sweeper in Palace's fine run to the FA Cup semi-finals in 1975-76. RIGHT: The FA Youth Cup winning side of 1977 celebrate with their tankards and the trophy.

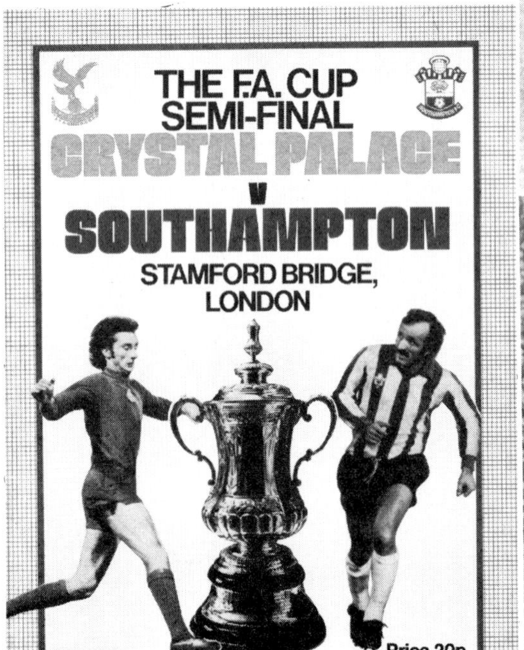
THE F.A. CUP
SEMI-FINAL
CRYSTAL PALACE
v
SOUTHAMPTON
STAMFORD BRIDGE,
LONDON
Kick-off 3p.m.
Saturday, April 3rd, 1976.
Price 20p
Official Souvenir Programme

Eagles On The Ebb

Although the half-decade 1979-84 was to become an extremely painful one for everybody connected with Crystal Palace FC, it began brightly enough and with no hint of what was to follow.

First, in the aftermath of promotion and the 2nd Division championship, there were the significant summer signings, which each raised the level of the Club's record transfer fee, of former England captain Gerry Francis from QPR for £465,000, then of England B international striker Mike Flanagan for £650,000 from Charlton. These moves certainly indicated that Palace meant serious business in the top flight but it has to be admitted that neither man lived up to their huge fees or the expectations that Palace fans rightly had for them in their times at Selhurst Park.

Palace's 1st Division return took place where our previous sojourn had ended, at Manchester City, on 18 August 1979, but the occasion was heavy with irony because former City and Palace manager Malcolm Allison, was now again in charge at Maine Road. As might have been anticipated, an intriguing tactical battle ensued but, while neither side could complain about the outcome — a 0-0 draw — the fans would have preferred a goal or two. It was left to Dave Swindlehurst to notch Palace's first strike upon our return to the senior section, to ensure another draw at Middlesbrough a week later, but on 1 September Palace ran riot and beat Derby County 4-0. Vince Hilaire's dazzling footwork matched the brilliant sunshine and once County's Gordon Hill had been dismissed they were always struggling. Vince made three of Palace's goals, Mike Flanagan netted two with glorious headers; Peter Nicholas and Dave Swindlehurst completed the annihilation.

A draw at Wolves was followed by a 2-0 success over Aston Villa on the first occasion where we had met the club that had been so heavily involved in our foundation at 1st Division level. These were heady days for Palace and their fans and we edged into second place in the table, following a terrific 2-1 win at Stoke where we came from behind, with exquisite second half goals from a Vince Hilaire chip and a Jim Cannon header. The following Saturday, 29 September, we had reached the top! After dismissing and finally outplaying Ipswich our 4-1 success was sufficient to put us ahead of Manchester United and Nottingham Forest on goal difference. Palace were three ahead after little more than half an hour and the fourth, a tremendous angled volley by skipper Jim Cannon on the hour, gave us the single goal advantage over our rivals. It was absolutely wonderful for Palace and their fans to bask in the glory of this exalted position and we can wonder how long it may be before it is equalled, for of course it remains unique in our history.

It was at this time that some of the media pundits dubbed Palace the 'team of the eighties'. Although it was not a title the Club either initiated or desired, it appeared in retrospect to have had a harmful effect, because our performances never again reached this level of sophistication or effectiveness. In the end, of course, the sobriquet became a jibe and it must be admitted that, while there were some further excellent victories, like consecutive ones over

LEFT: Terry Venables. BELOW: The programme for Palace's 1976 FA Cup semi-final. ABOVE: Jeff Bourne — his nine goals from fifteen games at the end of 1976-77 helped Palace gain promotion. RIGHT: Jim Cannon, captain of the 1978-79 championship side. CENTRE: Palace parade the old 2nd Division champions' cup at a pre-season match at the start of 1979-80. Kenny Sansom is missing but; back (l-r): Burridge, Cannon, P. Hinshelwood, Fenwick, Murphy, Francis, Flanagan; front: Swindlehurst, Kember, Nicholas, Gilbert and Hilaire. RIGHT: Part of the record crowd of 51,482 that packed Selhurst Park for the final match of 1978-79 to watch Palace win the 2nd Division championship.

Manchester City (2-0) and Arsenal (1-0) in November (the latter providing the Club's 500th post-war Football League success), the story of Palace's 1st Division tenure from then on was sadly one of accelerating decline. We managed to remain in the top five places until Christmas but 0-3 losses at Liverpool and Brighton followed by defeat at Selhurst Park by Middlesbrough, then a goalless home draw with Norwich took us to midtable, and we were knocked out of the FA Cup at the first hurdle by Swansea in a second replay at Cardiff. In the end Palace finished in thirteenth place in Division One but the last ten matches provided only a solitary victory, at home against Leeds on 12 April when Vince Hilaire netted inthe last minute, veering past four defenders and exploding a venomous right-footed shot, which soared past the straining John Lukic and in at the far post in front of our Whitehorse Lane end fans.

By this time Palace men were starring in the international sides of the home countries for, while Scotland continued unaccountably to ignore Jim Cannon, Kenny Sansom was appearing regularly and creditably for England and Ian Walsh and Peter Nicholas for Wales, with Jerry Murphy also in the Republic of Ireland side, but by mid-summer there were stories appearing that Palace would listen to offers for Kenny Sansom, who needed a big-money move for his own reasons.

Already the promotion-winning side of 1978-79 was breaking up, for Dave Swindlehurst had moved to Derby County in the spring the Rams' record fee of £400,000, though he still managed to finish as Palace's top scorer, with seven League goals from his 25 outings. His Palace career total of 73 strikes in the League puts him comfortably among our top goalscorers. Also departing from Selhurst Park in this 1979-80 season was Ian Evans. Our former skipper had made a splendid and courageous recovery against the odds from his broken leg, but could not force his way back into Palace's senior side, and in December he joined Barnsley, where he helped the Tykes win promotion from Division 3, before re-joining Palace as assistant manager in 1984.

August 1980 saw sensational transfer activity at Selhurst Park, for Kenny Sansom joined Arsenal in a £1 million exchange deal, which brought former Queens Park Rangers striker Clive Allen to Palace after only two months at Highbury, along with goalkeeper Paul Barron for a further investment of £400,000. The loss of Sansom was to prove significant, for Palace's defence suffered badly in 1980-81, whereas Allen, like Francis and Flanagan, never justified his massive fee while with the Eagles. He hit nine goals for us from 25 games in 1980-81 but moved back to QPR the following June for a greatly reduced sum.

For everyone connected with the Club, 1980-81 was simply dreadful: Palace began with a 0-3 reverse at Liverpool and lost nine of the first ten games up to mid-October, although we had miserable misfortune at Coventry on 6 September, when none of the officials saw a smashing Clive Allen shot hit then rebound from the stanchion inside the net, and the 'goal' was refused. At the same time, with the Eagles firmly rooted to the foot of the table, there were stories of disagreement between manager Terry Venables and the Palace board, and sure enough, to the dismay of many, Venables deserted Palace on 14 October to take charge of QPR. Terry was to have a highly successful subsequent managerial career and of course he *had* lifted Palace from the anonymity of Division 3 to the top flight but, when he left us, we were in a perilous condition and it had become evident that he was either unable or unwilling to remedy the problems.

Howard Kendall came to London to discuss the possibility of taking charge but Palace gave the manager's job to long-serving Ernie Walley, initially on a temporary basis before making it permanent — only to replace him with Malcolm Allison from 1 December! Five days later Palace, with Gerry Francis labouring in a sweeper's role, crumbled 0-3 at Nottingham Forest and, as if all this was not bad enough, as Christmas approached it became obvious that a take-over of the Club was imminent. At the same time that John Burridge, Terry Fenwick and

Mike Flanagan were all moving across to Loftus Road for a combined total fee of just £325,000 in Malcolm Allison's final transfer deal as our manager, Fulham chairman Ernie Clay put in a bid to buy the Palace club. So did a group of wealthy, loyal Palace fans, and there were stories of a possible merger with Brighton, but by mid-January forthright Ron Noades, then the chairman of Wimbledon, together with a small, enterprising consortium, had emerged as the most favoured contenders and contracts were exchanged towards the end of 1980 with completion taking place on 26 January 1981.

Malcolm Allison was dismissed as manager on the morning of the transfer of ownership and replaced by Dario Gradi, the former Wimbledon boss and England amateur international, thus becoming Palace's sixteenth post-war manager and our fourth in three turbulent months at Selhurst Park. Palace's first result after the change of ownership was a 0-2 defeat at Middlesbrough on 31 January, where Jim Cannon and Tony Sealy were both sent off and Clive Allen missed a penalty, and there followed the departure of Gerry Francis to QPR in February for a mere £150,000, though there was one, rare, bright spot when centre-half Terry Boyle scored on his international debut for Wales against Eire in Dublin on 24 February.

Palace actually lost their first seven matches under the new administration, but before this we were a club and a team indisputably heading for relegation and completely lacking in morale. Now young players were drafted in to replace the departing stars and we were hit by suspensions and injuries, but the manager did not help matters by claiming that it was not part of his responsibility to keep Palace in Division One, although he later explained that in saying this he was merely seeking to alleviate the pressure felt by some of his team.

On the transfer deadline day in early March there were further hectic dealings as part of the early attempts by Mr Noades to bring financial sanity to the Club's overstretched resources. Great favourite Peter Nicholas moved to Arsenal for £500,000 with experienced, Caterham-born David Price joining us from the Gunners for £80,000. Brian Bason came from Plymouth for a similar sum and striker Tommy Langley from QPR for £120,000, with Tony Sealy joining Palace exiles at Loftus Road for £80,000. All three new men appeared in the home fixture against Sunderland on 14 March, but Palace still lost to a goal conceded just before the half hour, though a David Price equaliser earned the new manager his first point, when we travelled to Leicester a week later.

Two further defeats, at home to Leeds and at Manchester United (both 0-1), were sufficient to make survival statistically impossible a full month before the end of the season but, frankly, this was almost a relief to the long-suffering supporters and, when the season finished with a thirteen point gap between us and the twenty-first placed club, no-one at Selhurst Park was in the least sorry to see it end.

As the first executive boxes at Selhurst Park were being built during the summer of 1981 Clive Allen left the Eagles in June, inevitably for QPR, in a deal which brought 6ft 3 inches centre half Steve Wicks to Palace but cost the Club an additional £200,000, but Steve was troubled initially by injury and then Palace had to sell him (back to Rangers) for little more than half his valuation of £675,000 in March in order to raise much needed money.

The first match of 1981-82 was at home to Cambridge United and Paul Hinshelwood (Palace's Player of the Year in both our 1st Division seasons 1979-81) was twice on target in little more than half an hour from penalties (the first after only 55 seconds for surely the fastest penalty awarded at our ground). The game was unusual because Cambridge also replied from the spot after the interval! Meanwhile at Loftus Road, Palace reserves were engaged in the first competitive matches to be played on an artificial surface, as QPR pioneered the fad of plastic pitches which plagued the League for a decade or more.

It was not until our fourth match that Palace scored a goal from open play; Ian Walsh was twice on target either side of the break to beat Charlton while Steve Wicks excelled in our defence, so that it was soon evident that we needed greater striking power if we were to make any impact upon the division. Shrewsbury began their lengthy hoodoo over Palace at the end of September, winning 1-0 at Selhurst Park to leave the Eagles in the bottom third of the table and Dario Gradi complaining about our 'woeful finishing'.

Teenager Shaun Brooks, captain of the England Youth team at the time, came into the side and scored in the next home game, a welcome 3-1 success against Rotherham, and Palace won the next match as well, 1-0 at Wrexham, thanks to full-back Steve Lovell, to secure the first away win in 32 matches and 19 months!

An exciting new arrival at the end of October was Bristol City striker Kevin Mabbutt, secured from Ashton Gate for £200,000, but we lost on his debut at Luton and it was only when that intelligent and articulate young man scored his first Palace goals on 24 November against Norwich City (2-1), that Palace won another League match and by then we were under new management.

Dario Gradi was not the most fortunate of Palace managers but on Tuesday 10 November 1981, with Palace 15th in Division Two, he was dismissed and replaced by ever-popular Steve Kember, who was our Youth Team coach at the time. Dario has subsequently proved his managerial qualities and few at Palace blamed him for our predicament, but the Club of November 1981 undoubtedly needed a lift and it was inevitable that he should go.

Steve Kember immediately provided precisely that! He led Palace to an unexpected victory at the tough venue of Roker Park, where a Jim Cannon goal just before the hour beat 1st Division Sunderland in a third round League Cup-tie, and Palace made a good start in the League under the new boss, drawing at Oldham, then beating Norwich and Bolton at Selhurst Park to move into the top half of the table.

However, it would not be accurate to suggest that overall results under Steve Kember were any improvement on those secured under his predecessor. Apart from a 4-0 beating of high-ranking Oldham in mid-April they were not, and we finished 1981-82 in 15th place which was precisely the position we had been in when Steve took over in November, and with a goal tally (34) that barely improved on the Club's worst-ever in this respect (secured back in the dreadful season of 1950-51) but which included two own-goals! In fact the highlight of the second half of the season was an FA Cup run to the quarter finals, where victories over Enfield (3-2), Bolton (1-0) and Orient (1-0 after a scoreless first match at Selhurst Park) took us into the last eight and a tie at eventual finalists — QPR. Playing before easily the biggest crowd to watch us all season, 24,653, we lost a match that was strangely lacking in passion on the artificial pitch, to a goal scored by Clive Allen just three minutes before the end.

Steve Kember's final contribution to the Palace as manager was to sign versatile defender Henry Hughton on a free transfer from Orient. While Henry was to prove a most useful fellow to a couple of Palace managers he was not given the opportunity to benefit Kember's cause because, little more than a week later, Palace announced the appointment of Alan Mullery as our new man in charge.

Mullery was a big name in football in the early 1980s. He had had a distinguished playing career with Fulham, 'Spurs and England, been awarded the MBE, then gained substantial success in management at Brighton. However, Alan's two years at Crystal Palace were bitterly disappointing to the Club, the fans and, no doubt, to him. Palace concluded 1982-83 in 15th place (again!) and dropped to 18th in 1983-84. His formerly proven ploy of securing experienced men nearing the end of their careers for modest fees or on free transfers failed to produce any cohesion, or the beginnings of a settled, effective side. There was little if any money available to strengthen the team by major transfers because, while the commercial aspects of the Club had been greatly and successfully expanded under Ron Noades, the income from our gates had fallen alarmingly to their lowest post-war average level in 1981-82 and of course the continued lack of success meant that they dropped even further during his managership.

On the strength of two draws, then two victories at the start of 1982-83, Palace were a top six side for the first five weeks of the season but, by the end of October, we had slipped into the bottom half of the table and, by the time we approached the last match of the term, there was still a chance that we might even be relegated. Our Selhurst Park opponents, by a black coincidence, were Burnley: only four years earlier we had beaten them to gain the 2nd Division championship, but this evening we had to salvage at least a point to retain our 2nd Division status. A crowd of nearly twenty-three thousand loyal Palace fans — almost three times the average — came to help their favourites survive and saw Ian Edwards, Mullery's first signing for the Club, from Wrexham back in June, steer the ball home just after the hour from a Henry Hughton cross. The relief was evident and huge as the fans swarmed onto the pitch and the champagne flowed in the dressing room at the close of the game.

Other incoming transfers during the season were strikers Chris Jones, from Manchester City on a free in November, who scored after only four minutes on his debut (but Palace still lost at home to Wolves (3-4)) and Ally Brown from West Bromwich Albion in March. But perhaps Mullery's best signing for Palace that season was full-back Gary Locke, who came to us from Chelsea, initially on loan in January, and stayed to play 101 matches for Palace over the ensuing three years and more.

Another player to make a major contribution that season was Gavin Nebbeling, who teamed up with Jim Cannon at the centre of defence when Billy Gilbert was having to fill in at full-back, then had a spell at number three himself. Gavin was still learning at this stage but he was to play a useful role in Palace's recovery later in the '80s.

Palace had a Cup-tie against 1st Division opponents in this season and beat Birmingham City 1-0 in the FA Cup fourth round, before going out in a replay at Burnley in round five (from where the match programme is one of the most sought after modern issues for Palace collectors because of the small number that the Clarets had printed).

If 1982-83 was disappointing for Palace and their fans 1983-84 was worse. Not once were we so much as near the top third of the table; in fact we were never in the upper half. During the summer months Paul Hinshelwood left us to join rising Oxford United, after playing 276 League games for us and becoming the fifth highest man in our all-time charts with 319 first class Palace matches. Arriving were big, 32-year-old Sheffield Wednesday striker Andy McCulloch, who cost us £20,000, 29-year-old Les Strong, a full-back from Fulham, Sunderland's winger Stan Cummins, and 28-year-old John Lacy, a tall centre-half from 'Spurs, while 33-year-old George Wood, the former Arsenal and Scotland goalkeeper, was certainly Mullery's best acquisition from among his many experienced signings. Best of all was to be young Phil Barber, signed from Aylesbury Town in February 1984, who was to assist the Club to promotion, then in the 1st Division and the 1990 FA Cup Finals.

Bleak news however, even before the season began, was that leading scorer Kevin Mabbutt, who had missed four months of the previous term with a pelvic injury, had gone down within minutes of a friendly against Southampton with a complicated injury to his left knee. In fact poor Kevin's career was blighted from that moment, even if he did play a few games for us later this term and during 1984-85 and in fairness to the manager, Kevin's unavailability was a severe handicap. Mullery's reaction was to sign unsettled striker Tony Evans from Birmingham.

The immediate impact of the new arrivals was minimal. Apart from a League Cup 1st round, 1st leg victory over 4th Division Peterborough, Palace went to 27 September before winning a game — and by then we were in the relegation places and dismissed from the League Cup. Peterborough had reversed the 3-0 result from the first leg and then, to our distress, dismay, chagrin then woe, knocked us out in the ensuing penalty competition. Appearing for Palace in that match at London Road, quite unproductively and without showing any hint of the player he was to become, was John Fashanu, on loan from Norwich City.

Peter Nicholas returned from Arsenal in an unusual transfer whereby he was still registered at Highbury and Palace did not have to find the £150,000 fee till the close season, and there was a brief improvement in Palace's fortunes during November, when a late header by substitute Jerry Murphy despatched Cardiff in midweek, Andy McCulloch and Murphy again put paid to Oldham the following Saturday, Tony Evans was on target at Chelsea, where the feature of the match was a 12th minute scorching drive by Gary Locke from twenty-five yards against his former colleagues, and then a David Giles effort beat Sheffield Wednesday, who were resurgent under Howard Wilkinson and previously undefeated all season.

But it was all too short-lived. We lost six of the next seven League games and, if we did beat 1st Division strugglers Leicester City 1-0 in the FA Cup third round with a late Billy Gilbert header, West Ham knew too much for us in the next round, took us back to Upton Park and knocked us out there.

1983-84 saw the South Suburban Co-op become Palace's first-ever sponsors and we wore 'Red Rose' on our shirts to promote their superstores from mid-October, but in the end it took till our penultimate home match, against Swansea on 5 May, before our 2nd Division survival was assured. Two first-class set pieces doomed already relegated Swansea — who included former Palace striker Ian Walsh — with Jim Cannon (playing through the pain barrier with a hamstring injury) on target after 24 minutes and Kevin Mabbutt seconds before half-time, so that the only happy Welshman at Selhurst Park that afternoon was Peter Nicholas, who was making his 150th appearance for the Eagles. A Phil Barber beauty completed a Palace come back at Carlisle on the May Bank holiday after David Giles had reduced our arrears. Phil ran with the ball from inside the Palace half, beat two defenders for pace, kept his nerve as the goalkeeper advanced, and slipped it past him for 2-2 and the provision of clear evidence of his burgeoning talent.

However, with several senior players absent, Palace lost their last game of the season, at home to Blackburn and, two days later, manager Mullery found that he had lost his job too, dismissed for the first time in his career. It was no surprise. Although not without interest, Alan's second season in charge had been extremely poor with, in fact, the home supporters suffering most, for Palace scored only 18 goals at Selhurst Park in their 21 League games, to equal our lowest-ever total in these matters at that time.

There followed the brief, extraordinary three day flirtation between the Club and Dave Bassett before on 4 June 1984 Steve Coppell and Ian Evans took charge.

LEFT: Former England skipper, Gerry Francis, was a record signing at £465,000, here against Nottingham Forest (1-0) on 8 December 1979. RIGHT: Kenny Sansom was an England regular in 1979-80. (Photo: Mark Leech) BELOW: Manager Ernie Walley. RIGHT: Dave Swindlehurst notches Palace's spectacular first goal in the 4-1 demolition of Ipswich on 29 September 1979 which put the Eagles top of Division One.

LEFT: Clive Allen came to Crystal Palace in the summer of 1980, here in action in the controversial game at Coventry on 6 September . . . BELOW . . . in which his stunning shot beat Coventry's defensive wall and the goalkeeper but rebounded back into play so quickly that none of the officials saw it and allowed play to continue. The picture demonstrates the validity of Palace's claims. RIGHT: Ron Noades and his consortium took control of Crystal Palace Football Club on 26 January 1981 and OPPOSITE: immediately installed Dario Gradi as our manager.

ABOVE: This picture spans the generations; Paul Hinshelwood receives a Mecca loyalty award from former Palace manager Arthur Rowe after completing 200 League appearances. Looking on is Tony Hutchinson, a staunch Palace fan and Mecca executive. LEFT: Hugely popular Steve Kember became Palace's manager on 10 November 1981. CENTRE: Manager Alan Mullery MBE. RIGHT: Goalkeeper George Wood was a valuable acquisition by manager Mullery. BELOW: Crystal Palace FC 1983-84; back: Hughton, Murphy, Strong, Wood, Phillips, Locke, Stebbing, Evans; middle: Cripps (coach), Nicholas, Cannon, Wilkins, Lacy, McCulloch, Gilbert, Nebbeling, Shellito (coach); front: Giles, Mabbutt, Mr A. Mullery (manager), Cummins, Hilaire.

LEFT: Manager Steve Coppell was in charge for nine years from 1984. CENTRE: Steve's initial assistant boss was Ian Evans. RIGHT: Midfielder Geoff Thomas came in the summer of 1987 and became an inspirational captain. (Photo: Sporting Pictures UK Ltd) BELOW: At his peak Phil Barber became an invaluable top flight player. Here he outstrips Arsenal's Steve Bould at Highbury and aims a drive at the Gunners' target. RIGHT: Alan Irvine's famous goal that defeated Nottingham Forest in the 3rd round FA Cup-tie at Selhurst Park on 11 January 1987.

Dignity Restored

Steve Coppell had been a brilliant penetrative outside-right for Manchester United and England before his playing career was blighted, then terminated by an agonising knee injury, initially incurred while playing for his country against Hungary at Wembley in November 1981. It eventually became necessary for him to retire in 1983 and, some twelve months later, following a meeting with Chairman Ron Noades, Steve was appointed manager of Crystal Palace. It was at Mr Noades' suggestion that Steve invited former Palace star Ian Evans to assist him and there was no little irony that the duo, who were to do so much to rebuild the playing fortunes of our Club — although they were to face a tough baptism — should both have had their own careers cut short by disgraceful tackles.

The immediate prospects of changing Palace from a struggling team into possible promotion candidates were hampered when Billy Gilbert and Vince Hilaire both moved on to other clubs, but Steve Coppell's riposte was to make his first signing for the Eagles by securing big Trevor Aylott, a 6ft 1 inch striker, from Luton Town, as part of the deal which took Vince Hilaire to Kenilworth Road. Another valuable signing was that of perky left-back Brian Sparrow from Arsenal but, without question, Steve's most effective early signing was that of £30,000 Alan Irvine from Everton. Alan, a winger with pace and guile, was also intelligent and articulate, and for obvious reasons his manager appreciated all these qualities.

Blackburn Rovers provided the opposition at Selhurst Park for manager Coppell's first senior match in charge of Crystal Palace on 25 August 1984, but Palace, missing skipper Jim Cannon, who had fractured his jaw in a pre-season game, could only scratch out a 1-1 draw thanks to an equaliser from Stan Cummins a quarter of an hour from the end, and the auguries for our future under the new manager appeared bleak, as we took a heavy beating a week later at Shrewsbury (1-4), then lost 0-2 at home to a powerful Birmingham side. Another defeat at Brighton left us ensconced at the bottom of Division Two — but it was from such depths that Palace were eventually to rise, phoenix-like to restored status and dignity.

The 1984-85 season was salvaged by two important victories, at Sheffield United (2-1), where Jerry Murphy's sophisticated display, particularly his equaliser on the hour, drew rhapsodies of praise from his manager, and at home to Leeds (3-1) on 22 September, when Alan Irvine was the Peacocks' chief destroyer. Alan was involved in all our goals and scored our third one himself, to provide a fitting result for an afternoon of significance in Palace's history. This was the occasion of Jim Cannon's 480th Palace appearance and the big Scotsman thereby equalled Terry Long's record, established some fifteen years before. Terry came along to Selhurst Park to make a presentation to the new record holder on behalf of the Club, before our match against Fulham (2-2) at the end of October, and hundreds of '50s and '60s Palace fans were delighted to see their old favourite alongside his worthy successor.

However, no immediate recovery in Palace's fortunes was in sight as we limped along near the foot of the table. We had considerable difficulty in scoring goals while being usually unable to prevent opponents from netting. Phil Barber had his first sustained run of appearances, largely in midfield, while George Wood, badly if unintentionally injured in the midweek game against Shrewsbury Town (2-2), refused to allow his impressive sequence of games to be interrupted and Palace fans were amazed, and not a little anxious, when he was back in our team, with his leg heavily bandaged and obviously causing considerable pain, the following Saturday when Huddersfield Town (1-1) were our visitors.

Unheralded by the media Steve Coppell signed two coloured strikers in the autumn months of 1984, Steve Galloway from Sutton United and Andy Gray from Dulwich Hamlet.

The signing of Andy Gray was to be the first indication of a supreme talent of manager Steve Coppell which was to be deployed greatly to Palace's advantage several times in the coming years. Steve was able to discern true footballing potential, even when it was in a raw state, and his successful recruitment of men from the lower divisions of the League, reserve team football or non-league teams, then the refinement of them into quality players, was a feature of his managerial tenure at Crystal Palace. In quick succession Steve also secured central defender Ken O'Doherty from University College, Dublin, and Tony Finnigan. The tall, academic Irishman's value to us was limited, but 'Finn' provided his manager with a versatile and creative additional resource, for he began in midfield but within twelve months had settled down at right-back, and was later to play on the other flank, both wings and at centre-forward!

In late January Peter Nicholas left Palace for Luton Town in a £150,000 deal. The loss of the fiery Welsh international was a blow so that several of our results in the early weeks of 1985 were extremely disappointing and not a little worrying. Worst of these was the 0-5 thrashing we took from Wimbledon on their first senior encounter against us at Selhurst Park, which enraged many Palace supporters.

It was a credit to Steve Coppell that, with such limited experience of management, he was able to remedy such a desperate situation. In order to do so he signed two proven players, midfield dynamo Kevin Taylor joining Palace from Derby, with veteran, giant centre-half Micky Droy coming across from Chelsea. 'Ticker' Taylor cost us £15,000 but proved a real asset in the ensuing relegation struggle and over the next two years, while the commanding Droy scored on his debut and paired up with Jim Cannon to play a crucial role in the vital run-in to the season.

Two matches within three days at the end of April held the key to our survival, a visit from promotion-hunting Portsmouth, complete with Billy Gilbert and Vince Hilaire, then a daunting re-arranged trip for a night game at promotion favourites Blackburn. Palace beat Pompey in front of our best crowd of the season at Selhurst Park, with Micky Droy spearheading our 2-1 success with an early opener and a back header to enable Andy Gray to deliver the 76th minute winner. At Blackburn Micky was again involved in the decisive strike, flicking on a rare Palace corner just before the hour, for Alan Irvine to rise unchallenged at the far post and head home. Those victories virtually secured Palace's 2nd Division status and Micky Droy quickly became a great favourite with our fans, but Jim Cannon was unquestionably the only choice for Player of the Year and the future for Palace now looked rosier, for Steve Coppell had off-loaded several of the fading but highly paid men recruited by his predecessor, even if many fans were saddened by Jerry Murphy's determination to leave us for Chelsea.

Still, Micky Droy's willingness to re-sign for Palace for 1985-86 was great news for the Club as was the addition of tall, angular Steve Ketteridge from Wimbledon for £15,000 to add midfield steel, but it was also during the summer of 1985 that manager Coppell acquired a player from the non-league ranks who was to become a household name across the nation and assist Palace to glory — 21-year-old Ian Wright from Greenwich Borough. Maybe later in his managerial reign Steve's sure touch in the transfer market deserted him to our cost, but it should never be forgotten just how brilliantly he served Palace in these matters through the mid- and late '80s.

It was in the wind and rain at Shrewsbury that Palace's 1985-86 League season began. The Gay Meadow has not often been a happy venue for Crystal Palace but here on Sunday 18 August we recorded our first opening day success for four years (2-0) and our fans were heard to sing Steve Coppell's name as we controlled the second half. Fancied Sunderland were beaten by a Micky Droy header twenty minutes from time the following Saturday, but this momentum faltered: we gained a 2-2 draw at Carlisle in another wind and rain affected match and then lost 2-3 at home to Huddersfield. However, the early autumn was highlighted by a memorable League Cup second round tie against Manchester United.

Everyone anticipated the first leg at Selhurst Park with huge relish. Playing confidently and pushing forward with commendable determination, Palace unquestionably surprised United but, after a scoreless first half, United's goalkeeper, Gary Bailey (whose father, Roy, had graced the Palace goalmouth 119 times thirty years or more earlier), denied Phil Barber with a fabulous save. A few minutes later Peter Barnes beat George Wood at the near post and in those moments the tie was won and lost. Norman Whiteside increased United's advantage just 21 seconds into the second leg at Old Trafford and Steve Coppell quipped afterwards 'The form United are in, I'm surprised we were able to hold out for so long! But', Steve added, 'we responded wonderfully well and goalkeeper George Wood did us proud'. In fact George had perhaps his best game for us, making three outstanding saves reminiscent of his Scottish international days.

Well as Palace had acquitted themselves over the two legs of the Cup-tie, we continued to flounder along in Division Two. We lost 1-3 at Charlton in a game of four penalties — but the news of lasting significance from the Valley that afternoon was that Charlton would be leaving their headquarters and moving into Selhurst Park as Palace's tenants, in a unique ground-sharing arrangement!

It was on 12 October, when Palace were at home to promotion candidates Oldham Athletic, that most Eagles fans first saw the potential value of Ian Wright. With four minutes remaining, Palace's injury-depleted side was trailing by the odd goal in three. In a desperate late rally Kevin Taylor equalised and substitute Wright headed in a cross from Alan Irvine, to produce an unexpected result and an early demonstration of his match-winning prowess.

Ian made astonishing progress in this 1985-86 season, going on to finish as our joint second top scorer with nine goals and Steve Coppell was happy to call the former plasterer's labourer his 'super-sub' so that, with Ian's burgeoning talent and the further stiffening of the defence with the arrival of West Ham full-back Paul Brush, we did slowly begin to become a side that looked as if it might challenge for the promotion places, although overall we lacked the necessary consistency. A Trevor Aylott brace gave us victory at Hull on 7 December but a dreadful Christmas-New Year with defeats by Wimbledon (1-3) on a Selhurst Park quagmire and at Brighton (0-2) set us back again, and it was not until we strung three consecutive home wins together in March and early April that we entertained serious hopes of snatching third position. Matters went awfully wrong when we travelled to Grimsby Town on 12 April. We were soon in arrears, had Kevin Taylor sent off in only the 24th minute and fell further behind. The referee then awarded the Mariners a 90th minute penalty for good measure, so that our new expectations were effectively sunk without trace up at Blundell Park on the edge of the North Sea.

In the last analysis Palace finished fifth and manager Coppell aptly summed matters up by saying that this 'placing was probably a true reflection of our ability over the season — good, but not good enough'.

For the record two developments during 1985-86 are worth noting. The Full Members Cup made its first appearance, although Palace's involvement in it was minimal, with defeats by Brighton and West Bromwich Albion in the inaugural group stage, but of immediate significance to our Club was the introduction of the popular 'Palace Lifeline' which was launched at the Fairfield Halls on 3 April and quickly produced important funds to assist Steve Coppell in his team-building. But there was sadness on the last day of the season among players and fans alike when it was learned that John Matthews, the popular and knowledgeable *Croydon Advertiser* sports editor, who had covered the Palace for his paper for fully thirty years, had suddenly died. The news was relayed to our crowd at half-time and the team were told at the end of the 1-1 draw with Sheffield United.

With Palace's generally improved performances towards the end of 1985-86 there were justifiably high hopes for a more successful term in1986-87 and augmented, if temporarily, by Anton Otulakowski, a much travelled left-winger from Millwall, Palace opened the season with an impressive 3-2 win at Barnsley with a make-shift team in which versatile Gary Stebbing featured at left-back and thereby completed the unusual record of appearing in every number of the Club's eleven outfield shirts!

Palace fell into arrears at Oakwell to the quickest goal of the day but we replied through Phil Barber and Paul Brush either side of the dismissal of Larry May for a punch thrown at Alan Irvine and, if Barnsley equalised for 2-2 with little more than twenty-five minutes played, the Eagles settled the outcome midway through the second half with a spectacular jack-knife header by Ian Wright.

Stoke were beaten 1-0 on the Selhurst Park pitch where a new, much-improved drainage system had been installed in the summer, and then a third victory was gained at Odsal over Bradford City (2-1), but Palace were brought crashing back to earth by a single, penalty, goal defeat at resurgent Derby County. For the next match, at home to Huddersfield, many of our players had an uncomfortable evening because they were wearing new boots, a thief having stolen all the first team's footwear from our Mitcham training ground the previous weekend. Still, Micky Droy scored the all-important goal six minutes into the second half via his unbroken, left foot size twelve, which had only been secured for him on the morning of the game!

Palace had a chance to go top of the 2nd Division for the first time since our championship of May 1979 when Sheffield United came to town on 13 September but the talented Blades were rather too sharp for us and cut us down with a 2-1 scoreline. However, three weeks later we *did* claim the top spot after beating Millwall 2-1, coming from behind in a real thriller, with second half goals from Anton Otulakowski and Tony Finnigan.

Unfortunately, from there on matters were largely downhill for the Palace and, after a sequence of four consecutive defeats, Steve Coppell found it necessary to dispense with Micky Droy. Micky had served us wonderfully well but had now begun to find it increasingly difficult to cope with talented, mobile strikers so that, although the fans were sorry to a man to see him go to Brentford, they recognised that the tough decision was unquestionably the right one. Gavin Nebbeling took over the vacated berth at the heart of our defence and performed as well as anyone in the remainder of the season, as Palace chased a place in the newly introduced play-offs.

Two new players assisted in this cause. 24-year-old Mark Bright joined Palace from Leicester City for £75,000 and scored on the stroke of half-time in his Palace debut, in a thrilling 3-3 draw with Ipswich at Selhurst Park. Mark immediately became Palace's joint top-scorer this season and matured into a class top-flight striker on the fringe of international honours, while his partnership with Ian Wright developed into the most prolific in the Club's history. It was another brilliant signing by manager Coppell.

Later in the season, at the turn of the year, we were joined by former 'Spurs and Brighton centre-half, Gary O'Reilly. Because of injuries Garry seldom had a prolonged spell in our first team, but his experience was valuable and he was to prove a key member of our side in several vital games.

In fact it was in midwinter that Palace again began to look as if we might make a serious impact on the division. Hull City were swamped 5-1 on 13 December, then two strikes from Mark Bright accounted for Huddersfield at Leeds Road. Brighton were beaten 2-0 at Selhurst Park on Boxing Day; then, after a significant reverse at Ipswich, we brought back all the spoils from the Hawthorns clash against West Bromwich Albion on New Year's Day with a late winner from Mark Bright, and we edged past Derby two days later back at the Palace.

Our best spell of the season concluded with a splendid victory, probably the best of season given the pedigree of the opposition, when we beat 1st Division Nottingham Forest in the FA Cup third round. Palace adapted to a frozen pitch much better than Forest and the match was settled by a spectacular strike from Alan Irvine, after 24 minutes on the occasion of Gary O'Reilly's debut.

But Palace's impressive form now wavered. Tottenham beat us in the FA Cup fourth round when nothing whatever would go right for us. Then we found ourselves back in eleventh place in Division Two after losing at Reading on 21 February. However, a better showing, including a 6-0 drubbing of Birmingham City at Selhurst Park, took us to the fringes of the play-off positions. For a spell in March and April, it was our defence which took the honours and for five games we did not concede a single goal, in a remarkable sequence which modern Palace sides have seldom equalled. But then, following a disappointing 1-1 draw with West Bromwich Albion on Easter Saturday, we put up our worst showing of the entire season at Brighton on the bank holiday Monday and lost 0-2.

Palace recovered somewhat by beating Oldham and promotion-bound Portsmouth at Selhurst Park so that we retained a slim hope of a play-off place right up to the final game of the season, which took us to Hull. A victory there, allied to a defeat for Ipswich, would enable us to snatch the fifth place in the table and take part in the knock-out competition for promotion . . . but inside ninety seconds Alex Dyer (who was to sign for Palace some eighteen months later!) had us in arrears and he scored again early in the second half to dash our hopes completely.

Scotsmen Jim Cannon and George Wood were the winners and runners-up respectively in the supporters' Player of the Year award: both had appeared in every match and were the thoroughly deserving recipients of the honours but, with Selhurst Park rivals Charlton successfully and creditably defending their top-flight status in the play-offs, there was a huge and over-riding feeling of anti-climax here at the end of 1986-87.

Although Steve Ketteridge moved to Leyton Orient and Alan Irvine to Dundee United during the summer of 1987, with Kevin Taylor joining Scunthorpe in September, Crystal Palace made two exciting dips into the transfer market to secure midfielder Geoff Thomas, the former captain of Crewe, and Neil Redfearn, a strong-running wide man from Doncaster. Also to fill an important role in the forthcoming season was midfielder Alan Pardew, who had joined us in the previous March. Alan had been spotted at nearby Dulwich Hamlet but it was from Yeovil that Palace recruited him for a bargain £7,000.

Another change at the Palace at the start of 1987-88 was in our colours. For only the second time in twelve years we dispensed with the all-white strip wth the distinctive red and blue sash, in favour of regular red and blue stripes while, for the first time, the Football League would allow the use of *two* substitutes.

Palace's programme began on 15 August at Huddersfield where, alongside Thomas and Redfearn, John Salako was making his first full appearance for the Club. The Eagles romped to a two goal lead in 54 minutes, with Mark Bright on target each time, but the Terriers halved their deficit after 67 minutes and equalised in the last seconds of the game. Such profligacy, even as early as the first game, was to cost us dear at the end of the season, but the following Saturday, against Hull City at Selhurst Park, it was Palace who had to claw their way back from a two goal disadvantage. The Tigers actually scored twice in the opening six minutes and they were furious about our second half goals which both came from Andy Gray penalties.

Defeat followed at Barnsley (2-3) but Palace then revealed their credibility with a fine run of five victories and a draw which took us to within a point of the top of the table, after we had beaten Reading 3-2 at rain-soaked Elm Park. Palace's line-up had been consistent in the opening sequence of games but 19-year-old Richard Shaw made his debut in this match, replacing the hobbling Paul Brush.

The autumn matches in the League Cup were interesting and hugely contrasting: we met Newport County for the last time in round two and gained an aggregate 6-0 victory, then faced Manchester United at Old Trafford where we trailed 0-2 within half an hour, before Ken O'Doherty rifled a consolation for us just before the interval. At this stage of the season the Palace defence was augmented by the purchase of left-back David Burke. Formerly with Bolton, the club he re-joined after leaving us in 1990, 'Burky' came to Palace from Huddersfield and had played against us in the first game of the season. He had an impressive debut when we beat Millwall 1-0 on 10 October and was ever-present in the remainder of the season.

Palace's inconsistency on their travels and occasional lapses at home made it impossible for us to remain at the top of the Division, although an excellent run of six victories in seven games included successes at Bournemouth (3-2), where all the scoring took place before the break and we were two in arrears after just twelve minutes, and a remarkable 3-1 victory at Manchester City in a game of great controversy, in which City's goalkeeper, Eric Nixon, was dismissed and Palace scored three times in a quarter of an hour. Unfortunately, it was at this stage of the term that Palace's prospects were damaged by a row that erupted between manager Steve Coppell and volatile Andy Gray and eventually led to Andy's departure for Aston Villa amid much acrimony. Palace replaced the departed Gray with former Southend skipper, Glenn Pennyfather, and the little fellow scored for us in an important match at Leicester early in January, which was to prove the end of a Palace era, for we let slip a 4-2 interval lead following a rare blunder by George Wood. George had become a great favourite at Selhurst Park and missed but three League games in four and a half years but, like Micky Droy before him, his reflexes had just begun to slow so that he was no longer equal to the demands of the top end of Division Two. In recognition of his splendid services George was given a free transfer and he moved quietly down to Cardiff City. His replacement was England Youth and Under 21 international Perry Suckling, who joined Palace from Manchester City for £100,000.

As 1987-88 moved into its last stages, with Palace now bearing the logo of their new sponsors Virgin Atlantic Airways on their breasts, and following a first-ever appearance at Wembley in the Football League Centenary tournament, it became clear that the possibility of us gaining a play-off place was going to become extremely close-run. Indeed, everything hinged on the last game of the season, although we required a favour elsewhere. Our opponents were Manchester City: we had to beat them *and* rely on champions Millwall conceding no more than a point to Blackburn at the Den.

A season's best crowd of 17,555 came to the Palace for the showdown and saw the Eagles forge ahead in the 70th minute of a dour encounter, with a Gavin Nebbeling header from a David Burke free kick, then Geoff Thomas delivered a second strike a few minutes later. Now affairs at Millwall assumed paramount significance — and BBC radio announced that the Lions were drawing 3-3! Enough to put Palace fifth! But there was total confusion. Fans listening to BBC on their transistors were elated, but others tuned in elsewhere had different intelligence and were merely confused. The players, Steve Coppell, the bench and many fans were convinced that we had nicked a play-off place, but it was not the case and for the main protagonists it was only in the dressing room that the harsh reality emerged, that Blackburn had scored an emphatic 4-1 win so that, contrary to what had been announced, it was they, not we, who had taken the fifth place. There was bitter disappointment everywhere and no little anger about the spurious information, but there was nothing anyone could do. Palace had finished sixth in Division Two for the second season running and been denied a play-off place again.

Player of the Year this time went to Geoff Thomas, but there was some disquiet when it was announced that skipper Jim Cannon, who received a second testimonial this term and had played his 650th game for us during April, was leaving the Club. His contribution to Crystal Palace FC had been magnificent and it was understandable that many fans were sad to see him leave.

However, in an historical context, the most significant factor of 1987-88 was the hugely increased scoring rate. Palace hit 86 Division Two goals — the third highest post-war tally at our Club — while top scorer Mark Bright secured 24 in the Football League games and that had only been bettered by Johnny Byrne and Roy Summersby, in more matches, in 1960-61. This vastly improved scoring rate was soon to reap a rich harvest.

For 1988-89 Palace naturally based their playing policy on an attacking strategy but, in order to secure the defence, Steve Coppell signed 24-year-old Welsh international centre-half Jeff Hopkins from Fulham, for a tribunal-set fee of £240,000 and, although this sum represented manager Coppell's biggest outlay by some margin, it proved another shrewd purchase. Another defender who was to play a vital role was John Pemberton, who had joined Palace towards the end of 1987-88 from Crewe in a £60,000 deal, while midfielder Dave Madden came from Reading. Dave was to provide a cool head when Palace were awarded several penalties in crucial or even decisive games late in the season.

To begin with, Palace's 1988-89 season was dismal. We sat out the opening day because Swindon's ground improvement work had not been completed, then drew and lost at home to Chelsea and Watford respectively. Four more draws left us still without a win and in twelfth place at the end of September but, with Bright and Wright now finding the target regularly, and the defence becoming more settled after enforced absences, Palace were in the top half of the table by the end of October. It was on 8 October that Palace featured in one of the most astonishing matches in our history. Although we had fallen behind at Blackburn we were in front soon after half-time and Mark Bright extended our lead so that with twenty minutes remaining Blackburn were looking a beaten side. However, the referee granted them a second chance by awarding a seemingly gratuitous penalty, following an innocuous collision between Scott Sellars and Gary O'Reilly. At 2-3 Rovers took new heart, Simon Garner netted twice for them in as many minutes, only for Gary O'Reilly to nod a late Palace equaliser, but in the dying seconds Rovers scored a devastating fifth goal to deny us any consolation.

Palace got back to winning ways at Bradford City a week later but now Neil Redfearn announced that he wanted to leave. The issue simmered for about a month before he left us in mid-November for Watford at a fee of £150,000. Arriving at this time was Alex Dyer from Hull, but Alex was unlucky with injuries and made his major mark for us in the Full Members Cup, with a brace of goals against Walsall (4-2) and the winner at Southampton (2-1).

Palace beat Walsall again in the League match on 2 January, with Mark Bright's hat-trick the feature of a 4-0 win, but we went out of the FA Cup at Stoke (0-1) a week later and then had Geoff Thomas sidelined with an injury that proved difficult to diagnose. In fact Geoff was unable to play for Palace's senior team again for the rest of the season and his absence was a severe loss, but Steve Coppell made his last attempt to build a promotion side for 1988-89 by obtaining right-winger Eddie McGoldrick from Northampton Town for £200,000.

By mid-February Palace had risen to seventh in Division Two but, as a result of further Full Members Cup victories over 1st Division Luton Town (4-1) and at Middlesbrough (3-2), most Eagles' eyes were fixed on the prestigious semi-final at Nottingham Forest. Over three thousand fans were at the City Ground to see Ian Wright nullify Forest's early opener and then Palace threatened to create a major upset . . . but, with Forest rocking and just six minutes left, a bizarre refereeing decision saw acting captain David Burke sent off after he and Franz Carr had jostled one another some forty yards from goal. This handicap was inevitably too much against a side of Forest's pedigree and their England men Stuart Pearce and Neil Webb both netted in the last three minutes.

There now followed Palace's first change in our managerial team in more than four and a half years, for Ian Evans went to take charge at Swansea City. Steve Coppell's choice of replacement was the perky, knowledgeable Geordie, Stan Ternent, who had formerly managed Blackpool and been deputy at Bradford City.

A series of eight victories (interspersed with one poor display, at Shrewsbury) from the middle of March lifted Palace from mid-table into promotion challengers. Among these was an amazing Easter Monday match against Brighton (2-1) which made Football League history, for referee Kelvin Morton awarded *five* penalties! Palace, already ahead from a typical piece of Ian Wright brilliance, netted from the first of their four awards while the Seagulls replied from their own predictable spot-kick.

In the end three Dave Madden penalties ensured a 2-2 draw at Leicester in the last away game and a 1-0 success over Stoke to send us leaping into third place, with outright promotion still a possibility on the last day of the season, depending on Manchester City's result at Bradford City. Palace were soon in front against relegated Birmingham but visiting supporters then invaded the pitch and caused half an hour's delay, with dreadful scenes before the hooligans were controlled by police and stewards. Palace romped to a 4-0 lead with Ian Wright securing a hat-trick, but long before the end we knew that Manchester City had gained the single point they needed and Birmingham netted while we were assimilating the implications of this news.

By finishing third Palace were involved in the play-offs and the semi-final stage of these pitted us against Swindon. The first leg, in Wiltshire, was played in baking heat and Swindon failed to make anything of their home advantage, so that we returned to Selhurst Park with only a 0-1 defeat, and Palace's biggest crowd for more than five years came along to the second leg on a steamy, humid evening, anticipating a further Palace success. There was not long to wait: Mark Bright levelled the aggregates after only seven minutes and Ian Wright despatched a volley half an hour later to put us into the final against Blackburn Rovers.

At Ewood Park Blackburn dominated — and tucked away their chances, so that Palace retired with a 1-3 defeat and only Eddie McGoldrick's first goal for the Club as consolation. The finale was at Selhurst Park on 3 June and drew a full house of 30,000. With only sixteen minutes gone Palace reduced the overall arrears, when Ian Wright stabbed the ball home from close range, following a sweet cross from the left by Alan Pardew. Further reward did not come until after the interval, when Eddie McGoldrick was bundled over in the penalty area and Dave Madden converted the 47th minute award with aplomb. Ninety minutes was reached with the sides still locked together, so extra time had to be played, although Palace had the advantage because of our precious away goal. Only two minutes of the additional period remained when, with Rovers stretched after pressing up in a desperate attempt to net a winner, Eddie McGoldrick battled his way to the by-line and crossed, for Ian Wright to rise like a salmon, unchallenged, and head home! Pandemonium erupted as the ecstatic crowd invaded the pitch but order was soon restored; Blackburn had one last response but Perry Suckling clutched a cunning, curling effort from Scott Sellars and then came the final whistle. The euphoric fans engulfed the players as they struggled to reach the tunnel, but our heroes finally made an appearance in the Directors' Box to the strains of *Glad All Over*. Steve Coppell, as so often, had it perfectly analysed: 'Our performance here was nothing short of magnificent' he said — and remember, Steve was never a man to eulogize.

Remarkably then, Palace had won promotion to Division One for the third decade running, but it was no surprise when our supporters made Ian Wright our Player of the Year. His marvellous tally of 27 League goals had only been exceeded by Johnny Byrne since the War, and not even that splendid fellow could reach Ian's total of 33 in all competitions, while the combined total of 58 with his partner Mark Bright was the best by any Palace striking pair since 1936!

Steve Coppell audaciously brought back Andy Gray, from Queens Park Rangers for £500,000, to stiffen his midfield for top-flight duty but, while most supporters were initially amazed by Andy's return this was another hugely successful move by the manager, for Andy added power and strength to our cause while also improving sufficiently himself to gain a full England cap in November 1991.

Intriguingly, Palace's 1st Division return on 19 August was over at Andy's old club, Queens Park Rangers, but we were beaten by a side with considerable experience at this level and who scored twice after the break.

The first home game three days later was a terrific opener — Manchester United! Palace lit up their new electronic scoreboard at the Whitehorse Lane end before the match, only for United to dampen the exuberant atmosphere by taking the lead after 17 minutes through England captain Bryan Robson. Although Palace responded positively enough it looked as though we were heading for another defeat until, with barely ninety seconds remaining, a lightning strike by Ian Wright from Alex Dyer's deft touch brought delight as well as relief.

Dour, defensive Coventry stole the points with a deflected free kick on the second Saturday of the season but a rather spiritless Wimbledon were defeated with a goal in each half from Geoff Thomas and Ian Wright — and then came our infamous trip to Liverpool. Palace had the temerity to *attack* Liverpool and were punished severely. However, the ploy *might* have succeeded for we created several chances, hit a post and missed a penalty while the Reds' finishing was absolutely devastating. Palace's 0-9 defeat certainly highlighted the paucity of top-flight talent in our defence but, with changed personnel, the attacking tactic against Liverpool was to prove brilliantly correct in wonderfully exciting fashion later in the season.

Palace emphasised the fact that we were no worse than many 1st Division sides by gaining a creditable draw at Southampton four days later, courtesy of a Jeff Hopkins headed equaliser but, in the wake of the defeat at Anfield, manager Coppell now secured the country's first £1 million goalkeeper in Nigel Martyn from Bristol Rovers and then signed former Wimbledon centre-half, Andy Thorn, from Newcastle for £650,000. Andy's debut was at Manchester United on 9 December where Palace won 2-1 with a brace from Mark Bright gaining our first away victory of the season in the League, then Andy himself put us on the way to another 2-1 success in our 'away' match against Charlton at Selhurst Park.

Coinciding with the arrival of the two new players there had been another change at assistant manager level. Stan Ternent left to take over at Hull City and Palace wisely promoted long-serving reserve and youth team boss, Alan Smith, who had been with the Club since 1983 and helped to develop such stars as Richard Shaw and John Salako.

The strengthened Palace side climbed slowly to 1st Division security, even in the absence of Ian Wright with a broken leg sustained on 20 January in a home defeat by Liverpool and broken again against Derby (1-1) precisely two months later, but manager Coppell signed experienced striker Garry Thompson from Watford towards the end of March and an early, conclusive goal on his debut against Aston Villa provided an immediate dividend.

1989-90 will always be remembered by Palace fans as the season when the Eagles went to Wembley to play in the FA Cup Final! That possibility looked remote in early January when Portsmouth, our third round visitors, were leading and comfortably holding us at bay in the chill drizzle — but substitute Geoff Thomas equalised and then Palace were awarded a penalty in the last minute which was rapped home by Andy Gray. Huddersfield (4-0) posed scant problems but victory over Rochdale in round five was hard won, earned by a close-range strike from Phil Barber just after the hour and a brilliant Nigel Martyn save in the last minute, then a scrappy quarter final contest at Cambridge was settled by a scuffed Geoff Thomas goal fourteen minutes from time.

Palace's semi-final opponents were Liverpool, at Villa Park. The Reds seized a first-half lead but, providing magnificent entertainment, Palace had the powerful northern outfit in retreat after the break. Superb goals by Mark Bright and Gary O'Reilly rocked the opposition though they replied through Steve McMahon before a somewhat fortuitous late penalty converted by John Barnes appeared to have settled the matter against us, only for Andy Gray to steer a header past Bruce Grobbelaar to take the tie into extra time. In this period Palace matched Liverpool's sophistication but patently outwitted them, especially at set pieces, and proceeded to make Club history when Alan Pardew headed the 109th minute winner, after Andy Thorn had flicked on an Andy Gray left-side corner.

The 1990 FA Cup Final between Palace and Manchester United was acknowledged as among the best in the long history of the competition. Ian Wright was not sufficiently recovered to take his place in Palace's starting line-up but we still opened the scoring after a quarter of an hour, when Gary O'Reilly reached a Phil Barber free kick to loop a header over Jim Leighton. United replied before half time and took the lead themselves just after the hour but then Steve Coppell made his perfectly judged substitution, bringing on Ian Wright to replace Phil Barber after 69 minutes. Within three minutes Palace were level with a goal to match the finest the old stadium has ever seen! The lithe and eager Palace striker skipped clear of the lunging Phelan, turned inside Pallister and delivered a low shot past Leighton for 2-2. Another goal then would have settled it all but we could not find it until two minutes into extra time although again it was a beauty. Young John Salako, who caused United endless trouble with his marauding runs down the left, sent over a long, testing cross. Wright saw it early and volleyed the ball into the net while flying some five feet above the ground! What a Cup winner it would have been but regrettably United had time to regroup and show one more example of high-class finishing, Hughes making it 3-3 to require a replay the following Thursday.

With an equal distribution of tickets for the second match, Palace fans were at Wembley in full strength and gave their favourites incredible visual and vocal backing, but the replay was a totally different match — dour, uncompromising and even tough in parts. The media chose to blame Palace for what were claimed to be over-physical tactics, failing to recognise or (worse) report, the fact that the foul count between the sides was almost equal or that some of United's stars were apparently rehearsing for the histrionics of the World Cup which was to follow later in the summer!

The goal which won the Cup for United came right on the hour and this time even the introduction of Ian Wright proved powerless to change the course of the game. But the destination of the Cup had actually hinged on a few minutes earlier in the game, in the first half, when United's stand-in goalkeeper, Les Sealey, had the good fortune to save an Andy Gray free kick, which had shredded the defensive wall, with his legs as he dived the opposite way and then, crucially, the referee awarding a free kick several yards outside the penalty area after a foul on Geoff Thomas committed some five yards inside the box. It was apparent at the time what had happened and the marks of the incident were clearly visible on the turf — but the official refrained from awarding the spot-kick.

So the Palace had to be content with fulfilling their dream of appearing at Wembley in a major final, though they had come cruelly close to achieving the greater ambition of winning the FA Cup. One day, hopefully before too long, we shall return to the great stadium and bring the famous trophy home to Selhurst Park.

Arriving early in the 1990 close season to augment Palace's defence was John Humphrey, the former Charlton skipper, for £450,000, although unsettled John Pemberton chose to move to Sheffield United in July for £300,000. Palace's other major summer acquisition was giant Welsh international centre-half Eric Young from Wimbledon for £850,000. Quibbles about the size of the fee for the 30-year-old evaporated as the season progressed and Eric (soon dubbed 'Ninja' by the fans on account of his headband, which resembled those worn by the cartoon turtles of the time) dominated opposing strikers in awesome fashion at the heart of Palace's best defence for years.

Meanwhile, there was major restructuring at Selhurst Park where five thousand seats were installed to make the Arthur Wait Stand an all-seater, with new dressing rooms and a reception area being built into the much older main stand.

The 1990-91 season began on 25 August at Luton, on the Hatters' plastic pitch. Eric Young immediately endeared himself to those Eagles fans who had infiltrated the Kenilworth Road members-only security system, by heading us in front after a quarter of an hour, although Luton managed an equaliser on the stroke of half-time. The opening home game the following Tuesday evening was the all-London clash against Chelsea when the crowd of 27,101 paid the Club record receipts of some £226,000. Andy Gray thumped a 5th minute penalty but departed some afterwards when he and Dennis Wise were sent off following a brawl, and there was no way back for the Blues after Ian Wright lofted a great effort over Dave Beasant from twenty yards. A fierce Garry Thompson header disposed of visiting Sheffield United, then Palace routed Norwich 3-0 at Carrow Road to go to second in the table and, if the Palace charge was slowed by draws at home to Nottingham Forest (2-2) and at Tottenham (1-1), we were never out of the top five clubs all season and consistently held third place throughout the entire second half of the term.

Highlights of this excellent record were the single goal victory over Liverpool in a televised match on the Sunday after Christmas when, if the Reds found us at our peak, they simply had no answer to our challenge. It was probably on the strength of his electric performance in this game that Ian Wright was shortly afterwards awarded his first full England cap. Ian created our goal three minutes before half time, leaving Gary Gillespie floundering near the right corner flag, then speeding goalwards along the by-line, before flashing across a low centre which Mark Bright turned past Grobbelaar with aplomb from five yards.

Alright, there were occasions when Palace betrayed their inexperience, but other top clubs fell to our striking power: we won at Nottingham Forest on 2 February with a late Eric Young header to avenge an FA Cup defeat five days earlier and infuriate the Forest chairman, then at Leeds on 23 March when John Salako tapped home a late winner, Ian Wright having given us an early lead. Tottenham were beaten at the Palace in mid-April with another Eric Young goal in only the sixth minute, Ian Wright scored a virtuoso hat-trick at Wimbledon in the penultimate game, then Manchester United retired from Selhurst Park at the end of the season with a three goal beating.

In retrospect most Palace fans of the period will recall 1990-91 as the season in which we *won* a Wembley Cup Final. Fittingly, it was the Full Members Cup, the competition which had been the brainchild of Palace chairman Ron Noades. Played on a single match, knock-out basis, it had provided the smaller clubs with useful revenue and the prize of a Wembley final was its great lure. Palace reached Wembley by defeating Bristol Rovers, Brighton, Luton and Norwich and our Wembley opponents on Sunday 7 April were Everton. Having gone so close to winning the FA Cup Final the previous May there was no way we were going to be deprived this time. With magnificent support the Eagles powered their way to victory, to secure the Club's first major trophy and our first senior award since winning the 2nd Division championship in 1979. Ian Wright repeated his Wembley brace while John Salako netted our third with a header, all those goals coming in extra time, in which we were much too strong for the fading Everton.

Among our heroes at Wembley was 'Man of the Match' Geoff Thomas, who made an outstanding contribution to the contest. It was possibly because of Geoff's fine display, and his opening goal when he cleaved his way through Everton's defence to head home from a corner, that he was awarded his own first full England cap in the European Nations Championship tie in Turkey some three or four weeks later, and it was marvellous for Palace fans to have Geoff and Ian Wright in the England squad at the end of the season, with both of them appearing together against the USSR at Wembley on 21 May, by which time Geoff had been acclaimed again as Palace's Player of the Year.

Emerging towards stardom in this 1990-91 season had been the two youngest members of the Palace side, winger John Salako and defender Richard Shaw. The former scored a remarkable fifty yard goal during an FA Cup replay at Nottingham Forest, while Richard Shaw had netted early in the League game against Brian Clough's men in September. Salako had seized his opportunity with some style, become the regional Barclays Young Eagle of the Month twice in four months and was about to become the great success of England's Australasian tour.

Versatile Richard Shaw had been with Palace since his schooldays. He missed only two matches in this campaign but few would argue that his best performance had been in the League game at Forest, when he completely shackled the enigmatic but sometimes brilliant Nigel Clough.

Other products of the Palace youth scheme, Simon Osborn and Gareth Southgate, made debuts towards the end of the season, as did rangey striker Stan Collymore, signed from Stafford Rangers for £100,000. Just before the finale Palace revealed a new, lucrative sponsorship deal with Tulip Computers and then it was announced that, with Charlton on their way back to the Valley, we would be sharing Selhurst Park with Wimbledon from July.

The summer of 1991 saw the departure from the Palace of Phil Barber, who moved to Millwall for £100,000 after making 288 appearances for the Club, while Cup Final goalscorer Gary O'Reilly rejoined Brighton and Garry Thompson went to Queens Park Rangers, with reserve centre-half Tony Witter, in a double deal which netted Palace £½ million. Joining us were Welsh Under 21 defender Chris Coleman from Swansea for £275,000 and centre-half Lee Sinnott from Bradford City who cost £350,000.

By the start of the new season Steve Coppell had become Palace's longest-serving post-war manager, but 1991-92 was to prove controversial for Crystal Palace and Steve's popularity began to wane as he faced criticism about his judgement in the transfer market. To begin with, to the disappointment of our fans, Palace were unable to play their opening day home fixture against Leeds, because the £2 million ground improvements were not completed in time. Then, little more than three weeks into the season, Palace's relationship with the media, susceptible since the 1990 FA Cup Final replay, soured again after a stormy match at Everton. In an historical context the major event of 1991-92 and the beginning of the end of a Palace era, was the departure of Ian Wright to Arsenal on 23 September for £2½ million, forty-eight hours after he scored his last Palace goal in our 3-2 victory at Oldham. To a man, Palace fans were sad to see him go, but Ian had made clear his desire to play for a club involved in Europe and, in spite of inducements to stay, he chose to leave. He had scored 92 League goals for Palace, third highest in the Club's history, and 117 in all competitions. His had been an indelible contribution to our cause.

Palace's replacement for Wright was Marco Gabbiadini, who joined us from Sunderland for £1.8 million but, while Marco scored some valuable goals for us — his first helped us to victory at Coventry, his second to our biggest prize of the season, at Anfield — the move never really appeared satisfactory. Palace seldom played to Gabbiadini's strengths, while his fitness looked questionable. Thus, when Derby County offered £1.2 million at the end of January Palace accepted the bid — and this came only a short while after we had taken another big loss on a transfer that had not worked out, for Paul Bodin, recruited from Swindon the previous spring for £550,000, returnd to Wiltshire for less than half that sum.

In the wake of the departures and a spate of injuries, young players now came to the fore: David Whyte made a promising full debut, Simon Rodger and Simon Osborn were becoming first team regulars and so was Gareth Southgate, but then came further controversy when disgruntled Andy Gray left — again! — initially on loan to Tottenham, so that by the time of the last game of the season, at Queens Park Rangers, Palace fielded no fewer than eight new faces from the line-up that had appeared in the first match!

Out on the pitch it was an eventful season too. Palace gained a remarkable 3-2 victory over tenants Wimbledon, in our first home game in which three men were sent off, including our goalkeeper Nigel Martyn whose splendid deputy for almost an hour was John Salako. The re-arranged match against Leeds on 1 October brought another stirring victory, secured by a late Mark Bright header on Marco Gabbiadini's debut, but this evening will for ever remain etched in Palace memories for the sight of John Salako lying crumpled by the Holmesdale Road goal, having fallen badly after putting in a testing tenth minute header. An exploratory operation the following day revealed the severance of both cruciate ligaments behind his left knee, one of the worst injuries a footballer can sustain and one to deny Palace his presence for many months to come.

But the best and happiest moments of 1991-92 were our victories over Liverpool, for Palace did the 'double' over the Reds. With fabulous support from our colourful fans at Anfield on 2 November, Palace fell behind towards the end of the first half but took the second period with a display of passion, character and no little skill. Five minutes after the restart, Marco Gabbiadini scythed the ball past Bruce Grobbelaar, following a first class move down our right flank which had involved four other players, and culminated in a low cross from overlapping full-back Gareth Southgate. Providing compelling entertainment, and in spite of losing Paul Mortimer and Andy Gray to injuries in quick succession, Palace continued to attack so that, to mounting enthusiasm and anticipation among our packed supporters, we were able to dominate the home side and scored again after 72 minutes, when a corner was flicked on by Eric Young, then headed into the net by Geoff Thomas.

Eric himself became the Liverpool executioner in the return at a blustery, cool Selhurst Park on 14 March. Five minutes before the interval an Andy Thorn free kick created mayhem in the visitors' penalty area. Mark Bright soared above his marker to flick the ball on and it ran towards the corner of the goal area near the by-line in front of the Holmesdale Road terrace. Bruce Grobbelaar and Eric challenged for the ball but, as the extrovert goalkeeper sought to smother it, the Eagles' giant pivot stuck out a lanky leg and clawed the ball back from Bruce's attempted grasp before regaining his own balance and driving it into the far inside-netting of the goal from an acute angle . . . and that was sufficient to provide Palace with their fourth win over Liverpool in five matches and a superb first-ever 'double'.

Further encouraging evidence of the advances made by Crystal Palace in the period materialised as the Palace Youth team surged into the FA Youth Cup semi-finals for only the fourth time in the Club's history, and then overcame Wimbledon with a 2-1 victory in the first leg and a fabulous, titanic 3-3 draw in the second. By the time of the final our juniors were already champions of their division of the South East Counties League but, pitted against an outstanding team from Manchester United, we lost 1-3 at Selhurst Park and 2-3 at Old Trafford.

The FA generated huge publicity about the formation of its new Premier League in the summer of 1992 but regrettably the Eagle's initial participation in it was to be minimal, for although our 1992-93 season began in fine style when we opened our account with a pulsating 3-3 draw at sunful Selhurst Park against money-laden Blackburn Rovers, this term was to prove bitterly disappointing for everyone at Crystal Palace and end, ultimately, in the departure of manager Steve Coppell from Selhurst Park.

The draw with Blackburn was followed by three more: at Oldham (1-1) in some adversity, at Tottenham (2-2) amid controvery as Andy Thorn and Neil Ruddock were dismissed after skirmishing together, and at home to Sheffield Wednesday (1-1). Three defeats followed and then Mark Bright was transferred *to* Sheffield Wednesday with Palace receiving the talented if diminutive midfielder-cum-striker Paul Williams and £350,000 in return. Bright had craved a move for some time, but Palace fans regretted his departure because he was a proven goalscorer, even if his attention had appeared somewhat distracted this term. Only Ian Wright among our post-war marksmen could match Mark's Palace record of 92 Football/Premier League goals in our colours, but Williams' skill-factor clearly influenced Steve Coppell in this deal, because Palace had come under a lot of media criticism (not always well-informed, but strident nevertheless) about our direct style of play and this was now being echoed by some of our fans.

A new arrival at Selhurst Park early in this season was £1 million striker Chris Armstrong from Millwall. Manager Coppell was convinced that Chris had the predatory instincts and positional sense of a top-class striker and in this signing revealed again all his ability to recognise raw talent. Although this was to prove Steve's last successful import it was highly effective, for Chris quickly responded with important goals for Palace, and his 15 strikes from 35 League outings represented a haul of the highest pedigree from a man who had not performed at this level before. His first goals, a stunning right-footed volley and a spectacular header, within a minute of each other just after the hour on his debut, secured a point against visiting Oldham, and the following Saturday he netted another brace to provide Palace with our first victory in the Premier League, against Everton at Goodison Park. This time they both came early: a clever, diving, glancing header after eight minutes and a supreme effort when Chris rounded that great Welsh international goalkeeper, Neville Southall, ten minutes later. It was largely those two pairs of goals that brought Chris his first 'Barclays Young Eagle of the Month' award with Palace in September 1992, but the emerging midfield skills of Gareth Southgate brought *him* a similar award and the two Palace tyros received their silverware together before our home match against Manchester City (0-0) on 17 October.

However, in spite of Armstrong's commendable early return, it became apparent as the autumn progressed that Premier League survival would be the limit of our ambitions this term. We were not scoring sufficient goals, failing even from the penalty spot on three occasions; we were conceding them to the opposition with disturbing largesse and, with Andy Gray never replaced after his £1 million move to 'Spurs and Geoff Thomas looking a spent force even before he was sidelined by injury, we lacked sufficient authority in midfield. Seasoned supporters recognised these signs for what they were, evidence of a side that was in danger.

Just so, by the end of November Palace were next to bottom after a 0-5 thrashing at Liverpool but, immediately and delightfully, surprised the Anfield men by holding them to a 1-1 draw before their own supporters in the League Cup, with a makeshift side in which 18-year-old George Ndah was starting for the first time and 21-year-old Bobby Bowry achieved his senior debut. Liverpool manager Graeme Souness responded with one of his ill-tempered and unsporting outbursts — thus providing Palace with the stimulus needed to overcome his expensively assembled outfit in the replay in the week before Christmas!

In fact the League Cup was to provide Palace's only real pleasure this season for, following a passionate victory over the Reds in which young Grant Watts scored his first goal for the Club, and Andy Thorn secured the winner in extra time, and another over Chelsea (3-1) in January on a Selhurst Park quagmire, the Eagles reached the last four in this competition for the first time in our history. But even this relative success proved to be an illusion because we were beaten by Arsenal in both legs of the semi-final and were unable to use the victories we gained in the earlier rounds as stepping stones towards redeeming our ailing Premier League season.

Palace actually had their best spell of the entire campaign in December. As well as beating Liverpool in the League Cup we belatedly won our first home Premier League game by defeating Sheffield United (2-0) on 5 December, then scored three times in the second half at Loftus Road to secure an unlikely but welcome victory over Queens Park Rangers. An Andy Thorn header beat visiting champions Leeds in a Sunday game, tenants Wimbledon fell to goals early and late in the first half in a raw Boxing Day midday meeting and burgeoning Simon Osborn cracked a superb volley at bitterly cold Middlesbrough, to leave us in a healthy fifteenth place at the turn of the year.

But from that point our story was largely one of disappointment and decline so that, after a Good Friday afternoon 0-4 trouncing by Wimbledon, Palace were in obvious danger. Storming successes over Middlesbrough (4-1) on Easter Monday and again over Ipswich (3-1) on May Day appeared to have remedied the situation however, but the last relegation place was still unfilled and any one out of us, Sheffield United or Oldham could take it. Oldham won well at Aston Villa twenty-four hours later and the Blades secured a second away victory in four days to ensure their survival on the Tuesday.

On Wednesday 5 May Palace gained a 0-0 draw at Manchester City with a battling performance that gained high praise from Steve Coppell, but at the same time Oldham won again, beating a Liverpool side whose accumulated performance was woeful and their goalkeeper's nothing short of pathetic, so that now everything hinged on the final Saturday of the season: if Palace could avoid defeat at Arsenal we would be safe. Failure to do so would mean that an Oldham victory, however narrow, over Southampton at Boundary Park would doom us to relegation.

Palace's demanding task was made formidable when Ian Wright despatched an early chance and Eddie McGoldrick spurned the opportunity of an immediate riposte, so that, once we were aware that Oldham had gone ahead, the prospects were ominous. Palace created several possible openings, Arsenal certainly looked uneasy under pressure, but we could find no way through. Then we learned that Oldham were in control of matters in their game and, when we pushed up in a desperate search for the goal that might yet save us, Arsenal scored again ten minutes from time and right at the end.

It was all over. There was no way back — but for Palace fans the cruellest cut of all was that it had been Ian Wright's quick goal that had sunk us. Some of the team left the pitch in tears as Steve Coppell stepped on to the arena to offer each of them a consoling gesture.

It was to be Steve's last public act as our manager for, after a brief holiday, he announced his resignation saying that he felt 'devastated' by Palace's relegation. In fairness to Steve it should be stated that under the old system of two points for a win — still used in Scotland and in several other major footballing countries — Palace would have survived, and that only once before under the current system had a club been relegated from the senior section with 49 points. It was cruel — but academic. We were down and our manager had gone. Her Majesty the Queen had referred in her 1992 Christmas broadcast to the royal family's 'annus horribilus' — its 'horrible year'. If for totally different reasons, it was a description of events at *our* Palace throughout 1992-93 with which Palace fans everywhere would wholeheartedly agree.

ABOVE: Crystal Palace FC 1985-86; back (l-r): O'Doherty, Droy, Wood, Cannon, Galloway; middle: Finnigan, K. Taylor, Ketteridge, Aylott, Nebbeling, Hughton, Gray, I. Evans (assistant manager); front: Sparrow, Lindsay, S. Coppell (manager), Barber, Irvine. BELOW: An early look at Ian Wright, cracking the winning goal against Middlesbrough (2-1) on 8 March 1986.

LEFT: Mark Bright arrived from Leicester City in November 1986. CENTRE: John Salako made his first full Palace appearance at Huddersfield (2-2) on 15 August 1987. RIGHT: Goalkeeper, Perry Suckling. BELOW: Crystal Palace FC 1988-89; back (l-r): Nebbeling, Barber, Suckling, Parkin, Harris, Redfearn; middle: S. Coppell (manager), Bright, Hopkins, Thomas, O'Reilly, Madden, Bailey, Burke, I. Evans (assistant manager); front: Pemberton, Pennyfather, Pardew, Wright, Salako.

LEFT: Nigel Martyn, the country's first £1 million goalkeeper. (Photo: Mark Leech) RIGHT: And here's the goal that won the semi-final and took Palace to Wembley! Alan Pardew beats the 'Pool defenders and 'keeper Grobbelaar to earn everlasting glory at Selhurst Park! BELOW: Crowd scenes at Wembley on 7 April 1991 when Palace won the Full Members' Cup.

ABOVE: Eric Young became the Liverpool executioner in the return at Selhurst Park on 14 March 1992. Here's his angled shot into the inside side netting of the Holmesdale Road goal which separated the sides. BELOW: An evocative picture of Palace's redeveloped Whitehorse Lane end after the erection of the Executive boxes, but prior to the installation of seating in the summer of 1993.

LEFT: Palace manager Alan Smith (centre) and his coaches Steve Harrison (left) and former Eagles striker David Kemp (right) view the prospects for 1993-94 with optimism. BELOW: Crystal Palace FC 1993-94; back (l-r): P. McLean (physio), Stokoe, Patterson, Edwards, Vincent, Newman, Hawthorne, Clark, S. Hill (kit manager); second: Humphrey, Sparrow, Daly, Holman, Massey, Thorn, Watts, Ndah, Mortimer, Osborn; third: S. Harrison (coach) Sinnott, Salako, O'Connor, Woodman, Martyn, Glass, Thompson, Coleman, Barnes, D. Kemp (coach); front: Rodger, Whyte, Armstrong, Gordon, A. Smith (manager), Shaw, Young, Williams, Bowry, Southgate. RIGHT: Simon Rodger's efforts in midfield were a major factor in Palace's success this season.

New Worlds

Alan Smith, tall, stylish and urbane, a splendid communicator and motivator, and a football man through and through, was the obvious choice to succeed Steve Coppell as Palace's manager in the summer of 1993. He had been at Selhurst Park for almost ten years, and proved a thoroughly capable assistant to Steve since 1989 and it had been under his guidance and tutelage that Gareth Southgate, then more latterly 'The Bisto Kids' Simon Osborn and Simon Rodger were nurtured into first team players alongside their predecessors Richard Shaw and John Salako. However, Alan's task upon taking full charge at Crystal Palace was a highly demanding one, for the Club and many of its followers were greatly depressed by the experience of relegation. Yet, with a combination of energy, enthusiasm, commitment and flair, Alan and his coaching team of Steve Harrison, former Eagles striker David Kemp and the hugely popular Steve Kember, restored morale and set the Club's sights firmly upon the swiftest possible return to the top flight.

This goal was achieved, ultimately in an imperious manner, but initially he lost two of his troupe of international stars from the Palace squad, when Geoff Thomas and Eddie McGoldrick moved to Wolves and Arsenal respectively for big fees. These departures disappointed many Palace fans, although it was largely recognised that, if the players' loyalties could not be guaranteed, then it was better that they left us, but manager Smith had already generated a new optimism at the Club for season-ticket sales passed the 1992-93 Premier League total with over a month of the close-season remaining and, if financial restraints precluded any purchases being made to replace the duo, it was also evident that the restructuring of the Whitehorse Lane end was continuing on schedule to provide covered, all-seating accommodation in front of the executive boxes for the term ahead, along with new, more powerful, angled floodlights.

Again, Palace fans were encouraged by their manager's announcement that their favourites would be adopting a more sophisticated mode of play in their quest for an immediate return to the top flight. 'I've decided that we will use a "pass-and-move" style this season' said Alan. 'I think this will prove acceptable to everybody. People don't want to see the ball being constantly pumped through the middle' and, to be sure, the new-look Eagles were frequently much more refined than they had been for many years.

However, the early optimism surrounding our prospects for 1993-94 was somewhat muted by the two opening results, for Palace could only draw at home 0-0 with Tranmere on the first Saturday of the season then went down 0-2 at Bristol City a week later! These set-backs had the effect of putting the Palace establishment firmly on its mettle and thus there followed an emphatic riposte to the cynics and doubters which, over a period of eight days, certainly established the Eagles among the favourites for promotion. Nottingham Forest, who had invested heavily in their attempt to regain Premier League status, were dismissed from Selhurst Park in a superb evening game, when Eric Young's powerful header opened our season's account and Dean Gordon rifled the second. Playing at left-back, Gordon was to become a vital and attractive member of the Palace side this season, progressing rapidly to the England Under 21 side and contributing some fine goals in our cause. Then Portsmouth, another likely contender for honours, were routed 5-1 after scoring first and three days later Birmingham were beaten 4-2 at St Andrews, where our football was neat, sharp and highly incisive, clever Paul Williams setting us on our way with his first Palace goal.

With Palace flying high and looking increasingly serious promotion challengers, there occurred on Saturday 2 October 1993 one of those footballing occasions which might have come straight out of *Boys' Own*. John Salako, sidelined by a second cruciate ligament operation since the previous November and precisely two years and one day after the dreadful initial injury, returned to Palace's starting line-up for the first time for the visit of Stoke City, to score a devastating and spectacular hat-trick which absolutely delighted our fans on that rain-soaked afternoon and took Palace to the top of the table.

It was immediately after this success that Palace gained a new club sponsor in TDK Ltd, the manufacturers of audio and video tapes and, after appearing for two months with shirt fronts devoid of any motif, the Eagles paraded the company's logo for the first time in our televised home match against Wolves (1-1) on 17 October 1993.

It would be a mistake to pretend that Palace progress to the 1st Division championship was completely straightforward. It was not, because we had an Achilles heel in the matter of our away form and this fragility on our travels might have cost us dear. Autumn defeats at Derby and Notts County (the latter after we had secured a 2-0 lead!), then on a snow-flecked pitch in midweek at freezing Bolton, undid our hold on top place, then depressing midwinter ones at Millwall and Wolves implied that we might lack the ability to sustain our promotion challenge, but it was at this point that manager Alan Smith demonstrated his acumen by securing Liverpool's England international striker or midfielder Paul Stewart on loan. The signing was inspired, brilliantly effective and the catalyst which provoked Palace to an emotional and completely successful conclusion to the season. Stewart was majestic, out of his class at Division One level and a controlling influence both on particular matches and upon his team mates. With Stewart playing up front alongside the prolific Chris Armstrong, the Eagles rapidly matured into the strongest side in the section by a considerable distance and demonstrated an attractive brand of resilience, sophistication and fortitude, while Stewart himself quickly became a huge favourite with the Palace fans, so that a widening gap of several points was built between ourselves at the top of the table and our challengers.

The matter of away performances was confidently settled: Palace actually managed a total of eleven away League victories in this season — a tally only ever improved upon at our Club by Arthur Rowe's promotion-winning side of 1960-61 — and allied to this, Palace's defence tightened over the last third of the term into one of the best in the Club's history. It was in fact the meanest in the Division over the season but it conceded just nine goals during the last fourteen matches and during that period recorded no fewer than seven clean-sheets. Those statistics are impressive, but they become the more so when it is pointed out that Palace had lost their experienced skipper and central defender Andy Thorn with cartilage and hamstring problems back in November! Such an absence could have been crucial, but Chris Coleman moved to partner Eric Young at the heart of the back four, while Dean Gordon filled the vacated left-back berth with astonishing yet increasing maturity to great effect. These three men, along with experienced and proven Nigel Martyn in goal and John Humphrey at right-back gelled to provide a thoroughly redoubtable rearguard.

Assuming responsibility as captain was cultured, adaptable Gareth Southgate who was now performing in midfield. Articulate and a splendid Club ambassador, Gareth quickly became an influential and respected skipper, as well as the youngest in the history of the Palace over a prolonged period, at the age of twenty-three years. Meanwhile, in a season which contained a whole catalogue of spectacular Eagles goals, Gareth himself netted some terrific efforts among his nine League strikes (a total only surpassed over the past thirty years by a Palace midfield player by the great Steve Kember), although perhaps the most memorable goal of all was the astonishing one despatched by Chris Armstrong at Barnsley in November after just ten seconds' play!

The arrival of Damian Matthew, a £150,000 recruit from Chelsea in February and Alan Smith's first full signing for the Club, added a refined option to Palace's midfield then, as the promotion run-in gathered momentum, the Eagles invested £1.1 million to bring talented Watford winger Bruce Dyer to Selhurst Park. Now, with a squad of seventeen or eighteen men from whom to select, and unhampered by serious injuries (apart of course from the continuing absence of Andy Thorn) Palace really began to look the part of champions-elect.

A performance of fluency and panache at breezy Portsmouth on 5 March 1994 was crowned with a headed goal from Eric Young just after the hour and we saw periods of emphatic dominance which were to set the tone for the closing stages of the season, so that a trio of narrow but significant Easter victories over Oxford and Millwall at Selhurst Park and at a cramped and crowded Southend took the Eagles to the brink of promotion. Then, a single goal win at Luton, gained with a Chris Coleman volley following a first minute corner, followed twenty-four hours later by a 2-2 draw between our closest challengers Millwall and Nottingham Forest at the new Den, were sufficient to ensure our promotion.

Palace's objective now was the title itself and that quest continued with another one goal success over dour, visiting Barnsley in our penultimate home match on St George's Day (although our goalscorer, again, following a Simon Rodger corner, was Welsh international Eric Young!) and thus the stage was set for us to clinch the championship when we faced Middlesbrough at Ayresome Park on Sunday 1 May before a national television audience. Although Boro' scored first, top-quality headed goals from Gareth Southgate and David Whyte before the interval and an immaculate third just before the hour from Chris Armstrong ensured the prize was ours.

The season finished for Palace on Sunday 8 May with a home game against Watford. Inevitably, with the championship trophy to be awarded, there was a packed crowd — a season's best for the entire Football League in fact, at our capacity of 28,749 — but this was also an emotional and historic afternoon for another reason because the Holmesdale Road terrace was to be closed after the match for redevelopment to meet the requirements of the all-seater stadia demanded by the Taylor Report. Thousands of fans wanted to be present for 'The Last Stand' on the Holmesdale (even if we could not all get onto it at once!) and the occasion was turned into a pageant of massive proportions.

The celebrations were impressive: the imposing 106-year-old trophy and the players' medals were presented by Football League President, Mr Gordon McKeag, and Alan Smith received a second manager of the month award for the post-war record of six consecutive League victories Palace had achieved in April. The most spectacular welcome ever accorded to a Palace team greeted the players as they entered the arena, with thousands of balloons and a crescendo of noise being released to the strains of *Glad All Over* so that the atmosphere was festive in the extreme.

But, shades of thirty years previously, regrettably, Palace could not quite deliver the finale we all desired. Watford played bravely, sensibly and well. They survived intense periods of pressure in both halves and, like Oldham in 1964, scored the goals in the second period which won the game for them. Nevertheless, Palace's stars brought the championship trophy back on to the pitch after the final whistle and paraded it for all our fans to see in a rousing lap of honour.

Alan Smith's achievement in winning the title and taking Palace back to the Premier League in his first season in full charge at Selhurst Park was nothing short of outstanding, but further dignity was conferred upon the Club later in the week of the celebration when Nigel Martyn and Chris Armstrong both appeared as substitutes in an England B international side which beat Northern Ireland 4-2 at Hillsborough.

Having won promotion in such fine style and as emphatic champions, the Eagles and their supporters viewed Palace's return to the Premier League with confidence, boosted by the arrival of three signings in the summer of 1994. Vastly experienced former England skipper Ray Wilkins arrived from QPR, tough, resilient defender Darren Pitcher came from Charlton for £50,000 while former Stockport striker Andy Preece cost £350,000. There was pleasure and further assurance too when Palace returned to Highbury — the scene of our departure from the top flight in 1993 — in mid-August and emerged from Tony Adams' testimonial with an impressive 3-1 victory, to provide us all with an ideal prelude to the opening day fixture, at home to Liverpool. But it was now that we received a nasty shock which was to prove a thoroughly unpleasant augury of the disappointment the League season was to become.

With the Holmesdale Road now undergoing redevelopment the fans were confined to the three other sides of Selhurst Park and there was hardly an empty seat to be found when the Eagles and the Reds took the field to the strains of *Glad All Over* . . . but this was not an afternoon of any gladness at all for us, as Liverpool dispensed a 1-6 beating, among the heaviest we have ever suffered on our own grounds.

However, tense and faced with several controversies as the season ultimately became, it was certainly not without its thoroughly praiseworthy performances and exciting victories, even if in retrospect all Palace fans will agree that the regrettable and peculiar feature of 1994-95 was that too many of these triumphs were recorded in Cup-ties and we would willingly have forfeited them all if it had meant that we would have secured our Premiership survival. The frustration was intense: in the League our goal supply dwindled to a trickle at Selhurst Park, where Palace only reached double figures in our fifteenth home game, in mid-March, and we lost nine of the matches on our own soil. Yet in the cup-ties we were both rampant and prolific! Twice we put four goals past Premiership opposition; aspiring, wealthy Wolves were crushed with another four goal spree at Molineux and, perhaps most praiseworthy of all, we beat highly placed Premier League Nottingham Forest at the City Ground in the FA Cup 4th round. Had we been able to reproduce such form in the League we would have finished the season in the top third of the table! As it was, we became the only Club in the land to appear in the last four of both the major Cup competitions and barely lost the two-legged League Cup semi-final against Liverpool by the narrowest of margins. The inconsistencies of the team almost precisely mirrored the baffling form of striker Chris Armstrong: after Chris had netted two awesome goals in the 4-1 demolition of Wolves on 22 March to secure our place in the FA Cup semi-final, he had scored nine times in nine cup-tie appearances, yet in 30 outings in the Premiership he had scraped together just three!

Looking back on 1994-95, while the Cup successes were thoroughly impressive, probably the best and most satisfying performance of the entire season came early in the campaign on 1 October when, in wonderful style, the Eagles travelled to Highbury and recorded our first-ever League victory there in glorious and emphatic manner. Palace's chief executioner that afternoon was John Salako who, playing as a striker, scored both our goals in the 2-1 success precisely upon the third anniversary of the terrible cruciate ligament injury he had sustained in 1991. How the enclave of Palace fans cheered their favourites and derided their Arsenal counterparts as the home side struggled then failed to match our verve, enthusiasm and skill, while it was a particularly sweet occasion for those of us who over the years have witnessed many severe maulings for our team at the imposing north London ground.

In the final analysis the 1994-95 season hung upon the events of its last five weeks. Although Ray Wilkins' contribution to the Club had proved minimal due to injury, even before he departed in December to manage QPR, Palace had been boosted by the £700,000 additions of Northern Ireland striker Iain Dowie in January and Eire midfielder Ray Houghton in March. We lined up for the FA Cup semi-final against Manchester United at Villa Park on Sunday 9 April with a quiet confidence, in spite of our lowly position in the table, and produced a superb display which ranked alongside the 1990 performance against Liverpool at the same venue even if it did not, quite, achieve the same outcome. A pulsating, enthralling encounter of great skill and commitment ensued and for Palace fans the only disappointment was that our reward was merely a replay. Palace had much the better of the first half: Peter Schmeichel was certainly the busier 'keeper but even his telescopic arms could not reach the ball in the 32nd minute when John Salako leapt high at the far post, to head back a right side cross from Chris Armstrong and Iain Dowie was able to nod into the net from the closest range. United's first equaliser took a deflection from a free kick and the tie was into extra time before Chris Armstrong lobbed over Schmeichel from some fifteen yards, but United replied promptly and with neither side able to find a killer strike, a replay became necessary the following Wednesday.

However, it only became apparent on the morning after the game that Nigel Martyn had sustained a broken index finger of his left hand in a clash with United's David Beckham in only the second minute and, having played throughout in considerable pain, would now miss not just the replay but also several games of the crucial run-in to the Premiership season upon which so much depended.

While the semi-final was universally achnowledged to have provided an excellent advertisement for football in a troubled season, preparations for the replay were shrouded by the news of the death of Palace fan Paul Nixon, following a confrontation at a Walsall hostelry between groups of rival supporters prior to the Sunday game. Palace felt that the replay should be postponed for a week out of respect, but the FA insisted it should be played on schedule, only for most Eagles fans to follow the Club's recommendation and boycott it, Palace selling little more than twelve percent of their ticket allocation. The tragedy had added greatly to the intensity of feelings between followers of the two semi-finalists, which were already considerably strained following the infamous Eric Cantona kung-fu attack on a Palace supporter after the volatile Gaul had been dismissed in the League fixture (1-1) at Selhurst Park ten weeks earlier.

Deprived of Nigel Martyn's talents, Palace looked to Rhys Wilmot to deputise. Rhys had joined us at the start of the season from Grimsby in an £80,000 deal to provide cover for Martyn, but had only played three minutes of top-flight football for us since the move! It was also necessary for Dean Gordon to replace Chris Coleman in Palace's starting line-up but, as in the 1990 Cup Finals between the clubs, while the first game had been a fiesta the second was dour and tense while also, understandably, subdued. Palace conceded two set-piece goals in the last quarter of an hour of the first half without reply but the occasion was marred by the double sending-off of United's shamed Roy Keane for stamping on Gareth Southgate, and Darren Patterson for retaliation.

Meanwhile, in the Premier League, several other clubs haunted by fears of relegation had been losing important games, so that Crystal Palace retained an even if awkward chance of earning survival: eight matches remained, but only three of them were at home and the first was on the sunful afternoon of Good Friday, 14 April, against Tottenham. Like the semi-final replay, the match was preceded by a perfectly observed minute's silence in memory of Paul Nixon, then the action was absorbing as the initiative ebbed and flowed. Curiously, both goals of a 1-1 draw were scored from long range and against the run of play: as half-time approached Chris Armstrong ripped a low drive into the bottom left-hand corner from twenty-five yards, after 'Spurs had put Palace under a lot of pressure, while the equaliser was an 88th minute spectacular, if controversially awarded, Jurgen Klinsmann free kick into the diagonally opposite corner after Palace had taken the second half honours.

On the cool, blustery Easter Monday every game bar one in the Premiership fixture list had a bearing on matters at or near the foot of the table, but a thoroughly commendable single goal victory, gained with a crashing Iain Dowie header from Ricky Newman's left side corner as the hour approached, in a passionate clash at Queens Park Rangers, provided hope for the Eagles, even if we were still in the bottom four. Perhaps it was predictable that Palace then lost 1-2 to the powerful champions-elect, Blackburn, at Ewood Park, in a rare Thursday fixture, but the Lancashire fans were mighty relieved to hear the final whistle, for a Palace rally, sparked by Ray Houghton's first goal for us, came within the width of a post of bringing us a point.

So, to the run-in of five games in fifteen days upon which the Club's future status would depend, but 1994-95 was the season in which the Premier League was to be reduced to twenty clubs and so would consign a total of *four* sides — the largest number ever to be relegated from the top flight — to the Endsleigh League.

Palace went down by the odd goal in three to well-placed Nottingham Forest in our penultimate home game on 29 April, when our injury-ridden and suspension-hit side could not match the visitors' fire-power and it was certainly ironic that Forest's second, decisive goal, midway through the second half, was scored by former Palace reserve striker, Stan Collymore. Iain Dowie's response with thirteen minutes left set up an exciting finish, but the outcome inevitably left us still anchored inside the relegation places and, twenty-four hours later, fellow-strugglers West Ham gained a praiseworthy 2-0 victory over Blackburn to enhance the prospects of their own survival.

The re-arranged fixtures of the evening of Wednesday 3 May were inevitably going to be vital ones for four clubs still realistically involved in the relegation fracas, but Palace, the only one of the quartet to be playing away, lost 1-3 at Southampton despite a refined header from Gareth Southgate, while Aston Villa, West Ham and Everton all scratched their ways to inelegant but important draws. Palace's problems at the Dell began early: we conceded goals in the first and tenth minutes so that the task was too great even allowing for a spirited reply and the captain's graceful strike.

The final home match, against West Ham on the baking hot afternoon of Saturday 6 May, was Gareth Southgate's 150th League game for the Club but it was his fellow midfielder Ray Houghton who was Palace's inspiration, and the veteran Eire star set up the goal which provided the Eagles with our first-ever home victory over the Hammers in ten outings — and a slender Premiership lifeline in front of a packed, anxious but enthusiastic crowd. Palace dominated the proceedings throughout but the crucial moments came five minutes into the second half, when a Houghton shot struck the hands of Julian Dicks, but cannoned back to him. His second effort rebounded from Ludek Miklosko to Chris Armstrong, who responded to his critics by lashing the ball past the giant Czech 'keeper, under pressure and into the Whitehorse Lane net, from six yards.

The Club and its followers were also boosted by the news of the Youth Team's 6-1 victory earlier in the day at Brighton, which had earned them the South East Counties divisional title for the second year in succession; the trophy and medals were presented to the successful youngsters and their manager, Peter Nicholas, during the interval to the delight and acclaim of our fans.

Palace's season finished with two demanding and distant away games, at Leeds on Tuesday 9 May, then at Newcastle the following Sunday and victory at one or the other was essential to our quest. Regrettably both tasks proved beyond us. Our 1-3 defeat at Leeds, compounded by the other midweek fixtures, left us a remote possibility of survival but, even if Palace fans never gave up hope that it might turn out otherwise, and almost a thousand of us made the long, long trip to Tyneside, it was soon evident that there was to be no miraculous escape. Palace conceded the earliest goal of the Premiership proceedings, courtesy of a deflection,

LEFT: Gareth Southgate nets at West Bromwich Albion on 18 September 1993. Gareth took over as captain before the turn of the year and led the Palace to the 1st Division championship. CENTRE: Dean Gordon developed into a marvellously effective left-back during 1993-94 and was rewarded with England Under 21 caps. Here he beats a Millwall opponent on 9 April 1994. RIGHT: Captain Gareth Southgate proudly holds the 1st Division championship trophy prior to Palace's last match of the season, against Watford (0-2).BELOW: Clever Paul Williams contributed seven goals to the 1993-94 championship — all of them away.

and the match was all too soon beyond our reach, despite a defiant second half rally in pouring rain which brought goals from Chris Armstrong and Ray Houghton and at least ensured dignity to our departure from the top flight.

Relegation was a bitter pill for Palace to swallow. Its implications were obviously considerable, even if they must be expounded in a later volume, but it led, inevitably, to the departure by mutual consent of manager Alan Smith. Alan had been at loggerheads with chairman Ron Noades for several months, but discerning fans will recognise that the perverse fact is that his efforts for the Eagles and our ninetieth anniversary had only been shorn of at least some measure of glory by the closest of margins in two Cup semi-finals, and by the arbitrary and contentious ruling which relegated more clubs from the top division than ever before in the history of the game.

LEFT: Palace's outstanding Club President, Mr Stanley Stephenson, who died in May 1994. RIGHT: The Palace playing staf for 1994-95 parade the Football League Championship trophy: back (l-r): Spike Hill (kit manager), Paul Sparrow, Glen Littl Eric Smith, Peter McLean (physio); third row: Kevin Hall, Brian Launders, George Ndah, Eddie Dixon, Andy Preece, Ian Cox Andy Thorn, Bobby Bowry, Ricky Newman, Jamie Vincent, Tony Scully; second row: David Kemp (assistant manager), Bruc Dyer, Darren Patterson, Damian Matthew, Dean Gordon, Jimmy Glass, Nigel Martyn, Richard Shaw, Darren Pitcher, Pau Williams, Ray Lewington (coach); front: John Salako, John Humphrey, Chris Armstrong, Ray Wilkins, Alan Smith (manager) Gareth Southgate, Chris Coleman, Simon Rodger, Eric Young. CENTRE: The Holmesdale Road terracing erupts in a riot o red and blue as the players take the field before it for the last time. BELOW: The Holmesdale terrace as thousands of Palac fans remember it. (Paul Wright) RIGHT: The same scene just a few weeks later, with reconstruction work already under way (Paul Wright)

LEFT: John Salako was the destroyer-in-chief of Arsenal when his two goals brought Palace their first League victory at Highbury on 1 October 1994. BELOW: 'We were there!' Palace fans celebrate the win at Highbury. (Paul Wright) RIGHT: Chris Armstrong rises above former Palace defender Andy Thorn to reach this header during Palace's victory over Wimbledon in the League Cup-tie on 25 October 1994.

CRYSTAL PALACE F.C. – EVERY MAJOR CUP RESULT – FOOTBALL ASSOCIATION (FA) wef 1905-06, FOOTBALL LEAGUE (FL) 1960-61, FULL MEMBERS' (FM) 1985-86

(Crystal Palace score shown first on all occasions)

SEASON	05-06	06-07	07-08	08-09	09-10	10-11	11-12	12-13	13-14	14-15	19-20	20-21	21-22	22-23	23-24	24-25	25-26	26-27	27-28	28-29	29-30	30-31	31-32	32-33	33-34	34-35	35-36
NAME OF CUP	FA	FA	FA	FA	FA	FA	FA	FA	FA	FA	FA	FA	FA	FA	FA	FA	FA	FA	FA	FA	FA	FA	FA	FA	FA	FA	FA
ROUND REACHED	1	QF	3	2	1	1	2	3	2	1	1	2	2	1	3	2	5	1	2	5	3	4	2	1	4	1	2
VENUE	H A N1	H A N2	A	H A	H	H	H A	H A	H A	A A	A	H	H A	A	H A N1 N1	H A	H A	H A	H A	H A	A	H A N2	A	H	H A	A	A
ACCRINGTON STANLEY																											
ALDERSHOT																									10		
ARSENAL																									07		
ASHFORD																											
ASTON VILLA								05																			
BARNET																											
BARNSLEY																											
BARROW																											
BATH CITY																							12				
BIRMINGHAM CITY										22 03																	
BISHOP AUCKLAND																											
BLACKBURN ROVERS																											
BLACKPOOL	11 11 01																										
BOLTON WANDERERS																											
BOURNEMOUTH																											
BRADFORD CITY																											
BRENTFORD		11 10					40 00																				
BRIDGEWATER TOWN																											
BRIGHTON & HOVE ALBION																								12			
BRISTOL CITY																											10
BRISTOL ROVERS																				31							
BURNLEY				00 09																							
BURY								20																			
CAMBRIDGE UNITED																											
CARDIFF CITY																											
CARLISLE UNITED																											
CHARLTON ATHLETIC																											
CHELMSFORD CITY																											
CHELSEA	71																21										
CHESTER CITY																											
CHESTERFIELD																											
CLAPHAM	70																										
COLCHESTER UNITED																											
COVENTRY CITY			42																								
CREWE ALEXANDRA																											
DARLINGTON																											
DARTFORD																			31								
DERBY COUNTY																											
DONCASTER ROVERS																											
ENFIELD																											
EVERTON		11 04				04							60									06					
EXETER CITY																											
FINCHLEY																											
FULHAM		10 00																									
GATESHEAD																21											
GILLINGHAM																											
GLOSSOP								20																			
GREAT YARMOUTH																											
GRENADIER GUARDS	30																										
GRIMSBY TOWN			01																								
HALIFAX TOWN																											
HARTLEPOOL UNITED																											
HARWICH & PARKESTON																											
HEREFORD UNITED																											
HITCHIN																											
HUDDERSFIELD TOWN																				25							
HULL CITY												02				23											
IPSWICH TOWN																											
KETTERING TOWN																				20							
LEEDS UNITED																					18						
LEICESTER CITY																											
LEYTON ORIENT																											
LINCOLN CITY																											
LIVERPOOL																											
LUTON TOWN	10																			70 00							
MAIDSTONE UNITED																											
MANCHESTER CITY												20					4-11										
MANCHESTER UNITED																											
MANSFIELD TOWN																											
MARGATE																											13
MIDDLESBROUGH																											
MILLWALL													00 02							53 00							
NEWARK TOWN																						60					
NEWCASTLE UNITED		10									02																
NEWPORT COUNTY																											
NORTHAMPTON TOWN																	21 33										
NORWICH CITY									21									00 01							30		
NOTTINGHAM FOREST																											
NOTTS COUNTY															00 00 00 21												
OLDHAM ATHLETIC																											
OXFORD UNITED																											
PETERBOROUGH UNITED																											
PLYMOUTH ARGYLE			32																								
PORT VALE																											
PORTSMOUTH																											
PRESTON NORTH END																											
QUEENS PARK RANGERS														01													
READING																						11 11 20	10				
ROCHDALE																											
ROTHERHAM UNITED		40																									
SCARBOROUGH																											
SCUNTHORPE UNITED																											
SHEFFIELD UNITED																											
SHEFFIELD WEDNESDAY																											
SHREWSBURY TOWN																											
SOUTHAMPTON																											
SOUTHEND UNITED																											
STOCKPORT COUNTY																									21		
STOKE CITY																											
SUNDERLAND							00 01																				
SWANSEA CITY																											
SWINDON TOWN					13										12				12 00								
TAUNTON TOWN																						60					
TOOTING & MITCHAM																											
TORQUAY UNITED																											
TOTTENHAM HOTSPUR															20												
TRANMERE ROVERS																											
WALSALL																											
WALTHAMSTOW AVENUE																											
WALTON & HERSHAM																											
WATFORD																											
WEST BROMWICH ALBION																											
WEST HAM UNITED									02																		
WIGAN ATHLETIC																											
WIMBLEDON																											
WOLVERHAMPTON WANDERERS				42 22																							
WREXHAM																											
WYCOMBE WANDERERS																											
YEOVIL TOWN																										03	
YORK CITY																											

N = Neutral venue:- N1 = Villa Park N2 = Stamford Bridge

SEASON	36-37		37-38		38-39		45-46			46-47	47-48		48-49	49-50	50-51	51-52	52-53		53-54	54-55		55-56		56-57		57-58		58-59			59-60		60-61			61-62			62-63			63-64			64-65				65-66
NAME OF CUP	FA		FA		FA		FA			FA	FA		FA	FA	FA	FA	FA		FA	FA		FA		FA		FA		FA			FA		FA		FL	FA		FL	FA		FL	FA		FL	FA		FL		FA
ROUND REACHED	1		3		1		3			3	3		1	1	1	1	2		1	2		1		3		3		3			3		2		1	3		1	2		2	2		2	QF		4		3
VENUE	H	A	H	A	H	A	H	A	N1	A	H	A	H	H	H	H	H	A	A	H	A	H	A	H	A	H	A	H	A	N2	H	A	H	A	A	H	A	A	H	A	A	H	A	A	H	A	H	A	A
ACCRINGTON STANLEY				10																																												
ALDERSHOT																																																
ARSENAL																																																
ASHFORD																												10																			
ASTON VILLA																																				34											
BARNET																																																
BARNSLEY																																																
BARROW																																																
BATH CITY																																																
BIRMINGHAM CITY																																																
BISHOP AUCKLAND																			24																												
BLACKBURN ROVERS																																																
BLACKPOOL																																																
BOLTON WANDERERS																																																
BOURNEMOUTH																																																
BRADFORD CITY																																																
BRENTFORD																							32	11																							
BRIDGEWATER TOWN																																				30											
BRIGHTON & HOVE ALBION																																																
BRISTOL CITY											10	01																																			
BRISTOL ROVERS																																																
BURNLEY																																											02				
BURY																																												51			
CAMBRIDGE UNITED																																																
CARDIFF CITY																																																
CARLISLE UNITED																																																03
CHARLTON ATHLETIC																																																
CHELMSFORD CITY																														51																	
CHELSEA																																																
CHESTER CITY										01																																					
CHESTERFIELD																																																
CLAPHAM																																																
COLCHESTER UNITED																																																
COVENTRY CITY																																																
CREWE ALEXANDRA																																																
DARLINGTON																																		02													
DARTFORD																																																
DERBY COUNTY																																																
DONCASTER ROVERS																																																
ENFIELD																																																
EVERTON																																																
EXETER CITY																																																
FINCHLEY																	13																														
FULHAM																																																
GATESHEAD																																																
GILLINGHAM															01																																
GLOSSOP																																																
GREAT YARMOUTH																		01																													
GRENADIER GUARDS																																																
GRIMSBY TOWN																																																
HALIFAX TOWN																																																
HARTLEPOOL UNITED																																																
HARWICH & PARKESTON																																									82						
HEREFORD UNITED																																						20									
HITCHIN																																62															
HUDDERSFIELD TOWN																																																
HULL CITY																																																
IPSWICH TOWN																									01																						
KETTERING TOWN			22	40																																												
LEEDS UNITED																																								12				03			
LEICESTER CITY																																														12	00	
LEYTON ORIENT																																																
LINCOLN CITY																																																
LIVERPOOL			00	13																																												
LUTON TOWN																																																
MAIDSTONE UNITED																																																
MANCHESTER CITY																																																
MANCHESTER UNITED																																																
MANSFIELD TOWN																																						22	27								
MARGATE																										32				30	00																
MIDDLESBROUGH																																																
MILLWALL														14										02																							
NEWARK TOWN																																																
NEWCASTLE UNITED									26																																						
NEWPORT COUNTY													03																																		
NORTHAMPTON TOWN																																																
NORWICH CITY																																																
NOTTINGHAM FOREST																																												31			
NOTTS COUNTY																																																
OLDHAM ATHLETIC																																																
OXFORD UNITED																																																
PETERBOROUGH UNITED																																																
PLYMOUTH ARGYLE																																																
PORT VALE										21																																					
PORTSMOUTH																																			30												
PRESTON NORTH END																																																
QUEENS PARK RANGERS					11	03	00	00	01																													25										
READING																11	31																														
ROCHDALE																																																
ROTHERHAM UNITED																																																
SCARBOROUGH																																																
SCUNTHORPE UNITED																															01																
SHEFFIELD UNITED																												02																			
SHEFFIELD WEDNESDAY																											22	22	41																		
SHREWSBURY TOWN																																																
SOUTHAMPTON																					00	02			10																			21	20	
SOUTHEND UNITED	11	02																																														
STOCKPORT COUNTY																																																
STOKE CITY																																																
SUNDERLAND																																																
SWANSEA CITY																																																
SWINDON TOWN																				20																											
TAUNTON TOWN																																																
TOOTING & MITCHAM																																																
TORQUAY UNITED																																																
TOTTENHAM HOTSPUR																																																
TRANMERE ROVERS																																															20	
WALSALL																																																
WALTHAMSTOW AVENUE																							20																								
WALTON & HERSHAM																																																
WATFORD																																00	01														
WEST BROMWICH ALBION																																																
WEST HAM UNITED																																																
WIGAN ATHLETIC																																																
WIMBLEDON																																																
WOLVERHAMPTON WANDERERS																																																
WREXHAM																																																
WYCOMBE WANDERERS																																																
YEOVIL TOWN																																										13					
YORK CITY																																																

N = Neutral venue :- N1 = Craven Cottage N2 = Molineux

SEASON	65-66	66-67		67-68			68-69				69-70				70-71				71-72				72-73				73-74		74-75			75-76					76-77					77-78			78-79				
NAME OF CUP	FL	FA	FL	FA		FL	FA		FL		FA		FL		FA		FL		FA		FL		FA			FL	FA	FL	FA	FL		FA			FL		FA			FL		FA	FL		FA		FL		
ROUND REACHED	2	3	2	3		2	3		QF		5		4		3		QF		3		3		4			2	3	2	2	2		SF			2		3			2		3	2		5		3		
VENUE	H	A	A	H	A	A	H	A	H	A	H	A	H	A	H	A	H	A	H	A	H	A	H	A	N1	H	H	A	A	H	A	H	A	N2	H	A	H	A	N2	H	A	A	H	A	H	A	H	A	N3
ACCRINGTON STANLEY																																																	
ALDERSHOT																																																	
ARSENAL																	00	20																															
ASHFORD																																																	
ASTON VILLA																					22	02																									00	11	03
BARNET																																																	
BARNSLEY																																																	
BARROW						01																																											
BATH CITY																																																	
BIRMINGHAM CITY																																																	
BISHOP AUCKLAND																																																	
BLACKBURN ROVERS																																																	
BLACKPOOL													22	10																																			
BOLTON WANDERERS																																																	
BOURNEMOUTH																																																	
BRADFORD CITY																																																	
BRENTFORD																																											51	12					
BRIDGEWATER TOWN																																																	
BRIGHTON & HOVE ALBION																																					11	22	10										
BRISTOL CITY																														14															30			21	
BRISTOL ROVERS																																																	
BURNLEY										02																																							
BURY																																																	
CAMBRIDGE UNITED																																																	
CARDIFF CITY													31																																				
CARLISLE UNITED																																																	
CHARLTON ATHLETIC							02	00																																									
CHELMSFORD CITY																																																	
CHELSEA											14				22	02																	32																
CHESTER CITY																																																	
CHESTERFIELD																																																	
CLAPHAM																																																	
COLCHESTER UNITED																																			30	13													
COVENTRY CITY																																																	
CREWE ALEXANDRA																																																	
DARLINGTON																																																	
DARTFORD																																																	
DERBY COUNTY													11	03																																			
DONCASTER ROVERS																																				12													
ENFIELD																																					40												
EVERTON																			22	23																													
EXETER CITY																																																	
FINCHLEY																																																	
FULHAM			02																																														
GATESHEAD																																																	
GILLINGHAM																																																	
GLOSSOP																																																	
GREAT YARMOUTH																																																	
GRENADIER GUARDS																																																	
GRIMSBY TOWN	01																																																
HALIFAX TOWN																																																	
HARTLEPOOL UNITED																																										12							
HARWICH & PARKESTON																																																	
HEREFORD UNITED																																																	
HITCHIN																																																	
HUDDERSFIELD TOWN																																																	
HULL CITY																																																	
IPSWICH TOWN																																																	
KETTERING TOWN																																																	
LEEDS UNITED		03							21																								10																
LEICESTER CITY										10																																							
LEYTON ORIENT																																																	
LINCOLN CITY																	40																																
LIVERPOOL																																					23	00											
LUTON TOWN																					20																												
MAIDSTONE UNITED																																																	
MANCHESTER CITY																																																	
MANCHESTER UNITED																		24																															
MANSFIELD TOWN																																																	
MARGATE																																																	
MIDDLESBROUGH																																													10	11			
MILLWALL																																21	11																
NEWARK TOWN																																																	
NEWCASTLE UNITED																																																	
NEWPORT COUNTY																																																	
NORTHAMPTON TOWN																																																	
NORWICH CITY																																																	
NOTTINGHAM FOREST																																																	
NOTTS COUNTY																																																	
OLDHAM ATHLETIC																																																	
OXFORD UNITED																																																	
PETERBOROUGH UNITED																																																	
PLYMOUTH ARGYLE																													12																				
PORT VALE																																																	
PORTSMOUTH																																								22	10								
PRESTON NORTH END									31																																								
QUEENS PARK RANGERS																																																	
READING																																																	
ROCHDALE																	33	31																															
ROTHERHAM UNITED																																																	
SCARBOROUGH																																	21																
SCUNTHORPE UNITED																																																	
SHEFFIELD UNITED																																																	
SHEFFIELD WEDNESDAY																							11	11	23																								
SHREWSBURY TOWN																																																	
SOUTHAMPTON																							20											02									00	12					
SOUTHEND UNITED																																																	
STOCKPORT COUNTY																										01		01																					
STOKE CITY																																																	
SUNDERLAND																																	10																
SWANSEA CITY																																																	
SWINDON TOWN																																																	
TAUNTON TOWN																																																	
TOOTING & MITCHAM																													21																				
TORQUAY UNITED																																																	
TOTTENHAM HOTSPUR											10	00																																					
TRANMERE ROVERS																																																	
WALSALL				12	11						20																																						
WALTHAMSTOW AVENUE																																																	
WALTON & HERSHAM																																10																	
WATFORD																														51	11									13									
WEST BROMWICH ALBION																																																	
WEST HAM UNITED																																																	
WIGAN ATHLETIC																																																	
WIMBLEDON																																																	
WOLVERHAMPTON WANDERERS																																													01				
WREXHAM																											02																						
WYCOMBE WANDERERS																																																	
YEOVIL TOWN																																																	
YORK CITY																																																	

N = Neutral venue :- N1 = Villa Park N2 = Stamford Bridge N3 = Highfield Road, Coventry

SEASON	79-80		80-81		81-82		82-83		83-84		84-85		85-86			86-87			87-88			88-89			89-90
NAME OF CUP	FA	FL	FA	FL	FA	FL	FA	FL	FA	FL	FA	FL	FA	FL	FM	FA	FL	FM	FA	FL	FM	FA	FL	FM	FA
ROUND REACHED	3	3	3	3	QF	4	5	3	4	1	3	2	3	2	2	4	3	1	3	3	1	3	3	SF	F
VENUE	H A N1	H A	A	H A	H A	H A	H A	H A	H A	H A	H A	H A	H	H A	H A	H A	H A	A	A	H A	A	A	H A	H A	H A N2 N3 N3
ACCRINGTON STANLEY																									
ALDERSHOT																									
ARSENAL																									
ASHFORD																									
ASTON VILLA																									
BARNET																									
BARNSLEY																									
BARROW																									
BATH CITY																									
BIRMINGHAM CITY							10																		
BISHOP AUCKLAND																									
BLACKBURN ROVERS																									
BLACKPOOL																									
BOLTON WANDERERS				21 30	10																				
BOURNEMOUTH																									
BRADFORD CITY																									
BRENTFORD																									
BRIDGEWATER TOWN																									
BRIGHTON & HOVE ALBION															13										
BRISTOL CITY																									
BRISTOL ROVERS																							14		
BURNLEY							00 01																		
BURY																									
CAMBRIDGE UNITED																	00 10								
CARDIFF CITY																									10
CARLISLE UNITED																									
CHARLTON ATHLETIC														11 21											
CHELMSFORD CITY																									
CHELSEA																									
CHESTER CITY																									
CHESTERFIELD																									
CLAPHAM																									
COLCHESTER UNITED																									
COVENTRY CITY																									
CREWE ALEXANDRA																									
DARLINGTON																									
DARTFORD																									
DERBY COUNTY																									
DONCASTER ROVERS						20 01																			
ENFIELD					32																				
EVERTON																									
EXETER CITY																									
FINCHLEY																									
FULHAM																									
GATESHEAD																									
GILLINGHAM																									
GLOSSOP																									
GREAT YARMOUTH																									
GRENADIER GUARDS																									
GRIMSBY TOWN																									
HALIFAX TOWN																									
HARTLEPOOL UNITED																									
HARWICH & PARKESTON																									
HEREFORD UNITED																									
HITCHIN																									
HUDDERSFIELD TOWN																									40
HULL CITY																									
IPSWICH TOWN																									
KETTERING TOWN																									
LEEDS UNITED																									
LEICESTER CITY									10																
LEYTON ORIENT					00 10																				
LINCOLN CITY																									
LIVERPOOL																									43
LUTON TOWN													12											41	
MAIDSTONE UNITED																									
MANCHESTER CITY			04																						
MANCHESTER UNITED														01 01						12					33 01
MANSFIELD TOWN																									
MARGATE																									
MIDDLESBROUGH																								32	
MILLWALL											12 11														
NEWARK TOWN																									
NEWCASTLE UNITED																			01						
NEWPORT COUNTY																				40 20					
NORTHAMPTON TOWN												10 00													
NORWICH CITY																									
NOTTINGHAM FOREST																10	22 01							13	
NOTTS COUNTY																									
OLDHAM ATHLETIC																									
OXFORD UNITED																					01				
PETERBOROUGH UNITED								21 20		30 03×															
PLYMOUTH ARGYLE																									
PORT VALE																									
PORTSMOUTH								20 11										04							21
PRESTON NORTH END																									
QUEENS PARK RANGERS					01																				
READING																									
ROCHDALE																									10
ROTHERHAM UNITED																									
SCARBOROUGH																									
SCUNTHORPE UNITED																									
SHEFFIELD UNITED																									
SHEFFIELD WEDNESDAY								12																	
SHREWSBURY TOWN																									
SOUTHAMPTON																								21	
SOUTHEND UNITED																									
STOCKPORT COUNTY		70 11																							
STOKE CITY																						01			
SUNDERLAND						10						00 12													
SWANSEA CITY	33 22 12																								
SWINDON TOWN																							20 21		
TAUNTON TOWN																									
TOOTING & MITCHAM																									
TORQUAY UNITED																									
TOTTENHAM HOTSPUR				13 00												04									
TRANMERE ROVERS																									
WALSALL																								42	
WALTHAMSTOW AVENUE																									
WALTON & HERSHAM																									
WATFORD																									
WEST BROMWICH ALBION						13									12										
WEST HAM UNITED									11 02																
WIGAN ATHLETIC																									
WIMBLEDON																									
WOLVERHAMPTON WANDERERS		12																							
WREXHAM																									
WYCOMBE WANDERERS																									
YEOVIL TOWN																									
YORK CITY							21																		

N = Neutral venue :- N1 = Ninian Park, Cardiff N2 = Villa Park N3 = Wembley × Lost 2-4 on penalties

SEASON	89-90		90-91			91-92			92-93		93-94		94-95	
NAME OF CUP	FL	FM	FA	FL	FM	FA	FL	FM	FA	FL	FA	FL	FA	FL
ROUND REACHED	3	SF	3	4	F	3	QF	QF	3	SF	3	3	SF	SF
VENUE	H A	H A	H A R	H A	H A N1	A	H H A	H A	A	H A	A	H A	H A N2 N2	H A
ACCRINGTON STANLEY														
ALDERSHOT														
ARSENAL										13 02				
ASHFORD														
ASTON VILLA														41
BARNET														
BARNSLEY														
BARROW														
BATH CITY														
BIRMINGHAM CITY							11 21 11							
BISHOP AUCKLAND														
BLACKBURN ROVERS														
BLACKPOOL														
BOLTON WANDERERS														
BOURNEMOUTH														
BRADFORD CITY														
BRENTFORD														
BRIDGEWATER TOWN														
BRIGHTON & HOVE ALBION					20									
BRISTOL CITY														
BRISTOL ROVERS					21									
BURNLEY														
BURY														
CAMBRIDGE UNITED														
CARDIFF CITY														
CARLISLE UNITED														
CHARLTON ATHLETIC		20										31 10		
CHELMSFORD CITY														
CHELSEA		02 02						01		31				
CHESTER CITY														
CHESTERFIELD														
CLAPHAM														
COLCHESTER UNITED														
COVENTRY CITY														
CREWE ALEXANDRA														
DARLINGTON														
DARTFORD														
DERBY COUNTY														
DONCASTER ROVERS														
ENFIELD														
EVERTON					41							14 22		
EXETER CITY														
FINCHLEY														
FULHAM														
GATESHEAD														
GILLINGHAM														
GLOSSOP														
GREAT YARMOUTH														
GRENADIER GUARDS														
GRIMSBY TOWN														
HALIFAX TOWN														
HARTLEPOOL UNITED							61 11		01					
HARWICH & PARKESTON														
HEREFORD UNITED														
HITCHIN														
HUDDERSFIELD TOWN														
HULL CITY														
IPSWICH TOWN														
KETTERING TOWN														
LEEDS UNITED														
LEICESTER CITY	12 32					01								
LEYTON ORIENT				00 10										
LINCOLN CITY										31 11			51	30 01
LIVERPOOL										21 11				01 01
LUTON TOWN		41			31									
MAIDSTONE UNITED														
MANCHESTER CITY														40
MANCHESTER UNITED													22 02	
MANSFIELD TOWN														
MARGATE														
MIDDLESBROUGH														
MILLWALL														
NEWARK TOWN														
NEWCASTLE UNITED														
NEWPORT COUNTY														
NORTHAMPTON TOWN														
NORWICH CITY					20 11									
NOTTINGHAM FOREST	00 05		00 22 03				11 24						21	
NOTTS COUNTY														
OLDHAM ATHLETIC														
OXFORD UNITED														
PETERBOROUGH UNITED														
PLYMOUTH ARGYLE														
PORT VALE														
PORTSMOUTH														
PRESTON NORTH END														
QUEENS PARK RANGERS								32						
READING														
ROCHDALE														
ROTHERHAM UNITED														
SCARBOROUGH														
SCUNTHORPE UNITED														
SHEFFIELD UNITED														
SHEFFIELD WEDNESDAY														
SHREWSBURY TOWN														
SOUTHAMPTON				02						20				
SOUTHEND UNITED				80 21				42						
STOCKPORT COUNTY														
STOKE CITY														
SUNDERLAND														
SWANSEA CITY														
SWINDON TOWN		10					10							
TAUNTON TOWN														
TOOTING & MITCHAM														
TORQUAY UNITED														
TOTTENHAM HOTSPUR														
TRANMERE ROVERS														
WALSALL														
WALTHAMSTOW AVENUE														
WALTON & HERSHAM														
WATFORD													10 00	
WEST BROMWICH ALBION														
WEST HAM UNITED														
WIGAN ATHLETIC														
WIMBLEDON														10
WOLVERHAMPTON WANDERERS											01		11 41	
WREXHAM														
WYCOMBE WANDERERS														
YEOVIL TOWN														
YORK CITY														

N = : Neutral venue :- N1 = Wembley N2 = Villa Park

SUMMARY OF RESULTS

Part 1 of 2

Football Association Cup

	Pld	Home					Away					Neutral					Total				
		W	D	L	F	A	W	D	L	F	A	W	D	L	F	A	W	D	L	F	A
ACCRINGTON STANLEY	1						1			1	0						1			1	0
ALDERSHOT	1	1			1	0											1			1	0
ARSENAL	1								1	0	7								1	0	7
ASHFORD	1				1	0	1										1			1	0
ASTON VILLA	2								2	3	9								2	3	9
BARNET																					
BARNSLEY																					
BARROW																					
BATH CITY	1								1	1	2								1	1	2
BIRMINGHAM CITY	3	1			1	0		1	1	2	5						1	1	1	3	5
BISHOP AUCKLAND	1			1	2	4													1	2	4
BLACKBURN ROVERS																					
BLACKPOOL	3		1		1	1		1		1	1			1	0	1		2	1	2	3
BOLTON WANDERERS	1	1			1	0											1			1	0
BOURNEMOUTH																					
BRADFORD CITY																					
BRENTFORD	6	2	1		8	3	1	2		2	1						3	3		10	4
BRIDGEWATER TOWN	1						1			3	0						1			3	0
BRIGHTON & HOVE ALBION	4		1	1	2	3		1		2	2	1			1	0	1	2	1	5	5
BRISTOL CITY	4	1		1	3	1	2			2	0						3		1	5	1
BRISTOL ROVERS	1	1			3	1											1			3	1
BURNLEY	4		2		0	0			2	0	10							2	2	0	10
BURY	2	2			7	1											2			7	1
CAMBRIDGE UNITED	1						1			1	0						1			1	0
CARDIFF CITY																					
CARLISLE UNITED	1								1	0	3								1	0	3
CHARLTON ATHLETIC	2			1	0	2		1		0	0							1	1	0	2
CHELMSFORD CITY	1	1			5	1											1			5	1
CHELSEA	6	2	1	1	12	8	1		1	3	4						3	1	2	15	12
CHESTER CITY	1			1	0	1													1	0	1
CHESTERFIELD																					
CLAPHAM	1	1			7	0											1			7	0
COLCHESTER UNITED																					
COVENTRY CITY	1						1			4	2						1			4	2
CREWE ALEXANDRA																					
DARLINGTON																					
DARTFORD	1						1			3	1						1			3	1
DERBY COUNTY																					
DONCASTER ROVERS																					
ENFIELD	2	2			7	2											2			7	2
EVERTON	7		2	2	3	13	1		2	8	7						1	2	4	11	20
EXETER CITY																					
FINCHLEY	1								1	1	3								1	1	3
FULHAM	2	1			1	0		1		0	0						1	1		1	0
GATESHEAD	1	1			2	1											1			2	1
GILLINGHAM	1			1	0	1													1	0	1
GLOSSOP	1	1			2	0											1			2	0
GREAT YARMOUTH	1			1	0	1													1	0	1
GRENADIER GUARDS	1						1			3	0						1			3	0
GRIMSBY TOWN	1								1	0	1								1	0	1
HALIFAX TOWN																					
HARTLEPOOL UNITED	2								2	1	3								2	1	3
HARWICH & PARKESTON	1	1			8	2											1			8	2
HEREFORD UNITED	1	1			2	0											1			2	0
HITCHIN	1	1			6	2											1			6	2
HUDDERSFIELD TOWN	2	1			4	0			1	2	5						1		1	6	5
HULL CITY	2			1	0	2			1	2	3								2	2	5
IPSWICH TOWN	1			1	0	1													1	0	1
KETTERING TOWN	3	1	1		4	2	1			4	0						2	1		8	2
LEEDS UNITED	4			1	0	3	1		2	2	11						1		3	2	14
LEICESTER CITY	2	1			1	0			1	0	1						1		1	1	1
LEYTON ORIENT	3	1	1		1	0	1			1	0						2	1		2	0
LINCOLN CITY	1	1			5	1											1			5	1
LIVERPOOL	5		1	1	2	3		1	1	1	3	1			4	3	1	2	2	7	9
LUTON TOWN	4	2		1	9	2		1		0	0						2	1	1	9	2
MAIDSTONE UNITED																					
MANCHESTER CITY	3	1			2	0			2	4	15						1		2	6	15
MANCHESTER UNITED	4												2	2	5	8		2	2	5	8
MANSFIELD TOWN	2		1		2	2			1	2	7							1	1	4	9
MARGATE	4	1			3	0	1	1	1	4	5						2	1	1	7	5
MIDDLESBROUGH	2	1			1	0		1		1	1						1	1		2	1
MILLWALL	10	2	1	2	9	10		3	2	2	6						2	4	4	11	16
NEWARK TOWN	1	1			6	0											1			6	0
NEWCASTLE UNITED	4						1		3	3	9						1		3	3	9
NEWPORT COUNTY	1			1	0	3													1	0	3
NORTHAMPTON TOWN	2	1			2	1		1		3	3						1	1		5	4
NORWICH CITY	4	2	1		5	1			1	0	1						2	1	1	5	2
NOTTINGHAM FOREST	6	2	1		4	1	1	1	1	4	6						3	2	1	8	7
NOTTS COUNTY	4		1		0	0		1		0	0	1	1		2	1	1	3		2	1
OLDHAM ATHLETIC																					
OXFORD UNITED																					
PETERBOROUGH UNITED																					
PLYMOUTH ARGYLE	2						1		1	4	4						1		1	4	4
PORT VALE	1	1			2	1											1			2	1
PORTSMOUTH	2	2			5	1											2			5	1
PRESTON NORTH END																					
QUEENS PARK RANGERS	7		2		1	1		1	3	0	5			1	0	1		3	4	1	7
READING	6		2		2	2	2	1		5	2	1			2	0	3	3		9	4
ROCHDALE	1	1			1	0											1			1	0
ROTHERHAM UNITED	1											1			4	0	1			4	0
SCARBOROUGH	1						1			2	1						1			2	1
SCUNTHORPE UNITED	1								1	0	1								1	0	1
SHEFFIELD UNITED	1								1	0	2								1	0	2
SHEFFIELD WEDNESDAY	3		1		1	1		1		1	1			1	2	3		2	1	4	5
SHREWSBURY TOWN	3		1		2	2		1		2	2	1			4	1	1	2		8	5
SOUTHAMPTON	6	2	1		3	0	1		1	2	3			1	0	2	3	1	2	5	5
SOUTHEND UNITED	2		1		1	1			1	0	2							1	1	1	3
STOCKPORT COUNTY	1						1			2	1						1			2	1
STOKE CITY	1								1	0	1								1	0	1
SUNDERLAND	3		1		0	0	1		1	1	1						1	1	1	1	1
SWANSEA CITY	3		1		3	3		1		2	2			1	1	2		2	1	6	7
SWINDON TOWN	5			3	3	7	1	1		2	0						1	1	3	5	7
TAUNTON TOWN	1	1			6	0											1			6	0
TOOTING & MITCHAM	1						1			2	1						1			2	1
TORQUAY UNITED																					
TOTTENHAM HOTSPUR	4	2			3	0		1	1	0	4						2	1	1	3	4
TRANMERE ROVERS																					
WALSALL	3	1		1	3	2		1		1	1						1	1	1	4	3
WALTHAMSTOW AVENUE	1	1			2	0											1			2	0
WALTON & HERSHAM	1	1			1	0											1			1	0
WATFORD	4	1	1		1	0		1	1	0	1						1	2	1	1	1
WEST BROMWICH ALBION																					
WEST HAM UNITED	3		1		1	1			2	0	4							1	2	1	5
WIGAN ATHLETIC																					
WIMBLEDON																					
WOLVERHAMPTON WANDERERS	6	1	1	1	5	4	1	1	1	6	4						2	2	2	11	8
WREXHAM	1			1	0	2													1	0	2
WYCOMBE WANDERERS																					
YEOVIL TOWN	2								2	1	6								2	1	6
YORK CITY	1	1			2	1											1			2	1
TOTALS	227	54	29	24	193	109	28	27	49	109	186	6	3	7	25	22	88	59	80	327	317

Football League Cup

	Pld	Home					Away					Neutral					Total				
		W	D	L	F	A	W	D	L	F	A	W	D	L	F	A	W	D	L	F	A
ACCRINGTON STANLEY																					
ALDERSHOT																					
ARSENAL	4		1	1	1	3	1		1	2	2						1	1	2	3	5
ASHFORD																					
ASTON VILLA	6	1	2		6	3		1	1	1	3			1	0	3	1	3	2	7	9
BARNET																					
BARNSLEY																					
BARROW	1								1	0	1								1	0	1
BATH CITY																					
BIRMINGHAM CITY	3	1	1		3	2		1		1	1						1	2		4	3
BISHOP AUCKLAND																					
BLACKBURN ROVERS																					
BLACKPOOL	2		1		2	2	1			1	0						1	1		3	2
BOLTON WANDERERS	2	1			2	1	1			3	0						2			5	1
BOURNEMOUTH																					
BRADFORD CITY																					
BRENTFORD	2	1			5	1			1	1	2						1		1	6	3
BRIDGEWATER TOWN																					
BRIGHTON & HOVE ALBION																					
BRISTOL CITY	3			1	1	4	1		1	3	5						1		2	4	9
BRISTOL ROVERS	1								1	0	2								1	0	2
BURNLEY	1								1	0	2								1	0	2
BURY	2		1		0	0	1			1	0						1	1		1	0
CAMBRIDGE UNITED																					
CARDIFF CITY	1	1			3	1											1			3	1
CARLISLE UNITED																					
CHARLTON ATHLETIC	4	1	1		4	2	2			3	1						3	1		7	3
CHELMSFORD CITY																					
CHELSEA	1	1			3	1											1			3	1
CHESTER CITY																					
CHESTERFIELD																					
CLAPHAM																					
COLCHESTER UNITED	2	1			3	0			1	1	3						1		1	4	3
COVENTRY CITY																					
CREWE ALEXANDRA																					
DARLINGTON	1								1	0	2								1	0	2
DARTFORD																					
DERBY COUNTY	2		1		1	1			1	0	3							1	1	1	4
DONCASTER ROVERS	3	1			2	0			2	1	3						1		2	3	3
ENFIELD																					
EVERTON	2			1	1	4		1		2	2							1	1	3	6
EXETER CITY																					
FINCHLEY																					
FULHAM	1								1	0	2								1	0	2
GATESHEAD																					
GILLINGHAM																					
GLOSSOP																					
GREAT YARMOUTH																					
GRENADIER GUARDS																					
GRIMSBY TOWN	1			1	0	1													1	0	1
HALIFAX TOWN																					
HARTLEPOOL UNITED	2	1			6	1		1		1	1						1	1		7	2
HARWICH & PARKESTON																					
HEREFORD UNITED																					
HITCHIN																					
HUDDERSFIELD TOWN																					
HULL CITY																					
IPSWICH TOWN																					
KETTERING TOWN																					
LEEDS UNITED	2	1			2	1			1	1	2						1		1	3	3
LEICESTER CITY	4			2	2	4	1	1		3	2						1	1	2	5	6
LEYTON ORIENT	2		1		0	0	1			1	0						1	1		1	0
LINCOLN CITY	5	3			10	1		1	1	1	2						3	1	1	11	3
LIVERPOOL	4	1		1	2	2		1	1	1	2						1	1	2	3	4
LUTON TOWN	1	1			2	0											1			2	0
MAIDSTONE UNITED																					
MANCHESTER CITY	1	1			4	0											1			4	0
MANCHESTER UNITED	4			1	0	1			3	3	7								4	3	8
MANSFIELD TOWN																					
MARGATE																					
MIDDLESBROUGH																					
MILLWALL																					
NEWARK TOWN																					
NEWCASTLE UNITED																					
NEWPORT COUNTY	2	1			4	0	1			2	0						2			6	0
NORTHAMPTON TOWN	2	1			1	0		1		0	0						1	1		1	0
NORWICH CITY																					
NOTTINGHAM FOREST	6		3		3	3			3	2	10							3	3	5	13
NOTTS COUNTY																					
OLDHAM ATHLETIC																					
OXFORD UNITED																					
PETERBOROUGH UNITED	4	2			5	1	1		1	2	3						3		1	7	4
PLYMOUTH ARGYLE																					
PORT VALE																					
PORTSMOUTH	4	1	1		4	2	1	1		2	1						2	2		6	3
PRESTON NORTH END	1	1			3	1											1			3	1
QUEENS PARK RANGERS	1								1	2	5								1	2	5
READING																					
ROCHDALE	2		1		3	3	1			3	1						1	1		6	4
ROTHERHAM UNITED																					
SCARBOROUGH																					
SCUNTHORPE UNITED																					
SHEFFIELD UNITED																					
SHEFFIELD WEDNESDAY	1			1	1	2													1	1	2
SHREWSBURY TOWN																					
SOUTHAMPTON	5	1	1		2	0	1		2	3	4						2	1	2	5	4
SOUTHEND UNITED	2	1			8	0	1			2	1						2			10	1
STOCKPORT COUNTY	4	1		1	7	1		1	1	1	2						1	1	2	8	3
STOKE CITY																					
SUNDERLAND	3		1		0	0	1		1	2	2						1	1	1	2	2
SWANSEA CITY																					
SWINDON TOWN	3	1			2	0	2			3	1						3			5	1
TAUNTON TOWN																					
TOOTING & MITCHAM																					
TORQUAY UNITED																					
TOTTENHAM HOTSPUR	2			1	1	3		1		0	0							1	1	1	3
TRANMERE ROVERS	1						1			2	0						1			2	0
WALSALL																					
WALTHAMSTOW AVENUE																					
WALTON & HERSHAM																					
WATFORD	3	1		1	6	4		1		1	1						1	1	1	7	5
WEST BROMWICH ALBION	1			1	1	3													1	1	3
WEST HAM UNITED																					
WIGAN ATHLETIC																					
WIMBLEDON	1						1			1	0						1			1	0
WOLVERHAMPTON WANDERERS	1			1	1	2													1	1	2
WREXHAM																					
WYCOMBE WANDERERS																					
YEOVIL TOWN																					
YORK CITY																					
TOTALS	119	28	16	14	117	61	20	12	28	59	81	0	0	1	0	3	48	28	43	176	145

SUMMARY OF RESULTS

Part 2 of 2

	Full Members' Cup																					GRAND TOTALS (Pages 1-5)																							
	Pld	Home					Away					Neutral					Total					Home						Away						Neutral						Total					
		W	D	L	F	A	W	D	L	F	A	W	D	L	F	A	W	D	L	F	A	P	W	D	L	F	A	P	W	D	L	F	A	P	W	D	L	F	A	P	W	D	L	F	A
ACCRINGTON STANLEY																												1	1			1	0							1	1			1	0
ALDERSHOT																						1	1			1	0													1	1			1	0
ARSENAL																						2		1	1	1	3	3	1		2	2	9							5	1	1	3	3	12
ASHFORD																												1	1			1	0							1	1			1	0
ASTON VILLA																						3	1	2		6	3	4		1	3	4	12	1			1	0	3	8	1	3	4	10	18
BARNET																																								0					
BARNSLEY																																								0					
BARROW																												1			1	0	1							1			1	0	1
BATH CITY																												1			1	1	2							1			1	1	2
BIRMINGHAM CITY																						3	2	1		4	2	3		2	1	3	6							6	2	3	1	7	8
BISHOP AUCKLAND																						1			1	2	4													1			1	2	4
BLACKBURN ROVERS																																								0					
BLACKPOOL																						2		2		3	3	2	1	1		2	1	1			1	0	1	5	1	3	1	5	5
BOLTON WANDERERS																						2	2			3	1	1	1			3	0							3	3			6	1
BOURNEMOUTH																																								0					
BRADFORD CITY																																								0					
BRENTFORD																						4	3	1		13	4	4	1	2	1	3	3							8	4	3	1	16	7
BRIDGEWATER TOWN																												1	1			3	0							1	1			3	0
BRIGHTON & HOVE ALBION	2			1	1	3	1			2	0						1		1	3	3	3		1	2	3	6	2	1	1		4	2	1	1			1	0	6	2	2	2	8	8
BRISTOL CITY																						3	1		2	4	5	4	3		1	5	5							7	4		3	9	10
BRISTOL ROVERS	1	1			2	1											1			2	1	2	2			5	2	1			1	0	2							3	2		1	5	4
BURNLEY																						2		2		0	0	3			3	0	12							5		2	3	0	12
BURY																						3	2	1		7	1	1	1			1	0							4	3	1		8	1
CAMBRIDGE UNITED																												1	1			1	0							1	1			1	0
CARDIFF CITY																						1	1			3	1													1	1			3	1
CARLISLE UNITED																												1			1	0	3							1			1	0	3
CHARLTON ATHLETIC	1	1			2	0											1			2	0	4	2	1	1	6	4	3	2	1		3	1							7	4	2	1	9	5
CHELMSFORD CITY																						1	1			5	1													1	1			5	1
CHELSEA	3			2	0	3			1	0	2								3	0	5	7	3	1	3	15	12	3	1		2	3	6							10	4	1	5	18	18
CHESTER CITY																						1			1	0	1													1			1	0	1
CHESTERFIELD																																								0					
CLAPHAM																						1	1			7	0													1	1			7	0
COLCHESTER UNITED																						1	1			3	0	1			1	1	3							2	1		1	4	3
COVENTRY CITY																												1	1			4	2							1	1			4	2
CREWE ALEXANDRA																																								0					
DARLINGTON																												1			1	0	2							1			1	0	2
DARTFORD																												1	1			3	1							1	1			3	1
DERBY COUNTY																						1		1		1	1	1			1	0	3							2		1	1	1	4
DONCASTER ROVERS																						1	1			2	0	2			2	1	3							3	1		2	3	3
ENFIELD																						2	2			7	2													2	2			7	2
EVERTON	1											1			4	1	1			4	1	5		2	3	4	17	4	1	1	2	10	9	1	1			4	1	10	2	3	5	18	27
EXETER CITY																																								0					
FINCHLEY																												1			1	1	3							1			1	1	3
FULHAM																						1	1			1	0	2		1	1	0	2							3	1	1	1	1	2
GATESHEAD																						1	1			2	1													1	1			2	1
GILLINGHAM																						1			1	0	1													1			1	0	1
GLOSSOP																						1	1			2	0													1	1			2	0
GREAT YARMOUTH																						1			1	0	1													1			1	0	1
GRENADIER GUARDS																												1	1			3	0							1	1			3	0
GRIMSBY TOWN																						1			1	0	1	1			1	0	1							2			2	0	2
HALIFAX TOWN																																								0					
HARTLEPOOL UNITED																						1	1			6	1	3		1	2	2	4							4	1	1	2	8	5
HARWICH & PARKESTON																						1	1			8	2													1	1			8	2
HEREFORD UNITED																						1	1			2	0													1	1			2	0
HITCHIN																						1	1			6	2													1	1			6	2
HUDDERSFIELD TOWN																						1	1			4	0	1			1	2	5							2	1		1	6	5
HULL CITY																						1			1	0	2	1			1	2	3							2			2	2	5
IPSWICH TOWN																						1			1	0	1													1			1	0	1
KETTERING TOWN																						2	1	1		4	2	1	1			4	0							3	2	1		8	2
LEEDS UNITED																						2	1		1	2	4	4	1		3	3	13							6	2		4	5	17
LEICESTER CITY																						3	1		2	3	4	3	1	1	1	3	3							6	2	1	3	6	7
LEYTON ORIENT																						3	1	2		1	0	2	2			2	0							5	3	2		3	0
LINCOLN CITY																						4	4			15	2	2		1	1	1	2							6	4	1	1	16	4
LIVERPOOL																						4	1	1	2	4	5	4		2	2	2	5	1	1			4	3	9	2	3	4	10	13
LUTON TOWN	3	3			11	3											3			11	3	7	6		1	22	5	1		1		0	0							8	6	1	1	22	5
MAIDSTONE UNITED																																								0					
MANCHESTER CITY																						2	2			6	0	2			2	4	15							4	2		2	10	15
MANCHESTER UNITED																						1			1	0	1	3			3	3	7	4		2	2	5	8	8		2	6	8	16
MANSFIELD TOWN																						1		1		2	2	1			1	2	7							2		1	1	4	9
MARGATE																						1	1			3	0	3	1	1	1	4	5							4	2	1	1	7	5
MIDDLESBROUGH	1						1			3	2						1			3	2	1	1			1	0	2	1	1		4	3							3	2	1		5	3
MILLWALL																						5	2	1	2	9	10	5		3	2	2	6							10	2	4	4	11	16
NEWARK TOWN																						1	1			6	0													1	1			6	0
NEWCASTLE UNITED																												4	1		3	3	9							4	1		3	3	9
NEWPORT COUNTY																						2	1		1	4	3	1	1			2	0							3	2		1	6	3
NORTHAMPTON TOWN																						2	2			3	1	2		2		3	3							4	2	2		6	4
NORWICH CITY	2	1			2	0		1		1	1						1	1		3	1	4	3	1		7	1	2		1	1	1	2							6	3	2	1	8	3
NOTTINGHAM FOREST	1								1	1	3								1	1	3	6	2	4		7	4	7	1	1	5	7	19							13	3	5	5	14	23
NOTTS COUNTY																						1		1		0	0	1		1		0	0	2	1	1		2	1	4	1	3		2	1
OLDHAM ATHLETIC																																								0					
OXFORD UNITED	1								1	0	1								1	0	1							1			1	0	1							1			1	0	1
PETERBOROUGH UNITED																						2	2			5	1	2	1		1	2	3							4	3		1	7	4
PLYMOUTH ARGYLE																												2	1		1	4	4							2	1		1	4	4
PORT VALE																						1	1			2	1													1	1			2	1
PORTSMOUTH	1								1	0	4								1	0	4	4	3	1		9	3	3	1	1	1	2	5							7	4	2	1	11	8
PRESTON NORTH END																						1	1			3	1													1	1			3	1
QUEENS PARK RANGERS	1						1			3	2						1			3	2	2		2		1	1	6	1	1	4	5	12	1			1	0	1	9	1	3	5	6	14
READING																						2		2		2	2	3	2	1		5	2	1	1			2	0	6	3	3		9	4
ROCHDALE																						2	1	1		4	3	1	1			3	1							3	2	1		7	4
ROTHERHAM UNITED																																		1	1			4	0	1	1			4	0
SCARBOROUGH																												1	1			2	1							1	1			2	1
SCUNTHORPE UNITED																												1			1	0	1							1			1	0	1
SHEFFIELD UNITED																												1			1	0	2							1			1	0	2
SHEFFIELD WEDNESDAY																						2		1	1	2	3	1		1		1	1	1			1	2	3	4		2	2	5	7
SHREWSBURY TOWN																						1		1		2	2	1		1		2	2	1	1			4	1	3	1	2		8	5
SOUTHAMPTON	1						1			2	1						1			2	1	5	3	2		5	0	6	3		3	7	8	1			1	0	2	12	6	2	4	12	10
SOUTHEND UNITED	1	1			4	2											1			4	2	3	2	1		13	3	2	1		1	2	3							5	3	1	1	15	6
STOCKPORT COUNTY																						2	1		1	7	1	3	1	1	1	3	3							5	2	1	2	10	4
STOKE CITY																												1			1	0	1							1			1	0	1
SUNDERLAND																						2		2		0	0	4	2		2	3	3							6	2	2	2	3	3
SWANSEA CITY																						1		1		3	3	1		1		2	2	1			1	1	2	3		2	1	6	7
SWINDON TOWN	1	1			1	0											1			1	0	5	2		3	6	7	4	3	1		5	1							9	5	1	3	11	8
TAUNTON TOWN																						1	1			6	0													1	1			6	0
TOOTING & MITCHAM																												1	1			2	1							1	1			2	1
TORQUAY UNITED																																								0					
TOTTENHAM HOTSPUR																						3	2		1	4	3	3		2	1	0	4							6	2	2	2	4	7
TRANMERE ROVERS																												1	1			2	0							1	1			2	0
WALSALL	1	1			4	2											1			4	2	3	2		1	7	4	1		1		1	1							4	2	1	1	8	5
WALTHAMSTOW AVENUE																						1	1			2	0													1	1			2	0
WALTON & HERSHAM																						1	1			1	0													1	1			1	0
WATFORD																						4	2	1	1	7	4	3		2	1	1	2							7	2	3	2	8	6
WEST BROMWICH ALBION	1								1	1	2								1	1	2	1			1	1	3	1			1	1	2							2			2	2	5
WEST HAM UNITED																						1		1		1	1	2			2	0	4							3		1	2	1	5
WIGAN ATHLETIC																																								0					
WIMBLEDON																												1	1			1	0							1	1			1	0
WOLVERHAMPTON WANDERERS																						4	1	1	2	6	6	3	1	1	1	6	4							7	2	2	3	12	10
WREXHAM																						1			1	0	2													1			1	0	2
WYCOMBE WANDERERS																																								0					
YEOVIL TOWN																												2			2	1	6							2			2	1	6
YORK CITY																						1	1			2	1													1	1			2	1
© John McBride (MAFS) - 1995	23	9	0	3	27	14	4	1	5	13	18	1	0	0	4	1	14	1	8	44	33	177	91	45	41	336	184	174	52	40	82	182	285	18	7	3	8	29	26	369	150	88	131	547	495

CRYSTAL PALACE - Every Football League match played - home and away. (Palace score shown first)

SEASON	20-21	21-22	22-23	23-24	24-25	25-26	26-27	27-28	28-29	29-30	30-31	31-32	32-33	33-34	34-35	35-36	36-37	37-38	38-39	46-47	47-48
DIVISION / POSITION	3/1	2/14	2/16	2/15	2/21	3S/13	3S/6	3S/5	3S/2	3S/9	3S/2	3S/4	3S/5	3S/12	3S/5	3S/6	3S/14	3S/7	3S/2	3S/18	3S/13
VENUE	H A	H A	H A	H A	H A	H A	H A	H A	H A	H A	H A	H A	H A	H A	H A	H A	H A	H A	H A	H A	H A
ABERDARE ATHLETIC						01 02	00 32														
ACCRINGTON STANLEY																					
ALDERSHOT													30 13	41 40	30 22	21 31	30 22	11 01	30 12	00 20	10 02
ARSENAL																					
ASTON VILLA																					
BARNET																					
BARNSLEY		01 13	20 21	31 25	01 03																
BARROW																					
BIRMINGHAM CITY																					
BLACKBURN ROVERS																					
BLACKPOOL		10 31	11 04	31 02	12 10																
BOLTON WANDERERS																					
BOURNEMOUTH						31 16	22 11	61 22	13 02	11 12	10 00	11 14	30 23	41 11	10 11	20 52	22 13	01 01	30 11	01 04	20 00
BRADFORD CITY			20 11	30 10	41 00																
BRADFORD PARK AVENUE		11 00																			
BRENTFORD	42 40					20 23	43 03	02 12	10 42	21 02	51 28	10 11	21 02								
BRIGHTON + HOVE ALBION	32 20					21 23	20 11	11 24	10 51	22 21	01 11	20 30	50 21	21 14	30 03	40 12	20 01	32 12	10 00	10 01	00 11
BRISTOL CITY		11 21		10 00		52 01	42 45						22 33	01 22	31 10	61 02	10 01	11 00	32 11	00 03	40 02
BRISTOL ROVERS	30 12					02 13	74 14	32 11	52 11	30 32	02 12	50 16	20 32	12 10	20 35	53 42	30 01	32 01	00 21	21 12	00 11
BURNLEY																					
BURY		41 21	11 12	10 11																	
CAMBRIDGE UNITED																					
CARDIFF CITY												50 31	41 11	32 04	61 02	32 11	22 11	10 24	20 10	12 00	
CARLISLE UNITED																					
CHARLTON ATHLETIC						41 11	21 21	50 40	02 31					10 24	12 22						
CHELSEA					10 22																
CHESTER CITY																					
CHESTERFIELD																					
COLCHESTER UNITED																					
COVENTRY CITY		11 11	00 12	31 00	00 41		12 13	10 22	03 31	43 01	10 53	22 08	13 26	21 15	31 11	31 18					
CREWE ALEXANDRA																					
DARLINGTON																					
DERBY COUNTY		31 02	22 06	01 05	20 03																
DONCASTER ROVERS																					
EVERTON																					
EXETER CITY	21 11					32 10	10 13	20 22	10 21	11 16	72 34	30 10	22 11	00 21	01 60	22 01	80 23	22 22	32 44	10 12	12 02
FULHAM		20 11	00 12	11 01	12 13				21 22	43 21	52 02	20 04									
GATESHEAD		12 11	11 02	10 02	00 11																
GILLINGHAM	41 10					02 11	22 12	22 13	30 10	51 11	50 26	10 00	51 02	32 50	20 02	11 20	11 02	30 42			
GRIMSBY TOWN	20 01																				
HALIFAX TOWN																					
HARTLEPOOL UNITED																					
HEREFORD UNITED																					
HUDDERSFIELD TOWN																					
HULL CITY		02 01	11 11	00 22	10 05																
IPSWICH TOWN																			30 12	11 11	21 03
LEEDS UNITED		12 00	10 14	11 03																	
LEICESTER CITY		10 02	01 03	43 01	02 13																
LEYTON ORIENT		10 00	20 13	21 01	01 03					30 12	31 23	00 31	21 14	32 02	10 02	22 01	23 11	10 20	42 04	20 10	20 11
LINCOLN CITY																					
LIVERPOOL																					
LUTON TOWN	21 22					30 23	11 01	32 16	30 35	41 22	51 21	11 03	30 11	22 12	21 22	51 06	04 25				
MAIDSTONE UNITED																					
MANCHESTER CITY																					
MANCHESTER UNITED			23 12	11 15	21 01																
MANSFIELD TOWN												21 11						40 02	62 00	11 13	
MERTHYR TOWN	30 12					30 04	11 21	20 22	20 22	61 25											
MIDDLESBROUGH					22 00																
MILLWALL	32 10					12 01	16 01	04 11							11 23	50 04	10 03	00 22			
NELSON				11 24																	
NEWCASTLE UNITED																					
NEWPORT COUNTY	20 10					42 32	62 12	20 30	11 31	10 00	71 12		00 31	11 01	60 32	60 52	61 11	30 00	11 02		21 13
NORTHAMPTON TOWN	51 22					10 04	30 11	10 11	10 18	13 02	00 00	40 05	20 01	12 24	20 23	61 13	22 02	01 11	20 00	22 01	10 13
NORWICH CITY	10 10					20 34	71 10	21 14	21 10	32 22	21 12	31 23	40 03	01 02						01 32	20 13
NOTTINGHAM FOREST		41 12																			
NOTTS COUNTY		10 23	01 40								11 22					00 13	12 10	31 10	51 10	21 00	11 01
OLDHAM ATHLETIC				23 01	01 20																
OXFORD UNITED																					
PETERBOROUGH UNITED																					
PLYMOUTH ARGYLE	00 10					55 26	11 17	02 15	14 11	30 16											
PORT VALE		00 03	20 02	12 43	00 03														10 02	12 24	20 14
PORTSMOUTH	30 00				12 00																
PRESTON NORTH END																					
QUEENS PARK RANGERS	00 03					10 31	21 20	11 02	14 11	11 14	40 04	11 22	01 12	41 12	23 33	02 03	00 31	40 01	01 21	00 21	01 01
READING	20 01					30 12						11 03	11 32	00 00	31 16	20 10	31 11	31 23	00 13	21 240	21 00
ROCHDALE																					
ROTHERHAM UNITED		20 11	40 14																		
SCARBOROUGH																					
SCUNTHORPE UNITED																					
SHEFFIELD UNITED																					
SHEFFIELD WEDNESDAY		22 01	20 13	30 06	01 10																
SHREWSBURY TOWN																					
SOUTHAMPTON	11 11		10 20	00 01	31 02																
SOUTHEND UNITED	23 20					30 15	53 13	41 16	32 03	12 23	31 42	32 01	41 21	11 40	10 41	30 17	11 12	21 22	43 13	03 02	00 12
SOUTHPORT																					
STOCKPORT COUNTY			30 22	11 22	30 01																
STOKE CITY		02 15		51 11	01 11																
SUNDERLAND																					
SWANSEA CITY	01 00																				40 02
SWINDON TOWN	10 31					10 13	50 16	10 33	61 23	10 13	31 44	00 23	43 01	00 23	70 11	51 20	20 04	01 04	11 22	41 01	11 00
THAMES											21 20	21 31									
TORQUAY UNITED								32 20	20 21	42 22	50 13	70 13	21 12	41 12	22 17	10 23	00 03	41 00	13 21	61 12	21 33
TOTTENHAM HOTSPUR																					
TRANMERE ROVERS																					
WALSALL								51 11	11 13	51 00	63 12						31 01	31 11	40 11	11 33	23 11
WATFORD	22 11					40 03	01 21	21 12	30 33	11 11	61 20	21 21	03 01	43 13	00 02	12 23	20 13	41 21	20 14	20 01	12 50
WEST BROMWICH ALBION																					
WEST HAM UNITED		12 02	15 11																		
WIGAN ATHLETIC																					
WIMBLEDON																					
WOLVERHAMPTON WANDERERS		11 10	50 01		21 13																
WORKINGTON																					
WREXHAM																					
WYCOMBE WANDERERS																					
YORK CITY																					
GOALS F-A	70-34	45-51	54-62	53-65	38-54	75-79	84-81	79-72	81-67	81-74	107-71	74-63	78-64	71-67	86-64	96-74	62-61	67-47	71-52	49-62	49-49

SEASON	48-49	49-50	50-51	51-52	52-53	53-54	54-55	55-56	56-57	57-58	58-59	59-60	60-61	61-62	62-63	63-64	64-65	65-66	66-67	67-68	68-69
DIVISION / POSITION	3S/22	3S/7	3S/24	3S/19	3S/13	3S/22	3S/20	3S/23	3S/20	3S/14	4/7	4/8	4/2	3/15	3/11	3/2	2/7	2/11	2/7	2/11	2/2
VENUE	H A	H A	H A	H A	H A	H A	H A	H A	H A	H A	H A	H A	H A	H A	H A	H A	H A	H A	H A	H A	H A
ABERDARE ATHLETIC																					
ACCRINGTON STANLEY													92 32								
ALDERSHOT	21 03	21 00	02 03	02 03	30 10	00 21	32 03	10 11	21 12	11 14	41 21	11 01	21 12								
ARSENAL																					
ASTON VILLA																				01 10	42 11
BARNET																					
BARNSLEY														13 30	12 40	12 02					
BARROW											22 01	90 10	42 30								
BIRMINGHAM CITY																		10 12	21 13	00 01	32 10
BLACKBURN ROVERS																			21 12	10 12	10 21
BLACKPOOL																				31 02	12 03
BOLTON WANDERERS																	20 03	11 03	32 00	03 22	21 22
BOURNEMOUTH	21 02	10 02	01 05	22 21	10 24	31 02	21 14	13 01	11 22	30 13				00 01	10 03	21 34					
BRADFORD CITY																					
BRADFORD PARK AVENUE											20 05	10 13	41 13	00 02	60 12						
BRENTFORD							11 03	02 03	02 11	21 30				22 24		10 12					
BRIGHTON & HOVE ALBION	02 11	60 00	02 01	12 34	21 14	11 03	10 01	12 05	22 11	24 23					22 21						
BRISTOL CITY	40 02	11 02	10 02	21 02	13 05	12 04	12 03							23 22	32 11	10 11		21 11	21 10	20 12	21 11
BRISTOL ROVERS	10 01	10 00	10 11	01 04	10 02										21 02	10 31					
BURNLEY																					
BURY																	02 13	10 22	31 11		10 12
CAMBRIDGE UNITED																					
CARDIFF CITY																	00 00	00 01	31 21	21 24	31 40
CARLISLE UNITED											02 33	21 22	11 02		30 22			20 13	42 03	11 03	30 21
CHARLTON ATHLETIC																	31 21	20 01	10 11	30 10	33 11
CHELSEA																					
CHESTER CITY											33 23	34 10	51 03								
CHESTERFIELD																					
COLCHESTER UNITED			13 01	22 21	31 03	01 14	00 02	11 42	24 33	11 11					01 21	00 11					
COVENTRY CITY					22 24	31 00	10 14	30 31	11 33	20 22	11 02			22 20	00 01	11 15	22 00	01 10	11 21		
CREWE ALEXANDRA											62 14	40 11	00 21			10 20					
DARLINGTON											41 41	20 11	32 10								
DERBY COUNTY																	23 33	11 04	21 02	10 11	12 10
DONCASTER ROVERS												40 21	51 51								
EVERTON											—										
EXETER CITY	11 13	53 12	01 21	21 10	20 02	00 07	11 02	01 16	00 12	20 10	11 13	10 22	00 32								
FULHAM																					32 01
GATESHEAD											31 31	22 20									
GILLINGHAM			43 00	02 44	00 01	12 23	02 12	13 11	12 14	30 03	41 11	33 00	20 21								
GRIMSBY TOWN														41 00							
HALIFAX TOWN														43 11	00 22						
HARTLEPOOL UNITED											12 14	52 10	22 42								
HEREFORD UNITED																					
HUDDERSFIELD TOWN																	30 02	21 11	11 20	01 11	21 00
HULL CITY														12 42	11 00	22 11			41 16	01 11	20 02
IPSWICH TOWN	11 23	20 44	13 11	31 11	11 02	11 02		10 33	13 24								11 23	31 22	02 02	13 22	
LEEDS UNITED																					
LEICESTER CITY																					
LEYTON ORIENT	21 11	11 22	11 02	21 40	22 00	22 02	11 12	12 08									10 10	21 20			
LINCOLN CITY														13 23							
LIVERPOOL																					
LUTON TOWN																11 40					
MAIDSTONE UNITED																					
MANCHESTER CITY																	11 20	02 13			
MANCHESTER UNITED																					
MANSFIELD TOWN													41 21			31 11					
MERTHYR TOWN																					
MIDDLESBROUGH																	31 00	11 22		13 03	00 04
MILLWALL	11 01	10 32	11 01	11 13	01 00	23 22	11 25	22 11	22 03	01 03	40 12	12 01	02 20		30 11	21 10			12 11	22 15	42 20
NELSON																					
NEWCASTLE UNITED																	11 02				
NEWPORT COUNTY	01 05	10 22	11 42	11 01	21 23	30 31	21 10	10 10	21 22	22 00				20 12							
NORTHAMPTON TOWN	22 23	04 22	00 02	33 25	43 15	22 06	31 11	23 11	11 01	13 21	11 03	01 20	23 21	14 11	12 13		12 11		51 01		
NORWICH CITY	11 03	20 02	05 13	20 01	11 15	10 12	20 02	20 13	41 01	03 23							20 21	00 12	00 34	60 12	20 10
NOTTINGHAM FOREST		11 02	16 01																		
NOTTS COUNTY	15 15	12 10										11 17		41 00	11 20	20 11					
OLDHAM ATHLETIC											40 03	32 01	21 34			13 13					
OXFORD UNITED																					11 20
PETERBOROUGH UNITED													02 14	52 14	02 00	10 11					
PLYMOUTH ARGYLE			01 04	01 05					21 10	30 01							21 11	31 21	21 01	50 12	
PORT VALE	11 00	01 02	02 22	31 02						10 04	11 32			00 10	21 14	20 21					
PORTSMOUTH														12 12			42 11	41 11	02 11	22 22	31 33
PRESTON NORTH END																	10 01	11 02	10 01	20 00	12 00
QUEENS PARK RANGERS					42 11	03 11	21 01	11 30	21 24	23 24				22 01	10 14	10 43				10 12	
READING	01 15	11 21	03 11	12 13	03 14	10 14	11 05	23 01	11 21	22 22				34 12	21 10	41 00					
ROCHDALE												40 04	41 22								
ROTHERHAM UNITED																	21 01	22 03	11 10	10 30	
SCARBOROUGH																					
SCUNTHORPE UNITED																					
SHEFFIELD UNITED																					11 11
SHEFFIELD WEDNESDAY																					
SHREWSBURY TOWN				11 12	12 11	32 11	22 11	01 02	01 11	30 00	43 12			21 51	22 13	30 11					
SOUTHAMPTON						43 13	12 22	02 13	12 03	14 12							02 10	10 01			
SOUTHEND UNITED	21 10	21 00	02 25	10 04	00 22	42 21	22 23	12 34	20 11	20 11				22 22	23 01	30 12					
SOUTHPORT											10 20	22 13	50 33								
STOCKPORT COUNTY												31 10	21 25								
STOKE CITY																					
SUNDERLAND																					
SWANSEA CITY	11 03																33 12				
SWINDON TOWN	11 01	22 24	20 02	01 20	30 63	32 11	00 00	02 00	00 13	41 00				31 05	00 01		31 02				
THAMES																					
TORQUAY UNITED	01 02	13 01	21 14	11 51	22 11	41 01	11 22	30 11	11 03	11 11	31 20	11 12		72 21							
TOTTENHAM HOTSPUR																					
TRANMERE ROVERS																					
WALSALL	13 13	20 13	10 00	21 03	41 42	10 01	31 41	20 04	30 21	41 12	13 20	12 03				10 22					
WATFORD	31 02	20 00	11 01	20 02	10 02	11 14	11 17	12 20	00 41	42 12	30 22	81 24		11 23	01 41	20 13					
WEST BROMWICH ALBION																					
WEST HAM UNITED																					
WIGAN ATHLETIC																					
WIMBLEDON																					
WOLVERHAMPTON WANDERERS																		01 01	41 11		
WORKINGTON											11 40	01 11	42 01								
WREXHAM													32 21		50 43	21 22					
WYCOMBE WANDERERS																					
YORK CITY											00 11		10 20								
GOALS F-A	38-76	55-54	33-84	61-80	66-82	60-86	52-80	54-83	62-75	70-72	90-71	84-64	110-69	83-80	68-58	73-51	55-51	47-52	61-55	56-56	70-47

SEASON	69-70	70-71	71-72	72-73	73-74	74-75	75-76	76-77	77-78	78-79	79-80	80-81	81-82	82-83	83-84	84-85	85-86	86-87	87-88	88-89	89-90
DIVISION/POSITION	1/20	1/18	1/20	1/21	2/20	3/5	3/5	3/3	2/9	2/1	1/13	1/22	2/15	2/15	2/18	2/15	2/5	2/6	2/6	2/3	1/15
VENUE	H A	H A	H A	H A	H A	H A	H A	H A	H A	H A	H A	H A	H A	H A	H A	H A	H A	H A	H A	H A	H A
ABERDARE ATHLETIC																					
ACCRINGTON STANLEY																					
ALDERSHOT						30 12	00 01														
ARSENAL	15 02	02 11	22 12	23 01							10 11	22 23									11 14
ASTON VILLA					00 12						20 02	01 12							11 14		10 12
BARNET																					
BARNSLEY													12 02	11 13	01 11	01 13	10 42	01 32	32 12	11 11	
BARROW																					
BIRMINGHAM CITY				00 11								31 01				02 03		60 14	30 60	41 10	
BLACKBURN ROVERS						10 11			50 03	30 11			12 01	20 03	02 12	11 10	20 21	20 20	20 02	22 45	
BLACKPOOL		10 13			12 01				22 13												
BOLTON WANDERERS					00 02				21 02		31 11		10 00	30 01							
BOURNEMOUTH						41 04													30 32	23 02	
BRADFORD CITY																	21 01	11 21	11 02	20 10	
BRADFORD PARK AVENUE																					
BRENTFORD																					
BRIGHTON & HOVE ALBION						30 01	01 02	31 11	00 11	31 00	11 03	03 23			02 13	11 01	10 02	20 02		21 13	
BRISTOL CITY					31 10						11 20										
BRISTOL ROVERS									10 03	01 10											
BURNLEY	12 24	02 12							11 11	20 12				10 12							
BURY						22 22	10 10	21 10													
CAMBRIDGE UNITED										11 00			21 00	00 01	11 31						
CARDIFF CITY					33 11		01 10		20 22	20 22			10 10		10 20	11 30					
CARLISLE UNITED					01 01									21 14	12 22	21 01	11 22				
CHARLTON ATHLETIC						21 01			11 01	10 11			20 12	11 12	20 01	21 11	21 13				20 21
CHELSEA	15 11	00 11	23 12	20 00									01 21	00 00	01 22					11 01	22 03
CHESTER CITY							20 12	12 12													
CHESTERFIELD						14 12	00 21	00 20													
COLCHESTER UNITED						21 11	32 30														
COVENTRY CITY	03 22	12 12	22 11	01 02							00 12	03 13									01 01
CREWE ALEXANDRA																					
DARLINGTON																					
DERBY COUNTY	01 13	00 01	01 03	00 22							40 21		01 14	41 11	01 03			10 01			11 13
DONCASTER ROVERS																					
EVERTON	00 12	20 13	21 00	10 11							11 13	23 05									21 04
EXETER CITY																					
FULHAM					02 31				23 11	01 00				11 01	11 11	22 22	00 32				
GATESHEAD																					
GILLINGHAM						40 13	01 21	31 30													
GRIMSBY TOWN						30 12	30 21	21 10					03 10	20 14	01 02	02 31	21 03	03 10			
HALIFAX TOWN						11 13	11 31														
HARTLEPOOL UNITED																					
HEREFORD UNITED						22 02	22 11														
HUDDERSFIELD TOWN		03 20	00 10			11 10									00 12	11 02	23 00	10 21	21 22		
HULL CITY					02 03				01 01								02 21	51 03	22 12	31 10	
IPSWICH TOWN	11 02	10 21	11 20	11 12							41 03	12 23						33 03	12 32	20 21	
LEEDS UNITED	11 02	11 12	11 02	22 04							10 01	01 01		11 12	00 11	31 14	30 31	10 03	30 01	00 21	
LEICESTER CITY			11 00	01 12						31 11		21 11	02 11	10 10					21 44	42 22	
LEYTON ORIENT					00 03				10 00	11 10			10 00								
LINCOLN CITY								41 23													
LIVERPOOL	13 03	10 11	01 14	11 01							00 03	22 03									02 09
LUTON TOWN					12 12				33 01	31 10			33 01								11 01
MAIDSTONE UNITED																					
MANCHESTER CITY	10 10	01 01	12 04	10 32							20 00	23 11			02 13	12 12			20 31	00 11	22 03
MANCHESTER UNITED	22 11	35 10	13 04	50 02							02 11	10 01									11 21
MANSFIELD TOWN							41 11	20 01	31 31												
MERTHYR TOWN																					
MIDDLESBROUGH					23 02						12 11	52 02		30 02	10 31	10 11	21 20		31 12		
MILLWALL					11 23		00 12		10 30	00 30							21 23	21 10	10 11		43 21
NELSON																					
NEWCASTLE UNITED	03 00	10 02	20 21	21 02						10 01			12 00	02 01	31 13						
NEWPORT COUNTY																					
NORTHAMPTON TOWN								11 03													
NORWICH CITY				02 12							00 12	41 11	21 01				12 34				10 02
NOTTINGHAM FOREST	11 00	20 13	11 10		01 21						10 04	13 03									10 13
NOTTS COUNTY					14 31				20 02	20 00						10 00					
OLDHAM ATHLETIC									00 11	10 00			40 00	10 02	21 23	30 01	32 02	21 01	31 01	20 32	
OXFORD UNITED					20 11			22 10								10 05				10 01	
PETERBOROUGH UNITED						11 11	11 02	00 00													
PLYMOUTH ARGYLE						33 10												00 13	51 31	41 20	
PORT VALE						11 12	22 00	20 14													
PORTSMOUTH					00 22			21 00							21 10	21 11	21 01	10 02		20 11	
PRESTON NORTH END					20 11	10 11	20 00	10 12		00 32											
QUEENS PARK RANGERS													00 01	03 00							03 02
READING								11 00										13 01	23 32		
ROCHDALE																					
ROTHERHAM UNITED							20 14	21 11					31 02	11 22							
SCARBOROUGH																					
SCUNTHORPE UNITED																					
SHEFFIELD UNITED			51 01	01 02					10 20	31 20						13 21	11 00	12 01	21 11		
SHEFFIELD WEDNESDAY	02 00				00 04		11 01	40 01					12 01	20 12	10 01						11 22
SHREWSBURY TOWN							11 42	21 11					01 01	21 11	11 11	22 14	01 20	23 00	12 02	11 12	
SOUTHAMPTON	20 11	31 06	23 01	30 02					12 02		00 14	32 24									31 11
SOUTHEND UNITED						11 10	11 21														
SOUTHPORT																					
STOCKPORT COUNTY																					
STOKE CITY	31 01	32 00	20 13	32 02					01 20	11 11	01 21	11 01					01 00	10 13	20 11	10 12	
SUNDERLAND	20 00				30 00				22 00	11 21		01 01					10 11	20 01		10 11	
SWANSEA CITY															20 01						
SWINDON TOWN					42 10	62 11	33 21	50 11											21 22	21 01	
THAMES																					
TORQUAY UNITED																					
TOTTENHAM HOTSPUR	02 02	03 02	11 03	00 12					12 22		11 00	34 24									23 10
TRANMERE ROVERS						21 02		10 01													
WALSALL						10 03	01 11	30 00												40 00	
WATFORD						10 21							03 11							02 10	
WEST BROMWICH ALBION	13 23	30 00	02 11	02 40	10 01						22 03	01 01						11 21	41 01	10 35	
WEST HAM UNITED	00 12	11 00	03 11	13 04						11 11											
WIGAN ATHLETIC																					
WIMBLEDON																05 23	13 11				20 10
WOLVERHAMPTON WANDERERS	21 11	11 12	02 01	11 11							10 11	00 02		34 01		00 12					
WORKINGTON																					
WREXHAM						20 00	11 31	21 42		10 00			21 10								
WYCOMBE WANDERERS																					
YORK CITY								10 12													
GOALS F - A	34-68	39-57	39-65	41-58	43-56	66-57	61-46	68-40	50-47	51-24	41-50	47-83	34-45	43-52	42-52	46-65	57-52	51-53	86-59	71-49	42-56

SEASON	90-91		91-92		92-93		93-94		94-95		GRAND TOTALS – 1920-21 to 1994-95 (68 seasons)																	
DIVISION/POSITION	1/3		1/10		P/20		1/1		P/19		HOME						AWAY						TOTAL					
VENUE	H	A	H	A	H	A	H	A	H	A	P	W	D	L	F	A	P	W	D	L	F	A	P	W	D	L	F	A
ABERDARE ATHLETIC											2	0	1	1	0	1	2	1	0	1	3	4	4	1	1	2	3	5
ACCRINGTON STANLEY											1	1	0	0	9	2	1	1	0	0	3	2	2	2	0	0	12	4
ALDERSHOT											24	16	6	2	44	16	24	6	4	14	25	40	48	22	10	16	69	56
ARSENAL	00	04	14	14	12	03			03	21	11	1	4	6	11	24	11	1	2	8	9	26	22	2	6	14	20	50
ASTON VILLA	00	02	00	10	10	03			00	11	11	4	5	2	9	5	11	2	2	7	8	19	22	6	7	9	17	24
BARNET											0						0						0					
BARNSLEY							10	31			16	5	2	9	16	19	16	6	2	8	27	31	32	11	4	17	43	50
BARROW											3	2	1	0	15	4	3	2	0	1	4	1	6	4	1	1	19	5
BIRMINGHAM CITY							21	42			11	8	2	1	24	8	11	4	1	6	16	17	22	12	3	7	40	25
BLACKBURN ROVERS					33	21			01	12	16	10	3	3	28	12	16	5	2	9	19	27	32	15	5	12	47	39
BLACKPOOL											9	4	2	3	14	11	9	2	0	7	6	19	18	6	2	10	20	30
BOLTON WANDERERS							11	01			11	7	3	1	18	10	11	0	5	6	5	17	22	7	8	7	23	27
BOURNEMOUTH											32	19	7	6	60	29	32	3	8	21	31	75	64	22	15	27	91	104
BRADFORD CITY											7	5	2	0	15	4	7	3	2	2	5	5	14	8	4	2	20	9
BRADFORD PARK AVENUE											6	4	2	0	14	2	6	0	1	5	3	15	12	4	3	5	17	17
BRENTFORD											15	10	2	3	27	18	15	3	2	10	21	36	30	13	4	13	48	54
BRIGHTON & HOVE ALBION											40	22	9	9	68	39	40	6	10	24	40	72	80	28	19	33	108	111
BRISTOL CITY							41	02			30	19	6	5	64	33	30	5	10	15	24	51	60	24	16	20	88	84
BRISTOL ROVERS											26	19	2	5	52	23	26	7	5	14	30	50	52	26	7	19	82	73
BURNLEY											5	2	1	2	5	5	5	0	1	4	6	11	10	2	2	6	11	16
BURY											10	7	2	1	16	8	10	3	4	3	13	14	20	10	6	4	29	22
CAMBRIDGE UNITED											4	1	3	0	4	3	4	1	2	1	3	2	8	2	5	1	7	5
CARDIFF CITY											21	14	5	2	45	18	21	8	8	5	29	25	42	22	13	7	74	43
CARLISLE UNITED											13	7	3	3	24	13	13	1	5	7	15	29	26	8	8	10	39	42
CHARLTON ATHLETIC							20	00			21	16	3	2	42	15	21	6	7	8	26	26	42	22	10	10	68	41
CHELSEA	21	12	00	11	11	13			01	00	14	3	6	5	12	16	14	1	8	5	12	19	28	4	14	10	24	35
CHESTER CITY											5	2	1	2	14	10	5	1	0	4	5	10	10	3	1	6	19	20
CHESTERFIELD											3	0	2	1	1	4	3	2	0	1	5	3	6	2	2	2	6	7
COLCHESTER UNITED											12	3	5	4	15	17	12	4	4	4	18	20	24	7	9	8	33	37
COVENTRY CITY	21	13	01	21	00	22			02	41	38	12	15	11	46	46	38	9	11	18	54	85	76	21	26	29	100	131
CREWE ALEXANDRA											4	3	1	0	11	2	4	2	1	1	6	6	8	5	2	1	17	8
DARLINGTON											3	3	0	0	9	3	3	2	1	0	6	2	6	5	1	0	15	5
DERBY COUNTY	21	20					11	13			21	8	6	7	27	19	21	3	4	14	16	51	42	11	10	21	43	70
DONCASTER ROVERS											2	2	0	0	9	1	2	2	0	0	7	2	4	4	0	0	16	3
EVERTON	00	00	20	22	02	20			10	13	11	6	3	2	13	8	11	1	4	6	9	23	22	7	7	8	22	31
EXETER CITY											30	15	11	4	54	26	30	9	6	15	44	65	60	24	17	19	98	91
FULHAM											16	6	6	4	26	21	16	3	6	7	17	25	32	9	12	11	43	46
GATESHEAD											6	2	3	1	8	6	6	2	2	2	7	7	12	4	5	3	15	13
GILLINGHAM											28	15	6	7	63	33	28	8	8	12	37	45	56	23	14	19	100	78
GRIMSBY TOWN							10	11			12	8	0	4	19	12	12	5	2	5	11	15	24	13	2	9	30	27
HALIFAX TOWN											4	1	3	0	6	5	4	1	2	1	7	7	8	2	5	1	13	12
HARTLEPOOL UNITED											3	1	1	1	8	6	3	2	0	1	6	6	6	3	1	2	14	12
HEREFORD UNITED											2	0	2	0	4	4	2	0	1	1	1	3	4	0	3	1	5	7
HUDDERSFIELD TOWN											13	5	5	3	15	13	13	5	5	3	13	11	26	10	10	6	28	24
HULL CITY											16	5	5	6	22	19	16	3	5	8	14	31	32	8	10	14	36	50
IPSWICH TOWN					31	22			30	20	26	11	9	6	43	31	26	5	8	13	37	54	52	16	17	19	80	85
LEEDS UNITED	11	21	10	11	10	00			12	13	20	8	9	3	24	14	20	3	4	13	14	37	40	11	13	16	38	51
LEICESTER CITY							21	11	20	10	14	9	1	4	22	16	14	2	7	5	14	21	28	11	8	9	36	37
LEYTON ORIENT											30	18	9	3	48	26	30	7	8	15	25	48	60	25	17	18	73	74
LINCOLN CITY											2	1	0	1	5	4	2	0	0	2	4	6	4	1	0	3	9	10
LIVERPOOL	10	03	10	21	11	05			16	00	11	3	4	4	9	16	11	1	2	8	4	33	22	4	6	12	13	49
LUTON TOWN	10	11	11	11			32	10			22	12	8	2	51	29	22	4	6	12	27	46	44	16	14	14	78	75
MAIDSTONE UNITED											0						0						0					
MANCHESTER CITY	13	20	11	23	00	00			21	11	17	5	5	7	17	20	17	5	5	7	19	25	34	10	10	14	36	45
MANCHESTER UNITED	30	02	13	02	02	01			11	03	14	4	4	6	23	24	14	2	2	10	7	26	28	6	6	16	30	50
MANSFIELD TOWN											9	8	1	0	29	8	9	2	4	3	9	11	18	10	5	3	38	19
MERTHYR TOWN											6	5	1	0	17	2	6	1	2	3	9	16	12	6	3	3	26	18
MIDDLESBROUGH					41	10	01	32			15	8	3	4	29	18	15	4	5	6	14	22	30	12	8	10	43	40
MILLWALL							10	03			35	14	12	9	52	45	35	9	8	18	39	59	70	23	20	27	91	104
NELSON											1	0	1	0	1	1	1	0	0	1	2	4	2	0	1	1	3	5
NEWCASTLE UNITED									01	23	10	5	1	4	11	11	10	1	2	7	5	15	20	6	3	11	16	26
NEWPORT COUNTY											26	18	7	1	65	18	26	11	6	9	41	37	52	29	13	10	106	55
NORTHAMPTON TOWN											35	14	10	11	64	49	35	3	11	21	30	81	70	17	21	32	94	130
NORWICH CITY	13	30	34	33	12	24			01	00	37	22	5	10	66	36	37	7	4	26	44	78	74	29	9	36	110	114
NOTTINGHAM FOREST	22	10	00	15	11	11	20	11	12	01	15	5	6	4	19	19	15	3	3	9	10	27	30	8	9	13	29	46
NOTTS COUNTY			10	32			12	23			21	10	5	6	32	24	21	8	6	7	26	30	42	18	11	13	58	54
OLDHAM ATHLETIC			00	32	22	11					18	12	3	3	35	17	18	3	4	11	16	28	36	15	7	14	51	45
OXFORD UNITED							21	31			6	4	2	0	9	4	6	3	1	2	7	8	12	7	3	2	16	12
PETERBOROUGH UNITED							32	11			8	3	3	2	11	10	8	0	5	3	5	13	16	3	8	5	16	23
PLYMOUTH ARGYLE											18	9	5	4	39	23	18	6	2	10	19	44	36	15	7	14	58	67
PORT VALE											19	8	7	4	22	14	19	4	3	12	18	44	38	12	10	16	40	58
PORTSMOUTH							51	10			16	11	2	3	34	17	16	2	11	3	15	17	32	13	13	6	49	34
PRESTON NORTH END											10	7	2	1	12	3	10	1	5	4	6	10	20	8	7	5	18	13
QUEENS PARK RANGERS	00	21	22	01	11	31			00	10	34	11	13	10	40	39	34	10	6	18	42	59	68	31	19	28	82	98
READING											28	11	9	8	44	37	28	6	7	15	28	63	56	17	16	23	72	100
ROCHDALE											2	2	0	0	8	1	2	0	1	1	2	6	4	2	1	1	10	7
ROTHERHAM UNITED											10	7	3	0	20	7	10	2	3	5	10	18	20	9	6	5	30	25
SCARBOROUGH											0						0						0					
SCUNTHORPE UNITED											0						0						0					
SHEFFIELD UNITED	10	10	21	11	20	10					12	7	2	3	20	12	12	5	4	3	11	8	24	12	6	6	31	20
SHEFFIELD WEDNESDAY			11	14	11	12			21	01	15	6	6	3	21	12	15	1	2	12	7	29	30	7	8	15	28	41
SHREWSBURY TOWN											21	7	7	7	33	29	21	3	10	8	24	29	42	10	17	15	57	58
SOUTHAMPTON	21	32	10	01	12	01			00	13	23	11	4	8	34	29	23	3	4	16	18	46	46	14	8	24	52	75
SOUTHEND UNITED							10	21			33	19	8	6	66	41	33	10	6	17	49	71	66	29	14	23	115	112
SOUTHPORT											3	2	1	0	8	2	3	1	1	1	6	6	6	3	2	1	14	8
STOCKPORT COUNTY											5	4	1	0	12	3	5	1	2	2	7	10	10	5	3	2	19	13
STOKE CITY							41	20			16	9	2	5	26	15	16	3	6	7	14	22	32	12	8	12	40	37
SUNDERLAND	21	12					10	01			10	7	2	1	15	5	10	1	5	4	5	8	20	8	7	5	20	13
SWANSEA CITY											5	2	2	1	10	5	5	0	1	4	1	8	10	2	3	5	11	13
SWINDON TOWN											36	23	10	3	85	30	36	6	12	18	43	70	72	29	22	21	128	100
THAMES											2	2	0	0	4	2	2	2	0	0	5	1	4	4	0	0	9	3
TORQUAY UNITED											27	16	8	3	70	30	27	6	7	14	35	52	54	22	15	17	105	82
TOTTENHAM HOTSPUR	10	11	12	10	13	22			11	00	12	1	4	7	12	22	12	2	5	5	10	18	24	3	9	12	22	40
TRANMERE ROVERS							00	10			3	2	1	0	3	1	3	1	0	2	1	3	6	3	1	2	4	4
WALSALL											26	19	2	5	64	25	26	4	11	11	27	42	52	23	13	16	91	67
WATFORD							02	31			36	19	8	9	67	36	36	11	6	19	51	67	72	30	14	28	118	103
WEST BROMWICH ALBION							10	41			11	5	2	4	14	12	11	3	2	6	16	17	22	8	4	10	30	29
WEST HAM UNITED			23	20					10	01	9	1	3	5	8	18	9	1	4	4	6	12	18	2	7	9	14	30
WIGAN ATHLETIC											0						0						0					
WIMBLEDON	43	30	32	11	20	04			00	02	7	4	1	2	12	13	7	2	2	3	8	11	14	6	3	5	20	24
WOLVERHAMPTON WANDERERS							11	02			14	5	6	3	21	14	14	1	4	9	8	19	28	6	10	12	29	33
WORKINGTON											3	1	1	1	5	4	3	1	1	1	5	2	6	2	2	2	10	6
WREXHAM											8	7	1	0	18	6	8	5	3	0	16	9	16	12	4	0	34	15
WYCOMBE WANDERERS											0						0						0					
YORK CITY											3	2	1	0	2	0	3	1	1	1	4	3	6	3	2	1	6	3
GOALS F-A	50-41		53-61		48-61		73-46		34-49		1463	749	390	324	2537	1542	1463	330	393	740	1591	2599	2926	1079	783	1064	4128	4141

Friendly Matches Played by Crystal Palace FC 1905-95

Date	*Opponents*	*Venue*	*Result*
1905-1919			
9.9.1905	Eltham	H	4-0
21.9.1905	Fulham	H	1-1
30.9.1905	2nd Grenadier Guards	H	1-0
30.11.1905	Norwich City	A	2-0
16.12.1905	Newcastle United Reserves	A	2-2
3.2.1906	Croydon Common	A	4-0
24.2.1906	West Beckenham	H	17-2
31.3.1906	Woolwich Aresenal Reserves	A	2-2
28.4.1906	Luton Town	A	1-0
12.9.1906	Chelsea	H	4.0
25.12.1906	West Norwood	A	3-1
26.12.1907	Plymouth Argyle	H	1-1
17.4.1908	Norwich City	A	0-3
29.4.1908	Croydon Common	A	3-2
16.5.1908	Slavia (Prague)	A	5-4
17.5.1908	Slavia (Prague)	A	4-1
20.5.1908	Snnichow (Prague)	A	7-1
21.5.1908	Slavia (Prague)	A	2-0
23.5.1908	Koniggratz	A	10-1
24.5.1908	Klando	A	6-1
9.4.1909	Nunhead	A	4-2
4.10.1909	Ton Pentre	A	1-3
5.10.1909	Cardiff City (at Cardiff Arms Park)		3-3
5.2.1910	Clapton Orient	A	3-2
14.12.1910	Reading	A	2-1
3.4.1911	Aberdare	A	0-1
14.4.1911	Nunhead	A	6-2
22.4.1911	East Anglian League XI (at Colchester)		4-2
24.4.1911	East Anglian League XI (at Yarmouth)		4-0
29.4.1911	Croydon Common	A	1-1
2.12.1911	Portsmouth	A	1-0
8.5.1914	Copenhagen Select XI	A	1-2
10.5.1914	Copenhagen Select XI	A	2-4
15.5.1914	Gothenburg	A	4-1
17.5.1914	Gothenburg	A	3-1
22.5.1914	Christians (Norway)	A	6-1
24.5.1914	Christians (Norway)	A	4-1
27.8.1914	Millwall	A	1-5
29.1.1916	Croydon Common	A	2-0
5.5.1917	Millwall (J. Williams Benefit)	A	4-1
13.4.1918	Queens Park Rangers	A	1-2
20.4.1918	Queens Park Rangers	H	3-1
27.4.1918	Clapton Orient (National War Fund)	H	2-0
4.5.1918	Clapton Orient (National War Fund)	A	2-0
11.5.1918	Millwall	A	0-0
31.8.1918	Millwall	H	4-1
26.4.1919	Tottenham Hotspur	H	2-1
3.5.1919	Millwall	A	2-0
10.5.1919	Millwall	H	0-4
1919-1939			
21.2.1920	Corinthians	H	4-3
2.10.1922	Northampton Town	A	2-0
3.2.1923	Corinthians (at Crystal Palace)	A	3-3
25.4.1923	Croydon & District XI (Phil Bates Benefit)	H	3-0
19.11.1924	Folkestone (Albert Feebery Benefit)	H	2-2
21.2.1925	Corinthians	H	4-0
29.4.1925	Corinthians (at Crystal Palace)	A	2-4
11.12.1926	Corinthians	H	2-4
8.1.1927	Bristol City	H	7-3
27.4.1927	Jack Little's XI (Benefit)	H	2-0
2.1.1929	Corinthians (at Crystal Palace)	A	1-4
13.3.1929	Corinthians (Albert Feebery, Jimmy Hamilton, Bob Greener Benefit)	H	3-3
25.1.1930	West Bromwich Albion	H	1-2
1.5.1930	Kettering Town (Kettering Hospital Cup)	A	1-0
15.4.1931	Oxford & Cambridge Universities (Billy Callender Benefit)	H	4-0
13.2.1932	Charlton Athletic	A	5-4
20.2.1932	Corinthians	H	2-3
27.4.1932	British Army (George Clarke, Billy Turner Benefit)	H	3-1
24.4.1933	Guildford City	A	1-7
26.4.1933	Fulham (Albert Harry 2nd Benefit)	H	2-2
3.5.1933	Beckenham (Phil Bates 2nd Benefit)	A	4-2
31.10.1934	Corinthians (Peter Simpson Benefit)	H	3-2
8.12.1934	Millwall	H	6-2
30.4.1935	Aberdeen	H	1-1
20.11.1935	Corinthians	H	3-1
25.1.1936	Millwall	H	3-2
28.10.1936	Corinthians	H	4-0
12.12.1936	Aldershot	H	4-1
24.2.1937	Dutch National XI (in Rotterdam)	A	2-2
10.4.1937	Grimsby Town	H	6-3
27.10.1937	Corinthians	H	10-2
16.2.1938	The Army (Cental Command Ground, Aldershot)	A	5-4
23.3.1938	Royal Netherlands Voetbalbond (at Sparta Rotterdam FC)	A	2-3
24.3.1938	Colchester United (Ronnie Dunn Benefit)	A	1-2
28.3.1938	Tunbridge Wells Rangers (C. Goddard Benefit)	A	1-3
20.8.1938	Brighton & Hove Albion (Jubilee Fund)	H	5-1
4.1.1939	Belgian National XI (in Brussels)	A	4-5
19.8.1939	Brighton & Hove Albion (Jubilee Fund)	A	3-3
23.9.1939	Guildford City	A	0-5
30.9.1939	Brentford	A	0-3
7.10.1939	Brighton & Hove Albion	H	2-2
14.10.1939	Brentford	H	1-1
26.4.1941	Royal Air Force	H	3-2
3.5.1941	Shorts Sports	A	3-2
25.4.1942	Leicester City	H	1-3
2.5.1942	Charlton Athletic	H	1-3
16.5.1942	Reading	A	2-1
25.5.1942	Tottenham Hotspur	H	3-5
17.4.1943	Brentford	A	4-3
24.4.1943	Brentford	H	2-2
26.4.1943	Millwall	H	4-2
1.5.1943	Shorts Sports	A	6-0
1.4.1944	Millwall	H	7-0
15.4.1944	West Ham United	H	4-1
7.4.1945	Tottenham Hotspur	H	3-1
5.5.1945	Portsmouth	A	5-4
19.5.1945	Leicester City	A	1-0
26.5.1945	Leicester City	H	1-4
20.10.1945	Gillingham	H	5-2
27.10.1945	Gillingham	A	4-6
17.11.1945	Norwich City	A	5-2
24.11.1945	Norwich City	H	4-0
8.12.1945	Clapton Orient	H	5-1
26.1.1946	Plymouth Argyle	A	7-4
27.4.1946	Bristol City	H	4-4
6.5.1946	Ipswich Town (Ipswich Hospital Cup)	A	4-0
1947-1958			
2.7.1947	Combined Sevices (at Wuppertal, Gemany)	A	2-2
5.7.1947	British Army (at Bad Geynhausen)	A	0-1
7.2.1948	Nottingham Forest	H	1-0
1.5.1948	Aberdeen	H	3-0
11.12.1948	Doncaster Rovers	A	1-0

Date	Opponents	Venue	Result
18.12.1948	Stockport County	H	2-0
2.5.1949	Sunderland (Jack Lewis Benefit)	H	2-0
10.12.1949	Leyton Orient	H	2-0
24.4.1950	Bath City (Ted Owens Benefit)	A	2-1
26.4.1950	King's Lynn (Culey Victory Cup)	A	6-2
3.5.1950	Hastings (Freeman Thomas Charity Shield)	A	2-1
16.5.1951	Nancy (Festival of Britain)	H	1-2
15.12.1951	Plymouth Argyle	A	0-4
12.5.1952	Dundee United	A	1-1
13.5.1952	Inverness Select XI (at Inverness Caledonian)	A	1-3
15.5.1952	Morayshire Select XI (at Elgin City)	A	4-1
5.11.1952	Gloucester City	A	2-2
6.5.1953	Hastings (Freeman Thomas Charity Shield)	A	1-2
28.9.1953	Chelsea	H	1-1
6.10.1953	Cardiff City	H	2-2
13.10.1953	Derby County	H	1-1
20.10.1953	Leeds United	H	0-3
27.10.1953	Stade Francais	H	4-2
12.12.1953	Colchester United	H	2-1
23.2.1954	F.C. Vienna	H	4-3
2.3.1954	Brentford	H	0-0
9.3.1954	Charlton Athletic	H	2-2
16.3.1954	Queen of the South	H	2-2
23.3.1954	Chelsea	H	0-2
30.3.1954	Fulham	H	0.5
30.4.1954	London XI (Wally Hanlon Benefit)	H	6-5
4.10.1954	Queen of the South	H	2-1
13.10.1954	Clyde	H	1-1
18.10.1954	Third Lanark	H	0-1
26.10.1954	WAS Vienna	H	2-2
1.11.1954	St. Mirren	H	0-1
6.12.1954	EFB Esbjerg	H	5-2
21.2.1955	Plymouth Argyle	H	0-0
21.3.1955	Rotherham	H	1-2
30.3.1955	Headington United	A	2-0
4.4.1955	Hamilton Academicals	H	4-1
5.10.1955	Wycombe Wanderers	A	5-0
17.10.1955	Leyton Orient (Jack Edwards and Roy Bailey Benefit)	H	2-2
7.11.1955	England Amateur XI	H	3-0
21.11.1955	West Ham United	H	2-1
10.12.1955	Gillingham	A	1-2
8.2.1956	Army XI	H	1-2
20.2.1956	Croydon Professional XI	H	7-2
9.4.1956	Walthamstow Avenue	H	3-2
16.4.1956	Fulham	H	3-3
5.5.1956	All Star XI	H	5-6
8.10.1956	Army XI	H	3-3
15.10.1956	Leyton Orient	H	2-0
29.10.1956	All Star XI	H	2-7
18.3.1957	Walthamstow Avenue	H	2-1
8.4.1957	Clyde	H	3-4
15.4.1957	Fulham	H	1-2
29.4.1957	Kingstonian	A	1-3
4.5.1957	International Managers XI	H	2-2
14.10.1957	Wycombe Wanderers	H	3-3
17.3.1958	England Amateur XI	H	1-0
28.4.1958	Walthamstow Avenue	H	4-0

1958-1969

Date	Opponents	Venue	Result
27.10.1958	Sutton United	H	6-1
6.4.1959	Everton	H	2-2
2.5.1959	Queens Park Rangers (Charlie Catlett Benefit)	H	2-1
14.10.1959	Caribbean XI	H	11-1
9.11.1959	Margate	A	6-1
23.11.1959	Sutton United	H	4-2
2.5.1960	Tottenham Hotspur	H	2-2
16.11.1960	Margate	A	6-2
15.3.1961	Ex-Palace XI (Roy Greenwood Benefit)	H	2-3
20.3.1961	Eastbourne United	A	3-1
4.4.1961	Bangu (Brazil)	H	0-2
9.8.1961	Reading	A	2-7
31.1.1962	Bratislava	H	3-2
18.4.1962	Real Madrid	H	3-4
30.4.1962	Bexleyheath & Welling (Terry Gill Benefit)	A	0-2
6.5.1962	Bermuda Football League (at Somerset, Bermuda)	A	6-0
8.5.1962	Bermuda FA (at Devonshire Recreation Field)	A	7-2
10.5.1962	Bermuda FA (at National Field)	A	7-3
13.5.1962	Toronto City (at Hamilton, Bermuda)	N	5-0
15.5.1962	West End Rovers (Bermuda)	A	11-2
8.8.1962	Reading	A	2-2
11.8.1962	Charlton Athletic	A	2-3
13.8.1962	Redhill	A	7-3
24.10.1962	Corinthian Casuals	H	5-2
3.12.1962	Chelmsford City (Benefit for Chelmsford trainer, A. Parry)	A	
(Match abandoned in the second half — score not known)			
2.3.1963	Gillingham	A	0-1
14.8.1963	Charlton Athletic (Ron Brett Testimonial Fund)	H	3-0
20.8.1963	Tottenham Hotspur (played behind closed doors)	A	6-2
24.2.1964	Poole Town	A	2-2
9.5.1964	Croydon Amateurs (Clubhouse opening)	A	4-0
15.5.1964	Italia Montreal (Canada)	A	1-0
17.5.1964	Hamilton Steelers (Canada)	A	7-0
19.5.1964	Bermuda FA XI	A	3-0
c22.5.1964	Bermuda XI	A	8-1
c24.5.1964	Bermuda XI	A	6-1
c27.5.1964	Bermuda XI	A	4-0
8.8.1964	Dover	A	2-0
19.8.1964	West Ham United (Inaugural match at the Crystal Palace Recreation Centre)	N	4-1
14.8.1965	West Ham United (at CPRC)	N	1-2
4.3.1966	Nottingham Forest	H	4-1
30.3.1966	Alkmaar (Holland)	H	1-0
12.5.1966	Stoke City	H	4-0
17.5.1966	Aberdeen	H	1-0
6.8.1966	DOS Utrecht	A	1-0
7.8.1966	Alkmaar	A	2-0
9.8.1966	Feyenoord	A	1-3
11.10.1966	International XI (Terry Long Testimonial)	H	5-7
16.2.1967	Leicester City	H	1-1
21.2.1967	Slovan Bratislava	H	1-0
5.4.1967	Metz (France)	A	3-1
17.4.1967	Dundee United	H	1-1
1.8.1967	MVV Maastricht	A	0-2
3.8.1967	Go Ahead (Deventer)	A	0-3
6.8.1967	Feyenoord	A	1-1
11.8.1967	Burnley	H	2-3
15.11.1967	International XI (George Petchey Testimonial)	H	6-3
8.3.1968	Millwall	H	1-3
22.4.1968	Oxford United (Oxfordshire Benevolent Cup)	A	1-1
24.5.1968	Horley	A	9-3
29.7.1968	West Ham United (at CPRC)	N	2-4
31.7.1968	Chelsea	H	1-1
2.5.1969	Morton	H	0-0
6.5.1969	Swindon Town (Peter Hilton Testimonial)	A	5-3
8.5.1969	Swindon Town	H	2-1
14.5.1969	Benidorm	A	4-2
21.5.1969	Aruella (Spain)	A	3-2
22.5.1969	Hercules (Alicante, Spain)	A	0-0

1969-1979

Date	Opponents	Venue	Result
28.7.1969	Chelsea (CPRC)	N	0-2

Date	*Opponents*	*Venue*	*Result*
30.7.1969	Asante Kotoko (Ghana)	H	3-1
2.8.1969	Morton	H	1-1
20.10.1969	Dallas Tornado	H	2-0
26.11.1969	International XI (Arthur Rowe Testimonial)	H	3-5
20.4.1970	Oxford United (Oxford Benevolent Cup)	A	1-0
7.5.1970	San Paulo (Spain) (Fisherman's Cup)	A	3-2
14.5.1970	Atletico Madrid XI	A	1-1
21.5.1970	Mahon (Minorca)	A	2-1
1.8.1970	St. Mirren	H	4-0
3.8.1970	Wrexham	A	1-1
5.8.1970	Paykaan (Iran)	H	8-1
7.8.1970	Arsenal CPRC)	N	0-2
23.9.1970	Croydon Amateurs (Floodlight opening)	A	5-1
19.1.1971	Israel National XI	A	0-0
12.2.1971	PSV Eindhoven	H	2-4
3.3.1971	A.D.O. (The Hague)	H	0-0
8.3.1971	First Tower United (Jersey)	A	2-1
10.5.1971	Gillingham (John Simpson Testimonial)	A	4-1
13.5.1971	Bruges (John Sewell Testimonial)	H	1-3
21.5.1971	Clyde	H	1-1
28.7.1971	Feyenoord	A	0-1
1.8.1971	A.D.O. (The Hague)	A	0-0
4.8.1971	PSV Eindhoven	A	3-2
6.8.1971	Maccabi Nathanya (Israel)	H	4-1
26.2.1972	Partick Thistle	H	2-0
2.5.1972	Oxford United (Oxford Benevolent Cup)	A	0-2
29.7.1972	Dundee United	H	3-1
30.7.1972	MVV Maastricht	A	0-1
5.8.1972	Dundee	A	4-1
24.10.1972	MVV Maastrict	H	2-1
8.11.1972	Persepolis (Tehran)	A	5-1
14.11.1972	Leningrad Zenit	H	1-1
5.12.1972	Lincoln City All Stars (Trevor Meath Testimonial)	A	1-3
9.1.1973	Aberdeen	A	0-2
22.7.1973	Sirius (Sweden) (Juli Cup)	A	1-1
c25.7.1973	Sandvikens (Sweden) (Juli Cup)	A	1-1
29.7.1973	Vasterhaninge (Sweden) (Juli Cup Final)	A	3-2
30.7.1973	'A top Swedish 2nd Division side'	A	1-0
11.8.1973	Brighton	A	1-2
15.8.1973	Charlton Athletic	A	1-0
18.8.1973	Southampton	A	1-2
11.12.1973	Chelsea (John Jackson Testimonial)	H	1-3
26.1.1974	Gillingham	A	1-0
3.5. 1974	Queens Park Rangers (Ron Hunt Testimonial)	A	1-2
21.7.1974	IF Helsingborg	A	1-1
23.7.1974	IF Saab	A	2-1
25.7.1974	IFK Norrkoping	A	2-2
6.8.1974	Maidstone United	A	0-1
10.8.1974	Wimbledon	A	0-1
12.8.1974	Millwall	A	1-1
3.9.1974	Queens Park Rangers (John McCormick Testimonial)	H	1-1
14.10.1974	Camberley (Floodlight opening)	A	1-1
2.8.1975	Charlton Athletic (Kent County Challenge Cup)	H	0-1
5.8.1975	Gillingham (KCCC)	A	1-1
9.8.1975	Millwall (KCCC)	A	1-1
11.8.1975	Epsom and Ewell	H	3-0
7.5.1976	Chelsea (Marvin Hinton Testimonial)	A	2-2
24.7.1976	Alemmannia Aachen	A	2-3
28.7.1976	S.C.Heracles Almelo	A	2-0
30.7.1976	Rijnsurgrse Boys	A	6-0
1.8.1976	Wageningen	A	2-1
7.8.1976	AFC Bournemouth	A	2-1
9.8.1976	Orient	H	3-1

Date	*Opponents*	*Venue*	*Result*
18.7.1977	Jersey Under 23 XI	A	2-0
21.7.1977	Jersey XI	A	9-3
30.7.1977	Derby County	H	0-2
6.8.1977	Gillingham	A	1-1
10.8.1977	Wolverhampton Wanderers	H	1-2
6.9.1977	Wimbledon (Ian Cooke Testimonial)	A	1-2
20.9.1977	Surrey County FA (Surrey FA Centenary)	H	1-0
18.2.1978	Hibernian	H	0-1
c20.5.1978	Corfu Select XI	A	3-1
c22.5.1978	Corfu Select XI	A	2-0
25.7.1978	Sandviken (Sweden)	A	3-0
27.7.1978	IK Brage Borlange (Sweden)	A	3-1
31.7.1978	Brommapofkarna (Sweden)	A	4-0
3.8.1978	IK Siraeus (Sweden)	A	1-0
8.8.1978	Wimbledon	A	5-0
12.8.1978	Arsenal	A	1-1
13.11.1978	Wycombe Wanderers	A	2-0
12.12.1978	Chelsea (Charlie Cooke Testimonial)	A	0-2
22.5.1979	Memphis Rogues	A	3-1
23.5.1979	Fort Lauderdale Strikers	A	2-0
1979-1989			
24.7.1979	Storm FK (Norway)	A	1-0
26.7.1979	FK Ørn (Norway)	A	1-1
28.7.1979	FK Jerv (Norway)	A	3-0
31.7.1979	Viking FA (Norway)	A	1-0
2.8.1979	Lillestrom (Norway)	A	2-1
7.8.1979	Wimbledon	A	1-0
11.8.1979	Chelsea	H	5-0
16.2.1980	Notts County	H	2-2
15.4.1980	Tottenham Hotspur (Martin Hinshelwood Testimonial)	H	2-3
29.4.1980	Tottenham Hotspur (Terry Naylor Testimonial)	A	2-0
5.5.1980	Chelsea (George Graham Testimonial)	A	3-1
7.5.1980	Charlton Athletic (Phil Warman Testimonial)	A	0-2
15.5.1980	Wimbledon (at Mitcham)	H	2-6
25.5.1980	Malaga	A	0-2
23.7.1980	Ornskoldsvik (Sweden)	A	5-0
25.7.1980	IKK Stromsund (Sweden)	A	3-0
27.7.1980	Kramfers-Allienson (Sweden)	A	4-0
30.7.1980	Edsbyn (Sweden)	A	8-0
2.8.1980	Oxford United	A	4-1
5.8.1980	Wimbledon	A	3-0
9.8.1980	Luton Town	A	1-2
25.11.1980	Vince Hilaire's XI (Jim Cannon Testimonial)	H	5-3
23.3.1981	Minnesota Kicks	H	1-1
3.8.1981	Milton Keynes	A	1-0
7.8.1981	Maidstone United	A	2-1
13.8.1981	Fulham (at Mitcham)	H	1-0
18.8.1981	Bristol City	A	0-1
21.8.1981	Birmingham City	H	1-0
(Match abandoned after 66 minutes because of floodlight failure)			
14.11.1981	Brighton & Hove Albion	H	1-1
30.12.1981	Folkestone	A	5-0
24.2.1982	IFK Gothenburg	H	1-3
30.7.1982	Combined Flensburg XI (Germany)	A	4-3
31.7.1982	SV Larup (Hamburg)	A	1-3
1.8.1982	SV Bornsen (Germany)	A	4-2
7.8. 1982	Brighton & Hove Albion	H	1-0
4.8.1983	Gravelines	A	5-1
6.8.1983	Calais	A	2-0
(Match abandoned after 88 minutes because of crowd disturbances)			
9.8.1983	Japan National XI	H	1-2
13.8.1983	Southampton	H	1-1
16.8.1983	Queens Park Rangers	H	1-2
20.8.1983	Wimbledon	A	2-0
30.4.1984	Queens Park Rangers (Paul Hinshelwood Testimonial)	H	4-1
31.7.1984	Aylesbury	A	0-0
7.8.1984	Wealdstone	A	0-2

Date	*Opponents*	*Venue*	*Result*
10.8.1984	Southend United	A	0-2
14.8.1984	Torquay United	A	2-1
15.8.1984	Plymouth Argyle	A	0-0
17.8.1984	Exeter City	A	1-1
20.8.1984	Hapoel (Tel Aviv)	H	3-0
26.1.1985	West Ham United	H	1-2
23.7.1985	Aldershot	A	1-1
27.7.1985	Luton Town	H	0-0
(Restricted admission and match played in three half-hour sessions)			
31.7.1985	Coventry City	H	1-1
3.8 1985	Chelsea	H	0-1
6.8.1985	West Ham United	H	2-1
9.8.1985	Torquay United	A	1-1
12.8.1985	Southend United	A	1-1
3.2.1985	Qatar Under 21 XI	A	0-0
28.7.1986	Northampton Town (played behind closed doors)	A	2-5
30.7.1986	Newcastle Town	A	1-0
2.8.1986	Southend United	A	0-1
6.8.1986	Aldershot	A	2-2
9.8.1986	AFC Bournemouth	H	3-0
16.8.1986	Chelsea	H	2-1
18.8.1986	Fulham	A	4-1
21.1.1987	Swansea City	A	3-1
24.2.1987	Worthing (Grandstand Appeal Fund)	A	2-2
18.7.1987	Northampton Town (at Mitcham)	H	2-0
(Match played in three half-hour sessions)			
26.7.1987	ISK Grangesberg (Sweden)	A	5-0
28.7.1987	Smedjebackens (Sweden)	A	3-0
29.7.1987	Frovi IK (Sweden)	A	8-0
c1.8.1987	Rossons IF (Sweden)	A	6-1
c.2.8.1987	Lycksele IF (Sweden)	A	8-0
c.4.8.1987	Sodertalje (Sweden)	A	1-0
9.8.1987	Watford (Len Chatterton Testimonial)	H	1-2
3.2.1988	Gillingham	A	1-1
2.3.1988	Tottenham Hotspur (played behind closed doors)	H	1-0
8.3.1988	Aldershot (played behind closed doors)	A	2-0
23.3.1988	Gillingham (played behind closed doors)	A	3-2
19.4.1988	Egham Town (25th Anniversary)	A	6-1
26.4.1988	Tottenham Hotspur (Jim Cannon Testimonial)	H	3-3
25.7.1988	FK Mjolner (Norway)	A	1-3
27.7.1988	Kemin Pallaseura (Finland)	A	5-1
28.7.1988	Hemingsmarks IF (Sweden)	A	2-1
30.7.1988	Gallivare SK (Sweden)	A	4-1
2.8.1988	Lulia FF — IFK (Sweden)	A	4-0
3.8.1988	Vasterhaninge (Sweden)	A	9-0
9.8.1988	Carshalton Athletic	A	4-0
13.8.1988	Millwall	A	1-0
16.8.1988	Crewe Alexandra	A	2-1
20.8.1988	Fulham	A	2-0
23.8.1988	Tel Aviv (behind closed doors)	H	1-0
26.8.1988	Tottenham Hotspur XI (at Mitcham)	H	2-0
17.2.1989	Southend United	A	2-2

1989-1995

Date	*Opponents*	*Venue*	*Result*
23.7.1989	IF Norvella (Sweden)	A	3-1
25.7.1989	Billesholms GIF	A	7-2
27.7.1989	Verderslov Danningelanda (Sweden)	A	5-1
29.7.1989	Virserums SGF (Sweden)	A	7-1
31.7.1989	Skera IF (Sweden)	A	7-1
1.8.1989	Sodra Vings IF (Sweden)	A	2-0
5.8.1989	Farnborough Town	A	2-1
8.8.1989	Aldershot	A	2-0
11.8.1989	Swansea City	A	4-1
13.8.1989	West Ham United (Alan Devonshire Testimonial)	A	1-3
30.8.1989	Derry City	A	4-2
20.5.1990	Caribbean XI (in Trinidad)	A	2-2
23.5.1990	Caribbean XI (at Port of Spain)	A	0-4
c27.5.1990	Caribbean XI (at Kingston, Jamaica)	A	2-0
23.7.1990	Hamrange GIF (Sweden)	A	6-0
24.7.1990	Vasby IK (Sweden)	A	5-0
26.7.1990	IF Sylvia (Sweden)	A	5-0
28.7.1990	Hallstammers Sk (Sweden)	A	8-1
30.7.1990	Nykverns Sk (Sweden)	A	6-0
31.7.1990	Alno IF (Sweden)	A	6-1
4.8.1990	Brentford (at Mitcham) (behind closed doors)	H	0-3
11.8.1990	Colchester United	A	1-0
14.8.1990	Hull City	A	2-2
17.8.1990	Bristol City	A	1-1
20.8.1990	Fiorentina (Baretti Tournament) (played at St. Vincent, N. Italy)	A	1-2
22.8.1990	Sampdoria (Baretti Tournament) (won 5-4 on penalties)	A	1-1
22.7.1991	Smigen (Sweden)	A	8-1
24.7.1991	Landskrona (Sweden)	A	3-1
25.7.1991	Benkeryd (Sweden)	A	8-0
27.7.1991	Molnlycke (Sweden)	A	4-0
29.7.1991	Sandesjord (Sweden)	A	1-1
30.7.1991	Fredriksted (Sweden)	A	2-2
1.8.1991	Carshalton Athletic	A	6-1
3.8.1991	Fulham	A	2-3
5.8.1991	AEK Athens (Coste Verde Tournament, Gijon, Spain)	N	2-2
13.8.1991	Levski Spartak (Bulgaria — Coste Verde Tournament)	N	3-1
14.8.1991	Sporting Gijon (Coste Verde Tournament)	A	2-2
20.8.1991	Millwall (Nicky Coleman, Sean Sparham Testimonial)	A	5-3
28.4.1992	Glenn Hoddle All Star XI (Dave Madden Testimonial at Maidstone)	A	4-2
18.7.1992	Kaiser Chiefs (Johannesburg)	A	3-2
19.7.1992	Orlando Pirates (Durban)	A	1-2
26.7.1992	Horred (Sweden)	A	1-0
28.7.1992	Karlskrona (Sweden)	A	1-0
29.7.1992	Oskarsham (Sweden)	A	7-2
30.7.1992	Benkeryd (Sweden)	A	11-2
1.8.1992	Malilla (Sweden)	A	5-0
7.8.1992	Brighton & Hove Albion (Gary Chivers Testimonial)	A	1-0
10.8.1992	Leyton Orient	A	3-1
28.8.1993	Tottenham Hotspur (Malcolm Allison Testimonial)	H	3-3
26.4.1993	Yeovil Town	A	2-4
27.7.1993	Crawley Town	A	7-1
31.7.1993	Brentford	A	3-1
3.8.1993	Brighton & Hove Albion	A	3-0
7.8.1993	Fulham	A	5-0
13.11.1993	Guernsey XI	A	8-0
26.1.1994	Derry City	A	2-1
17.5.1994	Gibraltar Select XI	A	1-0
19.5.1994	Marbella (Spain)	A	0-2
21.5.1994	Malaga (Spain)	A	1-0
30.7.1994	Carshalton Athletic (Jon Warden Testimonial)	A	5-0
2.8.1994	Charlton Athletic	A	1-0
6.8.1994	Fulham	A	3-0
13.8.1994	Arsenal (Tony Adams Testimonial)	A	3-1
25.4.1991	Gibraltar FA XI	A	2-2
8.5.1991	Brittannia FC (Ramsgate) (Charity match)	A	6-2
13.5.1991	West Ham United (Paul Hilton Testimonial)	A	2-3
15.7.1991	Crawley Town	A	6-0

Appearances and Goalscorers

KEY: † denotes goalkeeper
(L) after dates denotes player on loan
Italic type denotes current player at end of 1994-95

Name	Seasons Played	SL	Gls	FL	Gls	FAC	Gls	FLC & other Cups	Gls	Total	Gls
Addinall, Bert	1954-55			12	2					12	2
Alderson, Jack†	1919-24	42		150		13				205	
Allen, Clive	1980-81			25	9			4	2	29	11
James	1921-24			16						16	
Ronnie	1961-65			100	34	7	3	2		109	37
Anderson, Ben	1973-74			11	1	1				12	1
John 'Bob'†	1951-53			38						38	
Andrews, Cecil "Archie"	1952-56			104	12	1				105	12
Armstrong, Chris	*1992-*			*118*	*46*	*8*	*5*	*10*	*7*	*136*	*58*
Astley, Horace	1905-07	32	12			14	4			46	16
Aylott, Trevor	1984-86			50+3	12	2	1	5+1	1	61	14
Ayres, Ken	1974-75			3+3						6	1
Bailey, Dennis	1987-88			0+5	1					5	1
Roy†	1949-56			118		1				119	
Baker, Robert	1907-08	4								4	
Balding, Henry†	1907-09	7								7	
Banfield, Neil	1980-81			2+1						3	
Bannister, Jack	1965-69			117+3	7	3		6		129	7
Barber, Tom	1919-20	19	7			1				20	7
Phil	1983-91			211+27	35	14	1	28+8	5	288	41
Barker, H.	1908-09	6	1							6	1
Barnes, Andy	1991-92			0+1						1	
Howard	1934-35			1						1	
Victor	1926-28			4	1	2				6	1
Barnett, Tom	1958-61			14	2			1		15	2
Barrie, George	1929-34			77		3				80	
Barron, Paul†	1980-83			90		5		13		108	
Barry, Roy	1973-75			41+1	1	1		2		45	1
Bartram, Per	1969-70			8+2	2			1+1	1	12	3
Bason, Brian	1980-82			25+2				4		31	
Bassett, Bill	1945-49			70		4				74	
Bateman, Ben	1913-24	75	4	97	6	8	1			180	11
Bates, Phil	1919-21	25	1	40	2	3				68	3
Bauchop, James	1907-09	43	23			4	3			47	26
Baxter, Paul	1981-82			1						1	
Beech, Daniel†	1911-13	4								4	
Belcher, Jimmy	1954-58			127	22	10				137	22
Bell, Bobby	1971-74			31		4		1		36	
Bennett, Ken	1953-54			17	2					17	2
Ron	1951-53			27	5					27	5
Beresford, Frank	1936-37			3						3	
Reg	1948-49			7	1					7	1
Berry, Peter	1953-58			151	27	10	1			161	28
William	1932-33			17	4					17	4
Besagni, Remo	1952-53			2						2	
Betteridge, Walter	1928-29			1						1	
Bigg, Bob	1934-39			109	41	5				114	41
Birch, Billy	1963-65			6				1		7	
Birchenall, Alan	1970-72			41	11	2	1	5	2	48	14
Birnie, Ted	1905-06	22	2			7	1			29	3
Birtley, Bob	1935-39			65	15	4	1			69	16
Blackman, Jack	1935-39			99	52	7	3			106	55
Blackshaw, Bill	1949-51			32	5					32	5
Blake, William	1924-26			34						34	
Blakemore, Cecil	1922-27			133	54	8	2			141	56
Blore, Vincent†	1936-38			33		2				35	
Blyth, Mel	(1968-75, 1977-78 (L))			219+3	9	12+1	1	19	2	254	12
Bodin, Paul	1990-92			8+1				1		10	
Booth, Samuel	1935-38			25		4				29	
Bostock, Ben	1948-49			4						4	
Boulter, David	1981-82			16		5		1		22	
Bourne, Jeff	1976-78			32	10	1		4		37	10
W. J.	1911-13	9	4							9	4
Bowler, James	1914-15	1				1				2	
Bowry, Bobby	*1992-*			*36+14*	*1*	*1*		*10*		*61*	*1*
Boyd, A.†	1911-12	1								1	
Boyle, Terry	1977-81			24+2	1	2	1			28	2
Bradley, C. E.	1909-15	4								4	
Brearley, John	1907-09	70	3			7				77	3
Brennan, Steve	1976-78			2+1	1			0+1		4	1
Thomas	1930-31			2						2	
Brett, Ron	(1955-59, 1961-62)			44	13	5				49	13
Briggs, Harry	1948-55			150	4	7				157	4
Bright, John	1913-14	18	9			2				20	9
Mark	1986-93			228+3	92	13+1	2	41	19	286	113
Brooks, Johnny	1963-64			7						7	
Shaun	1979-84			47+7	4	5		5+2	1	66	5
Brophy, Hugh	1966-67			0+1						1	
Broughton, Ted	1948-53			96	6	4				100	6
Brown, Ally	1982-83			11	2					11	2
Bert	1957-58			3						3	
Charles	1932-34			29						29	
John	1927-28			8	2					8	2
Tom	1934-35			4						4	
Brush, Paul	1985-88			50	3	1		5		56	3
Bryden, W.	1905-06	1								1	
Buckley, Frank	1947-51			69		4				73	
Bulcock, Joe	1909-14	137	2			9				146	2
Bumstead, Charlie†	1948-52			53		2				55	
Burgess, Cam	1951-53			47	40	3				50	40
Burke, David	1987-90			84+1		3		9		97	
Burns, Tony†	1974-78			90		2		6		98	
Burnside, David	1964-67			54+4	8	5	2	1		64	10
Burrell, Lester	1945-48			19	5					19	5
Burridge, John†	1977-80			88		7		7		102	
Peter	1962-66			114	42	6	3	4	4	124	49
Butler, Hubert	1928-32			108	31	16	8			124	39
Byrne, Johnny	(1956-62, 1966-68)			239	90	18	11	2		259	101
Callender, Billy†	1923-32			203		22				225	
Cannon, Jim	1972-88			568+3	30	42	1	46+1	4	660	35
Carson, James	1934-36			52	17	2				54	17
Carter, Les	1980-81			1+1						2	
Cartwright, Joe	1921-23			19	4	2				21	4
John	1961-63			11	1	1				12	1
Caswell, Peter†	1976-78			3						3	
Charlesworth, George	1928-32			21	8					21	8
Charlton, Stan	1928-32			121	7	14	2			135	9
Chase, Charlie	1948-50			55	2	2				57	2
Chatterton, Nicky	1973-79			142+9	31	15	2	15	3	181	36
Cherrett, Percy	1925-27			75	58	6	7			81	65
Chesters, Arthur†	1937-39			78		7				85	
Chilvers, Geoff	1948-54			118	1	5				123	1
Choules, Len	1952-62			258	2	21	1	1		280	3
Clark, Charles	1909-10	31				1				32	
Clarke, George	1925-33			274	99	25	7			299	106
Wally	1933-34			16		4				20	
Clelland, David	1949-50			2						2	
Clifford, John	1931-33			12						12	
Clough, Jimmy	1947-49			67	12	4	1			71	13
Coates, John	1946-47			4						4	
Colclough, Horace	1912-15	81				4				85	
Coleman, Chris	*1991-*			*126+11*	*13*	*8*	*1*	*22+2*	*2*	*169*	*16*
Colfar, Roy	1958-61			41	6	3				44	6
Collier, James	1920-21			1						1	
Collins, Edward	1908-10	25				3				28	
James	1910-15	50	2			1				51	2
Nick	1934-39			143	7	9				152	7
Tony	1957-59			55	14	6	2			61	16
Collyer, Harry	1906-15	263	1			18				281	1
Collymore, Stan	1990-93			4+16	1			2+3	1	25	2
Comrie, Malcolm	1935-36			2						2	

Name	Seasons Played	SL	Gls	FL	Gls	FAC	Gls	FLC & other Cups	Gls	Total	Gls
Conaty, Thomas	1928-29			3						3	
Conner, John	1919-23	37	18	61	37	6	2			104	57
Cook, Micky	1967-68			1						1	
Cooke, Charlie	1972-74			42+2		3+1	1	0+1		49	1
Cooper, George	1954-59			69	27	5	1			74	28
Corbett, John	1946-47			1	1					1	1
Cotton, Fred	1956-57			4						4	
Coulston, Wally	1936-37			12	1					12	1
Coyle, Terrance	1925-27			29	2	4				33	2
Cox, Ian	*1994-*			*1+10*		*1+1*				*13*	
Cracknell, Dick	(1919-20 1923-26)	33	1	47		8				88	1
Craven, John	1971-73			56+7	14	5+1	1	3	1	72	16
Crilly, Tom	1928-33			116	1	10				126	1
Crompton, Arthur	1933-35			26	6					26	6
Cropper, Reg	1931-32			3	1					3	1
Cross, Charlie	1922-28			221		16				237	
Cubberley, Stan	1905-06	1								1	
Cummins, Stan	1983-85			27+1	7			6	1	34	8
Cushlow, Dick	1950-52			28						28	
Cutler, Paul	1964-66			10	1			1		11	1
Daniels, George	1937-39			7						7	
Dare, Kevin	1980-82			6				1		7	
Davidson, Alex	1948-49			11	2					11	2
Davies, W. C. "Bill"	1907-15	194	20			14	3			208	23
Wyn	1974-75 (L)			3						3	
Davis, Arthur	1928-29			5	2					5	2
Harold	1937-39			26	4	3	1			29	5
Dawes, Albert	(1933-36 1937-39)			149	91	7	1			156	92
Fred	1935-49			222	2	15				237	2
Dawkins, Trevor	1967-71			24+1	3	2+2		3		32	3
Deakin, Fred	1946-48			6						6	
Mike	1954-60			143	56	9	7			152	63
Delaney, Louis	1949-50			3						3	
Dennis, Mark	1989-91			8+1				1		10	
Devonshire, Les	1951-55			83	12	4				87	12
Dick, J.	1905-06	1								1	
Dodge, Bill	1962-63			3						3	
Doncaster, Richard	1932-33			15	4					15	4
Douglas, Edward	1922-23			2	1					2	1
Dowie, Iain	*1994-*			*15*	*4*	*6*	*4*			*21*	*8*
Downs, Ronnie	1952-54			23	2					23	2
Dowsett, Gilbert "Dickie"	1962-65			54	22			2		56	22
Dreyer, Henry	1921-23			55	2	3				58	2
Droy, Micky	1984-87			49	7	1		8		58	7
Dunn, Ronnie†	1931-36			167		8				175	
Dunsire, Andrew	1928-30			5	1					5	1
Duthie, John	1929-30			13	3					13	3
Dyer, Alex	1988-90			16+1	2	1+1		6+2	3	27	5
Bruce	*1993-*			*9+18*	*1*	*1+2*		*1+2*	*1*	*33*	*2*
Dyson, Barry	1966-68			33+1	9	1				35	9
Earle, James	1933-34			10	3	1				11	3
Eastman, Don	1946-47			1						1	
Easton, Harry	1959-62			8	1	1				9	1
Edwards, Ian	1982-83			16+2	4	3	1	4	2	25	7
J.	1906-07	1								1	
Jack	1949-59			223		16				239	
Leslie	1933-36			23	2	1				24	2
Matthew	1905-08	57	4			14				71	4
Elwiss, Mike	1978-79			19+1	7			4		24	7
Evans, Fred	1950-53			52	11	1				53	11
Gwyn	1958-63			80		8		1		89	
Ian	1974-78			137	14	16	2	10		163	16
Tony	1983-84			19+2	7	0+1		1		23	7
Farrell, Ray	1957-59			5						5	
Farrington, Roy	1947-49			3		1	1			4	1
Fashanu, John	1983-84 (L)			1				1		2	
Feebury, Albert	1914-24	66	1	92	7	6				164	8
Fell, Les	1952-54			65	6	4	2			69	8
Felton, Robert	1946-47			1						1	
Vivien	1954-56			2						2	
Fenwick, Terry	1977-81			62+8		7	2	4+1		82	2
Fielding, Horace	1936-38			22	1					22	1
Finn, Arthur	1933-34			9						9	
Finnigan, Tony	1984-88			94+11	10	2+1		9+1		118	10
Fishlock, Laurie	1929-32			18	2	1				19	2
Flanagan, Mike	1979-81			56	8	1		7	5	64	13

Name	Seasons Played	SL	Gls	FL	Gls	FAC	Gls	FLC & other Cups	Gls	Total	Gls
Fletcher, Charlie	1928-29			7						7	
Flood, Joe	1926-28			34	5	5				39	5
Forgan, Thomas	1909-10	1								1	
Forster, Bill	1906-08	50				11				61	
Stan	1962-64			2	1			1		3	1
Forward, Fred	1921-24			6						6	
Foulds, Albert	1953-54			17	4	1				18	4
Francis, Gerry	1979-81			59	7	1		6	2	66	9
Freeman, Alf	1948-49			2						2	
Frost, Jack	1930-31			4	2					4	2
Fry, Bob†	1955-56			6						6	
David†	1977-83			40		5				45	
Fuller, Bill	1962-65			3				1		4	
Gabbiadini, Marco	1991-92			15	5	1		9	2	25	7
Gaillard, Marcel	1947-50			21	3					21	3
Gallagher, Hugh	1926-28			35		2				37	
Galliers, Steve	1981-82			8+5						13	
Galloway, Steve	1984-86			3+2	1			0+1		6	1
Garratt, George	1908-13	173	7			12	1			185	8
Gavin, Johnny	1959-61			66	15	2	2			68	17
Gennoe, Terry†	1980-81(L)			3						3	
George, Ron	1948-54			123	2	3				126	2
Gibson, Robert	1909-10	2								2	
Gilbert, Billy	1977-84			235+2	3	17	1	19		273	4
Giles, David	1981-84			83+5	6	5+1		5+1		100	6
Gill, James	1928-29			10	3					10	3
Gillespie, Ian	1936-46			21	4	6	1			27	5
Girling, Howard	1946-47			26	6	1				27	6
Glazier, Bill†	1961-65			106		5		2		113	
Glover, F.†	1910-11	1								1	
Goddard, Charles	1932-36			24	8					24	8
Goldthorpe, Bobby	1971-72			1						1	
Goodchild, Gary	1979-81			0+2		0+2				4	
Goodcliffe, William	1932-36			2	1					2	1
Goodhind, George	1910-11	1								1	
Goodwin, Sam	1971-72			18+7				2		27	
Gordon, Dean	*1991-*			*85+15*	*7*	*6+1*	*1*	*12+4*	*2*	*123*	*10*
Graham, Dick†	1945-51			155		9				164	
Graham, George	1976-78			43+1	2	3	1	4	1	51	4
Grainger, John	1919-20	1								1	
Grant, A.	1905-06	15				2				17	
Walter	1926-28			21	5					21	5
Gray, Andy	(1984-88 1989-92)			178+10	39	14	2	38+2	10	242	51
Green, Albert	1919-20	9	3							9	3
Greener, Bobby	1921-32			293	5	24	1			317	6
Greenwood, Alex	1954-55			2						2	
Roy	1954-59			111		5				116	
Gregory, Fred	1937-46			43	9	3				46	9
Grieve, David	1954-55			22	3					22	3
Griffin, Michael	1909-10	34	2			1				35	2
Griffiths, Lewis	1928-30			36	20	6	3			42	23
Grimshaw, Colin	1952-53			32	3	3				35	3
Groves, Fred	1924-26			14	2	1	1			15	3
Gunning, Harry	1954-57			62	4	2				64	4
Guthrie, Jimmy	1946-47			5						5	
Hall, William†	1907-08	10								10	
Hallam, Charles	1927-28			2	2					2	2
Hamilton, James	1923-31			180	4	16	1			196	5
Hammond, Paul†	1972-77			117		17		8		142	
Hampton, Colin†	1925-26			3						3	
Hancox, Ray	1950-53			20	3					20	3
Hand, William	1920-26			101	15	9	1			110	16
Handley, George	1934-35			5						5	
Hanger, Harry	1909-15	167	6			10	1			177	7
Hanlon, Wally	1949-55			126	8	4	1			130	9
Hann, Ralph	1946-47			1						1	
Hanson, Fred	1935-36			1						1	
Harding, Ted	1946-54			151		5				156	
Hardwick, Steve†	1985-86 (L)			3						3	
Harker, Richard	(1905-07 1911-12)	66	19			17	9			83	28
Harkouk, Rachid	1976-78			51+3	20	1+3	2	4+1	3	63	25
Harper, Bill†	1924-26			57		2				59	
Harris, Mark	1988-89			0+2						2	
Harrison, Bernard	1955-59			92	12	8				100	12
Harry, Albert	1921-34			410	53	30	2			440	55
Hatton, Albert	1910-12	43				2				45	
Havelock, Harry	1927-31			67	39	9	4			76	43

Name	Seasons Played	SL	Gls	FL	Gls	FAC	Gls	FLC & other Cups	Gls	Total	Gls
Hawkins, Alf	1925-27			20	8	2	1			22	9
Haynes, Alfred	1933-36			48	1	3				51	1
Hayward, Jack	1933-34			19	1	1				20	1
Haywood, Adam	1908-09	9	2							9	2
Hazell, Tony	1978-79			5						5	
Hearn, Frank	1954-55			8	1					8	1
Heckman, Ron	1960-63			84	25	6	4	3		93	29
Hedley, Ralph	1924-26			4						4	
Hedman, Rudi	1988-92			13+11				1+1		26	
Heineman, George	1934-35			25		1				26	
Henwood, A.	1905-06	1								1	
Heppolette, Ricky	1976-77			13+2		3				18	
Herbert, Trevor	1950-51			8	2					8	2
Hewitson, Bob†	1905-07	60		15						75	
Hewitt, Charles	1910-15	151	39			11	2			162	41
Higginbottom, Andy	1985-87			16+7	2	0+2		5		30	2
Higgins, Fred	1952-54			11						11	
H.	1907-09	2								2	
Hilaire, Vince	1976-84			239+16	29	16+1	3	21	4	293	36
Hill, Mick	1973-76			43+2	6	1		3		49	6
Hilley, Cornelius	1926-28			43	4	2				45	4
Hinshelwood, Martin	1972-78			66+3	4	7		6		82	4
Paul	1973-83			271+5	22	26	4	17	2	319	28
Hoadley, Phil	1967-72			63+10	1	2+4		9	1	88	2
Hoddinott, Tom	1923-26			79	20	10	2			89	22
Hodges, Glyn	1990-91			5+2				2+2	1	11	1
Hodgkinson, Albert	1906-07	5	1							5	1
Holder, Phil	1974-78			93+2	5	11	1	4+2		112	6
Holmes, Eddie	1927-28			17		3				20	
Holsgrove, John	1964-65			18	2	4				22	2
Holton, Cliff	1962-65			101	40	6	8	5	1	112	49
Hone, Mark	1987-89			4				3+1		8	
Hooper, Alf	1914-15	18	2							18	2
Hopgood, Ron†	1957-60			14		2				16	
Hopkins, Henry	1926-28			40	14	3	3			43	17
Idris	1932-33			4						4	
Jeff	1988-90			74	2	4	1	15	1	93	4
Horobin, Roy	1964-65			4		3				7	
Horton, Jack	1937-39			38	7	3				41	7
Houghton, Ray	*1994-*			*10*	*2*	*2*				*12*	*2*
Howard, Terry	1985-86 (L)			4						4	
Howe, Bert	1958-67			192+1		12	1	7		212	1
Harold	1933-34			2						2	
Howells, Ray	1946-50			25	5	1				26	5
Hoy, Roger	1968-70			54	6	4	1	4		62	7
Hudgell, Arthur	1945-47			25	1	4				29	1
Hughes, Jimmy	1909-20	200	15			9				209	15
John	1971-73			20	4	3				23	4
Ken†	1985-86							1		1	
Stephen "Billy"	1981-82			3+4				2		9	
William†	1950-52			18						18	
Hughton, Henry	1982-86			113+5	1	6		12+1		137	1
Hullock, James	1908-10	7								7	
Humphrey, John	*1990-*			*153+7*	*2*	*8+1*		*31+3*		*203*	*2*
Humphreys, Gerry	1970-71			4+7				1		12	
Humphries, C.	1910-11	1								1	
Hunt, Rev. Kenneth	1912-14 1919-20	16								16	
Michael†	1925-28			3		1				4	
Hunter, Herbert†	1906-07	2								2	
Hyatt, John	1954-55			1						1	
Hynd, Roger	1969-70			29+1		4		4		38	
Imlach, Stuart	1962-65 1966-67			51	3			3		54	3
Imrie, James†	1928-31			35		1				36	
Innerd, Wilf	1905-09	111	4			22	3			133	7
Irvine, Alan	1984-87			108+1	12	4	1	14	1	127	14
Irwin, George†	1921-23			17						17	
Isley, Arthur	1919-20	8								8	
Ivey, Lawrence	1927-28			1						1	
Jackson, Cliff	1966-70			100+6	26	5		8+1	4	120	30
J. B.	1906-07	7								7	
John†	1964-74			346		18		24		388	
James, Wilfred	1927-29			4	1					4	1
Jamieson, Harold	1929-30			4						4	
Jeffries, Derek	1973-76			107	1	9		6		122	1
Jenkins, Ross	1971-73			15	2			2		17	2
Jewett, George	1931-32			1						1	

Name	Seasons Played	SL	Gls	FL	Gls	FAC	Gls	FLC & other Cups	Gls	Total	Gls
Johnson, Jeff	1973-76			82+5	4	5		5+1	1	98	5
Josh†	1907-15	276				19				295	
Joe	1922-25			29	6	2				31	6
Peter	1974-76			5+2						7	
Jones, Chris	1982-83			18	3	4				22	3
Edwin	1924-25			4						4	
Ivor	1946-47			1	1					1	1
J. T. "Tom"	1920-22			61	6	5				66	6
Ken	1960-61			4		1				5	
William	1950-51			17	3	1				18	3
Jordan, David	1937-39			7						7	
Jump, Stewart	1973-78			79+2	2	6+1		3		91	2
Keenan, Arnold	1925-26			4						4	
Keene, Percy	1912-15	15	3			2				17	3
Kellard, Bobby	1963-66 1971-73			121+2	10	7		7		137	10
Kelly, John†	1927-28			22		1				23	
Noel	1949-51			42	5	1	1			43	6
Kember, Steve	1965-72 1978-80			255+5	36	15	2	16		291	38
Kemp, David	1974-77			32+3	10	4	2	5	4	44	16
Kennedy, Andrew	1920-22			4		1				5	
Kerrins, Pat	1960-61			5				1		6	
Ketteridge, Steve	1985-87			58+1	6	3		8+1		71	6
Kevan, Derek	1965-66			21	5			1		22	5
Knox, Thomas†	1936-37			3						3	
Kurz, Fred	1945-51			148	49	6				154	49
Kyle, J.	1908-09	3								3	
Lacy, John	1983-84			24+3		1		2		30	
Lane, Harry	1914-15	16	5							16	5
John	1930-32			34	10					34	10
Langley, Tommy	1980-83			54+5	8	5+1	1	5+1	1	71	10
Launders, Brian	*1994-*			*1+1*				*0+1*		*3*	
Lawrence, Bill	1906-14	25	5		5	1				30	6
Lawson, Ian	1965-66			15+2	6					17	6
Lazarus, Mark	1967-70			63	17	3		4		70	17
Leahy, Steve	1980-82			3+1				3		7	
Ledger, Bill	1906-07	11				2				13	
Lee, Frank	1908-09	6	2							6	2
Legg, Harry	1930-31			1						1	
Levene, David	1935-37			22		1				23	
Lewis, Brian	1960-63			32	4			1		33	4
F.	1907-09	16				1				17	
Glyn	1945-48			60	4	6				66	4
Jack	1938-50			124	5	6				130	5
Liddle, James	1936-37			13	1	1				14	1
Lievesley, Les	1936-39			75	3	7				82	3
Light, Danny	1966-68			18+1	5	2		0+1		22	5
Lindsay, David	1983-86			18+3		1		2+1		25	
Mark	1973-75			27+3		1+1		4	1	36	1
Little, Jack	1919-26	42		200		19				261	
Roy	1961-63			38	1	3		2		43	1
Littlewort, Henry	1906-07	1								1	
Lloyd, Herbert	1912-13	3								3	
James	1930-32			14		2				16	
Locke, Gary	1982-86			84	1	9		8		101	1
Long, Terry	1955-69			432+10	16	30	1	8	1	480	18
Loughlan, John	1968-72			58+2		6		6+2		74	
Love, John	1974-75			1						1	
Lovell, Steve	1980-83			68+6	3	2+1	1	9+1	1	87	5
Lucas, Fred	1963-65			16		2		1		19	
Robert†	1946-47			4						4	
Lunnis, Roy	1959-63			25	1			2		27	1
Mabbutt, Kevin	1981-85			67+8	22	8		5	2	88	24
McBride, Andy	1973-74			1						1	
McCormick, James	1948-49			12	2					12	2
John	1966-73			194	6	10	1	21		225	7
McCracken, Roy	1920-26			175	1	15	1			190	2
McCulloch, Andy	1983-84			25	3	3	1	1		29	4
MacDonald, David†	1952-55			30		5				35	
McDonald, Gordon	1954-56			13		4				17	
Harry	1950-55			140	1	6				146	1
McGeachie, George	1951-52			46	5	1				47	5
McGibbon, Charles	1908-09	17	13							17	13
McGoldrick, Eddie	1988-93			143+8	12	5		30+3	5	189	17
McGregor, John	1932-33			4						4	
McKenna, John	1923-25			3						3	
McMenemy, Frank	1936-37			25	3	2				27	3

Name	Seasons Played	SL	Gls	FL	Gls	FAC	Gls	FLC & other Cups	Gls	Total	Gls
McNichol, Johnny	1957-63			189	15	15		1		205	15
Madden, Dave	1988-90			23+8	6	0+2				33	6
Mahoney, Tony	1984-85			17+1	4	2	1	2+2		24	5
Manders, Frank	1931-36			97	31	5	3			102	34
Marsden, Eric	1950-53			34	11					34	11
Martin, Neil	1975-76			8+1	1					9	1
Wayne	1983-84			1						1	
Martyn, Nigel†	*1989-*			*226*		*20*		*48*		*294*	
Massey, Stuart	1992-94			1+1				1		3	
Matthew, Damien	*1993-*			*13+3*	*1*	*1*		*1*		*18*	*1*
May, Harold	1931-34			31	11	1				32	11
Menlove, Bert	1919-22	12	5	48	12	5	3			65	20
Menzies, Harry	1906-07	4								4	
Michael, Arthur	1914-15	1								1	
Middlemiss, James	1924-25			1						1	
Middleton, William	1913-20	32	7			2	1			34	8
Millard, Bert	1922-24			34	4	1				35	4
Millbank, Joe	1946-48			38	1	3				41	1
Milligan, A. George	1920-21			2	1					2	1
Millington, Tony†	1964-66			16		3		1		20	
Mills, W.	1905-06	1								1	
Mitchell, Harry†	1910-11	1								1	
Moody, F.	1905-06	1	1							1	1
Moore, John	1925-26			1						1	
Moralee, Jamie	1991-92			2+4						6	
Morgan, Billy	1922-25			76	14	8	2			84	16
Ken	1955-56			1						1	
R.	1926-27			1						1	
Morris, Frank	1956-57			8						8	
Mortimer, Fredrick	1912-13	1								1	
Paul	1991-94			18+4	2	1		4		27	2
Morton, Keith	1953-54			5	3					5	3
Moss, Don	1953-57			56	2	2				58	2
Moult, Joseph "Jack"†	1909-10	1				1				2	
Moyle, Walter	1928-29			5	1					5	1
Moyse, Alex	1955-57			4	1					4	1
Mulcahy, Pat	1927-29			23	5					23	5
Mulheron, Peter	1948-50			38	2	2				40	2
Mullen, Jimmy	1948-49			11		1				12	
Mulligan, Paddy	1972-75			57+1	2	5		1		64	2
Murphy, Jerry	1976-85			214+15	20	17+1		22	5	269	25
Joe	1948-51			37						37	
John	1931-32			8	2	2				10	2
Murray, Jimmy	1955-58			37	13	1	1			38	14
Muxworthy, Graham	1957-58			2						2	
Mycock, Albert	1946-48			59	9	3				62	9
Myers, Ernest	1909-12	21	1			1				22	1
Nash, Edward†	1932-33			1						1	
Nastri, Carlo	1958-59			2						2	
Naylor, Bill	1946-47			18	9	1	2			19	11
(Changed surname from Bark to Naylor c1946)											
Ndah, George	*1992-*			*9+17*	*1*	*1+1*	*1*	*7+4*	*1*	*39*	*3*
Nebbeling, Gavin	1981-89			145+6	8	5		16+1		173	8
Needham, Archie	1905-09	103	24			19	2			122	26
Nelson, David	1951-53			12						12	
Newman, Ricky	*1992-*			*43+5*	*3*	*5+2*		*7*		*62*	*3*
Ron	1962-63			6		1				7	
Nicholas, George	1930-34			39						39	
Peter	(1977-81 1983-85)			174	14	11	1	14	1	199	16
Nicholson, George	1923-24			2						2	
Nixon, Joe	1921-27			29	1	2				31	2
Noakes, Alf	1955-62			195	14	14				209	14
Norris, Fred	1933-34			11	4	1				12	4
O'Connell, Brian	1966-67			20+1	2			1		22	2
O'Connor, Martyn	1993-94			2				1+1		4	
O'Conor, Eric	1911-13	10								10	
O'Doherty, Ken	1985-88			41+1		1		6+2	1	51	1
Oliver, Jimmy	1967-70			3						3	
O'Reilly, Gary	1986-90			66+5	2	7	2	5+2		85	4
Orr, Robert	1926-28			70	2	1				71	2
Osborne, Ernest	1923-26			30	3					30	3
Osborn, Simon	1990-94			47+8	4	2		12+3	1	72	5
Otulakowski, Anton	1986-87			12	1			2		14	1
Owens, Isaac	1907-08	22	8							22	8
Ted	1934-39			164		8	1			172	1
Page, David	1911-12	1								1	
Palethorpe, Jack	1936-38			39	11	5				44	11
Palmer	1905-06	1								1	
Pardew, Alan	1987-92			115+17	8	8	1	25+3	3	168	12
Parker, Edward	1933-34			2						2	
Parkin, Brian†	1988-90			20				5		25	
Parry, Oswald	1931-36			142		8				150	
Parsons, Frank†	1966-67			4						4	
Patterson, Darren	*1994-*			*22*	*1*	*6*		*4*		*32*	*1*
Paul, Tony	1980-81			0+1						1	
Payne, David	1964-73			281+3	9	16	1	18	2	318	12
George	1909-11	45	30			1	1			46	31
Pemberton, John	1987-90			80+2	2	8		14+1		105	2
Penn, Frank	1949-50			1						1	
Pennyfather, Glenn	1987-89			31+5	1	1		4		41	1
Perrin, Steve	1976-78			45+3	13	6		4	1	58	14
Petchey, George	1960-65			143	12	7		3		153	12
Pettitt, Harold	1924-26			2						2	
Philip, Iain	1972-74			35	1	4	1	1		40	2
Pierce, Barry	1955-59			85	23	8	4			93	27
Pinkney, Alan	1969-74			19+5		1		3+1		29	
Pitcher, Darren	*1994-*			*21+4*		*8*	*1*	*3*	*1*	*36*	*2*
Possee, Derek	1972-74			51+2	13	1+1		1		56	13
Potter, Ray†	1955-58			44		5				49	
Powell, Chris	1987-89			2+1				0+2		5	
Preece, Andy	*1994-*			*17+3*	*4*	*2+3*		*4+2*	*1*	*31*	*5*
Presland, Eddie	1966-69			61		3		1		65	
Price, David	1980-83			25+2	2	1+1	1	4+1		34	3
Ernest	1951-53			34	5	1				35	5
Priestly, Gerry	1958-60			28	2	7				35	2
Pritchard, Harvey	1937-38			30	6	5	2			35	8
Proudler, Arthur	1956-59			26	2					26	2
Provan, David	1970-71			1				1		2	
Purdon, James	1934-36			14	2					14	2
Pyke, Malcolm	1959-60			2						2	
Quayle, Charles	1936-38			10	3					10	3
Queen, Gerry	1969-73			101+7	24	7	1	11+1	5	127	30
Rainford, Johnny	1948-53			64	8	3	2			67	10
Randall, Ernie	1953-55			22	11	2	1			24	12
Ransom, Frank	1906-07	1								1	
Read, Tom†	1934-35			16						16	
Redfearn, Neil	1987-89			57	10	1		7		65	10
Redmond, Harold	1957-58			2		1				3	
Reece, Thomas	1938-48			76	5	5				81	5
Reed, George	1934-35			2						2	
Rees, William	1959-60			17	1	1				18	1
Reeve, Fred	1936-37			1						1	
Rhodes, Ernie	1913-23	47		89	1	6				142	1
Rivers, Walter	1929-33			81	2	8				89	2
Roberts, Charles	1932-34			47	18	3	1			50	19
Dickie	1905-09	82	20			17	5			99	25
Robertson, Peter†	1933-34			4						4	
Tom	1966-67			5						5	
Robson, Albert	1934-48			85	22	4	1			89	23
Roche, Johnny	1959-60			36	11	4	2			40	13
Rodger, Simon	*1991-*			*83+8*	*5*	*2+1*		*16+1*		*111*	*5*
Roffey, Bill	1972-74			24		1				25	
Rogers, Don	1972-75			69+1	28	5	2	2+1		78	30
Rooke, Ronnie	(1933-37 1949-51)			63	32	1				64	32
Ross, Alex	1948-51			33						33	
R.	1905-06	4	3			1				5	3
Rossiter, Abbott "Bud"	1933-34			24		3				27	
Rouse, Vic†	1956-63			238		17		2		257	
Rumbold, George	1935-36			5						5	
Rundle, Charles	1950-52			38	2	2				40	2
Russell, James	1946-48			43	6					43	6
Rutter, Brian	1954-55			3	1					3	1
Ryan, Charles	1906-09	82	2			12				94	2
***S**alako, John*	*1986-*			*172+43*	*23*	*20*	*4*	*30+8*	*7*	*273*	*34*
Salt, Harold	1927-29			42	1	2				44	1
Sanders, James	1955-59			46		4				50	
Sidney	1914-15	1								1	
Sans, Arthur	1906-07	2								2	
Sansom, Kenny	1974-80			172	3	11	1	14		197	4
Saunders, John	1954-56			59		2				61	
Saward, Len	1948-51			9	1					9	1
Scott, Jimmy	1969-72			36+7	5	2		5	1	50	6
Laurie	1951-53			28		2				30	
Sealy, Tony	1978-81			16+8	5	1		0+2		27	5

Name	Seasons Played	SL	Gls	FL	Gls	FAC	Gls	FLC & other Cups	Gls	Total	Gls
Sewell, John	1963-71			228+3	6	12	1	15	2	258	9
Sexton, Dave	1959-60			27	11	1	1			28	12
Shanks, Robert	1937-39			18						18	
Shaw, H.†	1914-15	6								6	
Richard	*1987-*			*178+14*	*3*	*18*		*36+3*		*249*	*3*
Stuart	1966-67					0+1				1	
Sherwood, Jack	1949-50			2						2	
Silkman, Barry	1976-79			40+8	6	5	1	1		54	7
Sille, Les	1948-49			3						3	
Simpson, Peter	1929-35			180	153	15	12			195	165
William	1952-55			38	13					38	13
Sinnott, Lee	1991-94			53+2		1		11+1		68	
Skingley, Brian	1958-59			11		1				12	
Smillie, Andy	1961-63			53	23	5	1	1	2	59	26
Neil	1976-82			71+12	7	7	1	7		97	8
Smith, Cyril	1919-20	7								7	
George	1907-08	9	2			2	1			11	3
George	1950-51			7						7	
Keith	1964-67			47+3	14	4	1	2		56	15
Lewis	1925-29			45	1	3	1			48	2
Ted	1911-22	155	109	25	11	12	4			192	124
Thomas	1932-33			9						9	
Trevor	1937-46			57	14	4				61	14
Wilf	1935-36			2						2	
William	1933-36			38	1	3				41	1
Smout, John†	1965-66			1						1	
Snowdon, Brian	1968-69			1+4						5	
Somerfield, Alf	1947-48			10	3	2				12	3
Southgate, Gareth	*1990-*			*148+4*	*15*	*9*		*29+1*	*7*	*191*	*22*
Sparrow, Brian	1984-87			62+1	2	2		7+1		73	2
Spottiswoode, Bob	1909-15	178	2			11				189	2
Stack, Bill	1965-66			2						2	
Stanbury, George H.†	1936-37			1						1	
Stebbing, Gary	1983-88			95+7	3	6		8+2		118	3
Steele, Ernest	1938-39			30	8	2				32	8
Stephenson, Alan	1961-68			170	13	8		7		185	13
Stevens, Les	1950-51			20	3	1				21	3
Stewart, Paul	1993-94 (L)			18	3					18	3
Stone, Edward	1961-62			1						1	
Storey, Thomas	1920-22			52	4					52	4
Strang, Dick	1924-26			24						24	
Strong, Les	1983-84			7						7	
Stubbs, Alf	1947-49			3						3	
Suckling, Perry†	1987-92			63		1		7		71	
Sullivan, Neil†	1991-92 (L)			1						1	
Summersby, Roy	1958-63			176	59	13	1	1		190	60
Surtees, Hubert	1949-50			5						5	
Swan, Chris	1929-30			6						6	
Swann, Hubert	1906-09	69	15			3	1			72	16
Swannell, John†	1960-61							1		1	
Swift, Arthur	1920-21			1						1	
Swindlehurst, David	1973-80			221+16	73	22	5	17	3	276	81
Tambling, Bobby	1969-70 (L) 1970-74			67+1	12	1	2	7	3	76	17
Taylor, Colin	1968-69			32+2	8	2		4	2	40	10
John	1948-49			1						1	
Kevin	1984-88			85+2	14	2	1	10		99	15
Peter	1973-77			122	33	11	4	9	2	142	39
Robert	1954-55			2						2	
Tony	1968-74			192+3	8	11+1		14+1	3	222	11
Telling, Hubert	1936-37			3						3	
Thomas, Bob	1952-55			96	31	6	2			102	33
Geoff	1987-93			192+3	26	13+1	2	39+1	7	249	35
John	1948-52			53	17	1				54	17
Thompson, Garry	1989-91			17+3	3			0+2	1	22	4
George	1905-06	10	4			1				11	4
Henry	1910-11	4								4	
Len	1933-34			2						2	
Thoms, Harold	1928-29			6	1	1				7	1
Thorn, Andy	1989-94			128	3	10		30	4	168	7
Thorpe, Albert	1935-36			4						4	
James	1908-09	17								17	
Thorup, Borge	1969-70			0+1						1	
Tilston, Tommy	1953-56			58	13	1				59	13
Tizzard, Charles†	1934-35			4						4	
Tomkins, Len	1967-70			18+2	2	1				21	2
Tonner, Jack	1927-28			24	8					24	8
Sam	1926-27			2		1				3	
Tootill, Alf†	1938-39			1						1	
Townsend, Don	1962-65			77		2		3		82	
Truett, Geoff	1957-62			38	5	1				39	5
Turnbull, Robert	1932-33			2						2	
Turner, Billy "Rubber"	1925-36			281	36	21	1			302	37
Turton, Geoff	1935-37			12		2				14	
Uphill, Dennis	1960-63			63	17	9	3	2		74	20
Vansittart, Tommy	1967-70			10+1	2	1				12	2
Venables, Terry	1974-75			14		2				16	
Waite, Norman	1921-23			16	3					16	3
Waldron, Ernie	1934-47			80	30	6	2			86	32
Walker, George	1905-06 1907-09	66	2			10				76	2
George	1936-39			102	1	9				111	1
Wall, Peter	1970-78			167+10	4	15		15+1		208	4
Wallace, Charles	1905-07	54	14			14	1			68	15
Willie	1971-73			36+3	4	2	2	1		42	6
Walley, Keith	1973-74			6+1	1					7	1
Walsh, Ian	1976-82			101+16	23	11	2	2+3	2	133	27
Tom	1928-29			8	1	1				9	1
Walters, Thomas	1932-33			14	4					14	4
Ward, Edward	1922-23			4						4	
Tom	1933-34			7		2				9	
Waterfield, George	1935-36			2						2	
Watkins, Walter	1905-06	15	7			6	6			21	13
Watson, George	1930-31			2						2	
Watson, John	1936-37			12	3					12	3
John "Jock"	1949-51			61	1	2				63	1
Watts, Grant	1992-93			2+2				3+1	2	8	2
Webb, Ron	1946-47			3						3	
Wells, Albert	1921-23			5						5	
Werge, Eddie	1961-65			82	6	6	1	2		90	7
Weston, W.	1906-07	6	1							6	1
Wetherby, Thomas	1928-31			65		6				71	
Wharton, Terry	1970-72			18+2	1					20	1
Whibley, John	1912-23	55	11	91	15	4	1			150	27
White, Tom	1966-68			37+2	13	1	1			40	14
Whitear, John	1956-57			5	1					5	1
Whitehouse, Brian	1963-66			82	17	6		4		92	17
Whittaker, Bill	1950-51			35	1	1				36	1
Whittle, Alan	1972-76			103+5	19	10+1	2	3	3	122	24
Whitworth, George	1921-25			111	48	7	2			118	50
Whyte, Chris	1984-85 (L)			13				4		17	
David	1989-94			17+10	4	0+1		5+6	3	39	7
Wicks, Steve	1981-82			14	1	5				19	1
Wiggins, R.	1919-20	1								1	
Wilcockson, Ernest	1930-32			5	1	1				6	1
Wilde, W. C. "Jimmy"	1928-37			270	5	23	1			293	6
Wilkins, Paul	1981-84			9+4	3					13	3
Ray	1994-95			1						1	
Willard, Jess	1953-55			46	5	1				47	5
Williams, Gary	1982-83			10				3		13	
James	1909-14	142	57			7	1			149	58
Paul	*1992-*			*38+8*	*7*			*6+1*	*2*	*53*	*9*
Williamson, Bill	1927-28			6	1					6	1
P.	1911-13	2								2	
Wills, Thomas	1906-07	17				1				18	
Wilmot, Rhys†	*1994-*			*5+1*		*1*				*7*	
Wilson, Albert	1905-09	11								11	
Albert	1938-46			20	6	3				23	6
Woan, Alan	1959-61			41	21	4	2	1		46	23
Wood, A	1919-22	13	2	34	9	4	1			51	12
Brian	1961-67			142+1	1	5	3	4		152	4
Fred†	1913-14	3								3	
George†	1983-88			192		9		20		221	
James	1935-36			10	4					10	4
Norman	1909-10	1								1	
Woodger, George "Lady"	1905-11	161	45			16	3			177	48
Woodhouse, Charles	1910-12	44	23			1				45	23
Woodruff, Bobby	1966-70			123+2	48	4		9+1		139	48
Woods, Charles	1964-66			49	5	1		1		51	5
Ray	1953-55			18						18	
Wright, Ian	1985-92			210+19	92	9+2	3	34+3	22	277	117
Wyatt, George	1948-49			7						7	
Yard, Ernie	1965-67			35+2	3	1		1+1		40	3
York, Ernest	1912-15	55	6			3				58	6
Young, Eric	*1990-*			*161*	*15*	*10*		*33*	*2*	*204*	*17*
John	1909-10	15	7							15	7

CRYSTAL PALACE F.C. - A complete record of every season played

Prior to their attaining Football League status in 1920, Palace played in the Southern League. Details of these eleven seasons appear below but are not included in the overall League totals at the foot of the chart.

Season	League: Divn	Posn	Prom or Rel.	Pld.	Home W	Home D	Home L	Home F - A	Away W	Away D	Away L	Away F - A	Total W	Total D	Total L	Total F - A	Goal diff.	Pts.	Avge. pts. per mtch. ※	Cup ⊗: P	W	D	L	F - A
1905-06	SL 2	1	P	24	10	1	1	42-7	9	3	0	24-7	19	4	1	66-14				7	4	2	1	20-4
1906-07	SL 1	19		38	7	4	8	29-28	1	5	13	17-38	8	9	21	46-66				8	4	3	1	9-6
1907-08	SL 1	4		38	10	4	5	35-28	7	6	6	19-23	17	10	11	54-51				3	2	0	1	7-5
1908-09	SL 1	16		40	10	4	6	42-23	2	8	10	20-39	12	12	16	62-62				4	1	2	1	6-13
1909-10	SL 1	7		42	13	3	5	48-20	7	3	11	21-30	20	6	16	69-50				1	0	0	1	1-3
1910-11	SL 1	4		38	11	5	3	35-23	6	8	5	20-25	17	13	8	55-48				1	0	0	1	0-4
1911-12	SL 1	7		38	11	5	3	43-14	4	5	10	27-32	15	10	13	70-46				4	1	2	1	4-1
1912-13	SL 1	5		38	13	3	3	38-13	4	8	7	17-23	17	11	10	55-36				3	2	0	1	4-5
1913-14	SL 1	2		38	12	5	2	41-13	5	11	3	19-19	17	16	5	60-32				2	1	0	1	2-3
1914-15	SL 1	15		38	8	4	7	24-25	5	4	10	23-36	13	8	17	47-61				2	0	1	1	2-5
1919-20	SL 1	3	P	42	15	5	1	44-15	7	7	7	25-28	22	12	8	69-43				1	0	0	1	0-2
1920-21	3	1	P	42	15	4	2	45-17	9	7	5	25-17	24	11	7	70-34	+ 36	59	1·98	2	1	0	1	2-2
1921-22	2	14		42	9	6	6	28-20	4	7	10	17-31	13	13	16	45-51	- 6	39	1·24	3	1	1	1	6-2
1922-23	2	16		42	10	7	4	33-16	3	4	14	21-46	13	11	18	54-62	- 8	37	1·19	1	0	0	1	0-1
1923-24	2	15		42	11	7	3	37-19	2	6	13	16-46	13	13	16	53-65	- 12	39	1·24	6	2	3	1	5-3
1924-25	2	21	R	42	8	4	9	23-19	4	6	11	15-35	12	10	20	38-54	- 16	34	1·10	2	1	0	1	4-4
1925-26	3 S	13		42	16	1	4	50-21	3	2	16	25-58	19	3	20	75-79	- 4	41	1·43	4	2	1	1	11-16
1926-27	3 S	6		42	12	6	3	57-33	6	3	12	27-48	18	9	15	84-81	+ 3	45	1·50	2	0	1	1	0-1
1927-28	3 S	5		42	15	3	3	46-23	3	9	9	33-49	18	12	12	79-72	+ 7	48	1·57	3	1	1	1	4-3
1928-29	3 S	2		42	14	2	5	40-25	9	6	6	41-42	23	8	11	81-67	+ 14	54	1·83	7	4	2	1	19-9
1929-30	3 S	9		42	14	5	2	56-26	3	7	11	25-48	17	12	13	81-74	+ 7	46	1·50	1	0	0	1	1-8
1930-31	3 S	2		42	17	2	2	71-20	5	5	11	36-51	22	7	13	107-71	+ 36	51	1·74	6	3	2	1	16-8
1931-32	3 S	4		42	14	7	0	48-12	6	4	11	26-51	20	11	11	74-63	+ 11	51	1·69	2	1	0	1	2-2
1932-33	3 S	5		42	14	4	3	51-21	5	4	12	27-43	19	8	15	78-64	+ 14	46	1·55	1	0	0	1	1-2
1933-34	3 S	12		42	11	6	4	40-25	5	3	13	31-42	16	9	17	71-67	+ 4	41	1·36	4	3	0	1	6-8
1934-35	3 S	5		42	15	3	3	51-14	4	7	10	35-50	19	10	13	86-64	+ 22	48	1·60	1	0	0	1	0-3
1935-36	3 S	6		42	15	4	2	64-20	7	1	13	32-54	22	5	15	96-74	+ 22	49	1·69	2	1	0	1	2-3
1936-37	3 S	14		42	11	7	3	45-20	2	5	14	17-41	13	12	17	62-61	+ 1	38	1·21	2	0	1	1	1-3
1937-38	3 S	7		42	14	4	3	45-17	4	8	9	22-30	18	12	12	67-47	+ 20	48	1·57	5	2	2	1	8-5
1938-39	3 S	2		42	15	4	2	49-18	5	8	8	22-34	20	12	10	71-52	+ 19	52	1·71	2	0	1	1	1-4
1945-46																				3	0	2	1	0-1
1946-47	3 S	18		42	9	7	5	29-19	4	4	13	20-43	13	11	18	49-62	- 13	37	1·19	1	0	0	1	2-6
1947-48	3 S	13		42	12	5	4	32-14	1	8	12	17-35	13	13	16	49-49	0	39	1·24	3	2	0	1	3-2
1948-49	3 S	22		42	7	8	6	27-27	1	3	17	11-49	8	11	23	38-76	- 38	27	0·83	1	0	0	1	0-1
1949-50	3 S	7		42	12	5	4	35-21	3	9	9	20-33	15	14	13	55-54	+ 1	44	1·40	1	0	0	1	0-3
1950-51	3 S	24		46	6	5	12	18-39	2	6	15	15-45	8	11	27	33-84	- 51	27	0·76	1	0	0	1	1-4
1951-52	3 S	19		46	9	7	7	32-28	6	2	15	29-52	15	9	22	61-80	- 19	39	1·17	1	0	0	1	0-1
1952-53	3 S	13		46	12	7	4	40-26	3	6	14	26-56	15	13	18	66-82	- 16	43	1·26	3	1	1	1	5-5
1953-54	3 S	22		46	11	7	5	41-30	3	5	15	19-56	14	12	20	60-86	- 26	40	1·17	1	0	0	1	0-1
1954-55	3 S	20		46	9	11	3	32-24	2	5	16	20-56	11	16	19	52-80	- 28	38	1·07	2	1	0	1	4-4
1955-56	3 S	23		46	7	3	13	27-32	5	7	11	27-51	12	10	24	54-83	- 29	34	1·00	2	0	1	1	0-2
1956-57	3 S	20		46	7	10	6	31-28	4	8	11	31-47	11	18	17	62-75	- 13	40	1·11	4	2	1	1	6-5
1957-58	3 S	14		46	12	5	6	46-30	3	8	12	24-42	15	13	18	70-72	- 2	43	1·26	3	2	0	1	4-3
1958-59	4	7		46	12	8	3	54-27	8	4	11	36-44	20	12	14	90-71	+ 19	52	1·57	5	2	2	1	9-7
1959-60	4	8		46	12	6	5	61-27	7	6	10	23-37	19	12	15	84-64	+ 20	50	1·50	4	2	1	1	8-2

- complete record continued :-

Season	League: Divn	Posn	Prom or Rel.	Pld.	Home W	Home D	Home L	Home F - A	Away W	Away D	Away L	Away F - A	Total W	Total D	Total L	Total F - A	Goal diff.	Pts.	Avge. pts. per mtch. ※	Cup ⊗: P	W	D	L	F - A
1960-61	4	2	P	46	16	4	3	64-28	13	2	8	46-41	29	6	11	110-69	+ 41	64	2·02	4	1	1	2	6-5
1961-62	3	15		46	8	8	7	50-41	6	6	11	33-39	14	14	18	83-80	+ 3	42	1·22	4	2	0	2	11-9
1962-63	3	11		46	10	7	6	38-22	7	6	10	30-36	17	13	16	68-58	+ 10	47	1·39	4	1	1	2	7-11
1963-64	3	2	P	46	17	4	2	38-14	6	10	7	35-37	23	14	9	73-51	+ 22	60	1·80	3	1	0	2	9-7
1964-65	2	7		42	11	6	4	37-24	5	7	9	18-27	16	13	13	55-51	+ 4	45	1·45	8	5	1	2	15-8
1965-66	2	11		42	11	7	3	29-16	3	6	12	18-36	14	13	15	47-52	- 5	41	1·31	2	0	0	2	0-4
1966-67	2	7		42	14	4	3	42-23	5	6	10	19-32	19	10	13	61-55	+ 6	48	1·60	2	0	0	2	0-5
1967-68	2	11		42	11	4	6	34-19	3	7	11	22-37	14	11	17	56-56	0	39	1·26	3	0	1	2	2-4
1968-69	2	2	P	42	14	4	3	45-24	8	8	5	25-23	22	12	8	70-47	+ 23	56	1·86	6	3	1	2	6-6
1969-70	1	20		42	5	6	10	20-36	1	9	11	14-32	6	15	21	34-68	- 34	27	0·79	9	4	3	2	11-11
1970-71	1	18		42	9	5	7	24-24	3	6	12	15-33	12	11	19	39-57	- 18	35	1·12	8	3	3	2	16-12
1971-72	1	20		42	4	8	9	26-31	4	5	12	13-34	8	13	21	39-65	- 26	29	0·88	5	1	2	2	8-9
1972-73	1	21	R	42	7	7	7	25-21	2	5	14	16-37	9	12	21	41-58	- 17	30	0·93	5	1	2	2	6-6
1973-74	2	20	R	42	6	7	8	24-24	5	5	11	19-32	11	12	19	43-56	- 13	34	1·07	2	0	0	2	0-3
1974-75	3	5		46	14	8	1	48-22	4	7	12	18-35	18	15	13	66-57	+ 9	51	1·50	5	2	1	2	10-9
1975-76	3	5		46	7	12	4	30-20	11	5	7	31-26	18	17	11	61-46	+ 15	53	1·54	11	7	1	3	16-12
1976-77	3	3	P	46	17	5	1	46-15	6	8	9	22-25	23	13	10	68-40	+ 28	59	1·78	9	3	4	2	14-11
1977-78	2	9		42	9	7	5	31-20	4	8	9	19-27	13	15	14	50-47	+ 3	41	1·29	5	1	1	3	8-7
1978-79	2	1	P	42	12	7	2	30-11	7	12	2	21-13	19	19	4	51-24	+ 27	57	1·81	8	3	3	2	8-7
1979-80	1	13		42	9	9	3	26-13	3	7	11	15-37	12	16	14	41-50	- 9	40	1·24	6	1	3	2	15-10
1980-81	1	22	R	42	6	4	11	32-37	0	3	18	15-46	6	7	29	47-83	- 36	19	0·60	5	2	1	2	6-8
1981-82	2	15		42	9	2	10	25-26	4	7	10	9-19	13	9	20	34-45	- 11	48	1·14	9	5	1	3	9-7
1982-83	2	15		42	11	7	3	31-17	1	5	15	12-35	12	12	18	43-52	- 9	48	1·14	9	5	2	2	11-6
1983-84	2	18		42	8	5	8	18-18	4	6	11	24-34	12	11	19	42-52	- 10	47	1·12	5	2	1	2	5-6
1984-85	2	15		42	8	7	6	25-27	4	5	12	21-38	12	12	18	46-65	- 19	48	1·14	6	1	3	2	4-5
1985-86	2	5		42	12	3	6	29-22	7	6	8	28-30	19	9	14	57-52	+ 5	66	1·57	7	1	1	5	6-11
1986-87	2	6		42	12	4	5	35-20	7	1	13	16-33	19	5	18	51-53	- 2	62	1·48	7	2	2	3	4-11
1987-88	2	6		44	16	3	3	50-21	6	6	10	36-38	22	9	13	86-59	+ 27	75	1·70	5	2	0	3	7-4
1988-89	2	3	P	46	15	6	2	42-17	8	6	9	29-32	23	12	11	71-49	+ 22	81	1·76	9	6	0	3	19-15
1989-90	1	15		38	8	7	4	27-23	5	2	12	15-43	13	9	16	42-66	- 24	48	1·26	16	9	2	5	26-22
1990-91	1	3		38	11	6	2	26-17	9	3	7	24-24	20	9	9	50-41	+ 9	69	1·82	14	8	4	2	27-12
1991-92	1	10		42	7	8	6	24-25	7	7	7	29-36	14	15	13	53-61	- 8	57	1·36	12	5	4	3	22-16
1992-93	P	20	R	42	6	9	6	27-25	5	7	9	21-36	11	16	15	48-61	- 13	49	1·17	9	4	2	3	13-11
1993-94	1x	1	P	46	16	4	3	39-18	11	5	7	34-28	27	9	10	73-46	+ 27	90	1·96	5	2	1	2	7-8
1994-95	P	19	R	42	6	6	9	16-23	5	6	10	18-26	11	12	19	34-49	- 15	45	1·07	15	8	3	4	27-12
Totals				2926	749	390	324	2537-1542	330	393	740	1591-2599	1079	783	1064	4128-4141	- 13	3169	1·37※	369	150	88	131	547-495

Notes: — ※ (Average points per match). In order to obtain an exact comparison throughout all seasons; the figures in this column assume that three points were always awarded for a win. (Prior to 1981-82, only two points were given). Also taken into account is the varying number of matches played, i.e. 38, 42, 44 & 46.

— ⊗ (Cup results). The figures incorporate all three major competitions: Football Association, Football League and Full Members'. A comprehensive summary of every cup result is given elsewhere in the book.

— x - This was formerly known as the 2nd Division.

INDEX

All figures in *italics* refer to illustrations.

Old photographs have been copied by Tony Davies from whom copies are available (5 Paddington Street, London NW1).

CRYSTAL PALACE
F.C.

CRYSTAL PALACE
F.C.
CRYSTAL PALACE
F.C.
CRYSTAL PALACE
F.C.
CRYSTAL PALACE
F.C.
CRYSTAL PALACE
F.C.
CRYSTAL PALACE
F.C.
CRYSTAL PALACE
F.C.
CRYSTAL PALACE
F.C.
CRYSTAL PALACE
F.C.
CRYSTAL PALACE
F.C.
CRYSTAL PALACE
F.C.
CRYSTAL PALACE
F.C.
CRYSTAL PALACE
F.C.
CRYSTAL PALACE
F.C.
CRYSTAL PALACE
F.C.